A HANDBOOK
FOR THE HUMANISTIC
ASTROLOGER

MICHAEL R. MEYER is the Director of the International Committee for a Humanistic Astrology and for many years a student of astrology and occult philosophy. His articles have appeared in every leading astrological periodical, including *Horoscope*, *The Aquarian Agent*, and *Aquarian Astrology*. He is currently living in Berkeley, California.

# a handbook
# for
# the humanistic
# astrologer

## MICHAEL R. MEYER

ANCHOR BOOKS
ANCHOR PRESS/DOUBLEDAY
GARDEN CITY, NEW YORK

Illustrations by Michael R. Meyer and Nancy Kleban

For

VIOLET UNDINE

may you fulfill the splendor
of your innermost being

# CONTENTS

## Appendixes:

# SAMPLE CHARTS

# FOREWORD

Astrology today offers significant answers to the very critical questions posed by contemporary men and women in search of a deeper meaning of life; at the same time, it is regarded with blatant prejudice by large segments of the academic and scientific communities. This situation, of course, is not entirely new. Astrology has probably been the most controversial, disputed, and maligned system of knowledge of the historical era. Much of the intolerance to astrology stems from simple misunderstandings and misrepresentations about its operative principles and the way in which astronomical data may be related to the destinies and free wills of human beings. The most detrimental point of contention is the popular misconception (widely believed by many astrologers and laymen alike) that astrology is founded upon the belief that the positions of celestial bodies *determine specific events,* on an individual as well as collective scale—a belief naturally unacceptable to modern science and religion.

To my mind, astrology should be primarily concerned with the cyclic process of unfoldment as it is operative within all forms of existence—as it can be observed by the annual cycle of seasons and by the cyclic motion of the planets; as it is observable in the most basic and inevitable cycle of human existence: birth to death to rebirth into a new phase of existence. By *correlating* the cyclic motions of the planets and the phenomena associated with their motion and interrelationship to the growth process (beginning with birth) of individual human beings, astrology is able to reliably describe the unique potential focused within each of us and decipher the "instructions" for setting into motion the process of their fuller actualization.

Less than a century ago Sigmund Freud encountered hysterical criticism and resistance in his effort to legitimatize the study of psychology by formulating it into a scientifically accurate body of knowledge. In much the same way, though hopefully dissimilar in terms of values, meaning, and goals, astrology is today experiencing a rebirth. There is a new approach to astrology which is re-examining the traditional concepts and principles and reformulating them around a new meaning and purpose. This new astrology hopes to assist men and women in fulfilling their individual potential and realizing the meaning of their individual selfhood in terms of individual, collective, and global significance.

*

My initial contact with Dane Rudhyar and his astrological work came during the early part of 1968, while I was living in Berkeley, California. I had been interested in astrology and had studied it for some time before then, but the traditional and sometimes sensational quality of nearly all available astrological literature during that time had discouraged my intense involvement.

It was during a visit to the San Francisco Theosophical Library that I first noticed a copy of Rudhyar's newly published *The Lunation Cycle,* among a small assortment of books offered for sale. I realized, after reading it, that Rudhyar's approach represented a significant break with traditional values. Rudhyar happened to be giving a series of lectures around the San Francisco Bay Area that summer, which enabled me to hear him speak and casually meet him before returning to New York.

On East Ninth Street, on New York's Lower East Side, I opened a small astrological-theosophical bookshop, in 1969, while at the same time reading, researching, teaching, and practicing astrology. Although several of Rudhyar's books were becoming available at that time, I thought a complete and concise textbook of astrology from the new approach Rudhyar was introducing would be of value.

After another two years of intense preparation, I began the mundane work on the project—at the Spring Equinox of 1971. Working with the vernal energies, I was able to complete much of the organization work for the text in a few months and began the actual drafts during the early summer of the same year in New York. Work continued in Cambridge, Massachusetts, during the midsummer of 1971 and in Berkeley, California, from September 1971 until now, May 20, 1973.

*

I have attempted to present the subject of astrology here in a manner useful to both the beginner and the more experienced student of astrology. The "cookbook" type of presentation (which gives a "meaning" or, more traditionally, "delineation" to every planet in each sign, house, aspect, etc.) has been purposely avoided to discourage dependence upon an extensive memorization of combined astrological factors and to encourage an organized understanding of the basic tools and frames of reference employed by astrologers, beginning with their most basic or essential meanings and progressing to an application of these meanings to all levels of personal existence, but essentially to the process of the fulfillment of human potentialities.

The text has been divided into four parts with several appendixes, for the convenience of the reader. Part One introduces the philosophical basis of astrological thought. Part Two presents the derivation and significance of astrological cycles and symbols. A scheme of interpretation for birth-charts and a presentation of various techniques related to the process of astrological interpretation are given in Part Three, while Part Four discusses the use of progressions and transits in the practice of astrology. In addition, I have chosen birth-charts of well-known and interesting persons to illustrate examples of certain configurations and factors throughout the text.

*

I would like to warmly thank all those who helped in making this book a reality.

Nancy Kleban was an invaluable help to me in preparing and illustrating the manuscript. My appreciation also goes to Robert Grantham, Marcia Poole, Pat Crawford, and F. Emptysky for their perceptive comments and helpful suggestions, and to Susan Meyer-Bear who first encouraged me to pursue the study of astrology.

I'm particularly indebted to Dane Rudhyar, whose inspiration and guidance are the foundation of this book.

# PREFACE

The inner urge to start the International Committee for Humanistic Astrology (ICHA) came to me rather unexpectedly in the late evening of February 26, 1969. The immediate incentive to make such a move was the reading of printed material that emphasized the need for using the scientific tool of statistical research, and indirectly if not explicitly downgraded any other approach to astrology. I realized that the time had come to publicize the fact that the scientific analytical and "event-oriented" approach to astrology was not the only and most significant one, even though it was most specifically appealing to the modern mentality, carrying an official stamp of "respectability," as well as (in the form of fortunetelling) most appealing to the general public.

I also realized that the situation resembled in many ways the one that led to the emergence of humanistic psychology, under the leadership of Abraham Maslow, Anthony Sutich, etc.—a psychology tracing its immediate origin to the work of Carl G. Jung, which in turn had ancient European and Asiatic roots. The humanistic psychologists spoke of their movement as a "third force" in order to situate it in relation to Freudian psychoanalysis and the experimental laboratory psychology developed in universities especially since the behaviorists and, in Russia, Pavlov. In a similar sense, my approach to astrology differs from the traditional type of predictive fortunetelling and the recent research movement based on empirical and statistical techniques. As a result, after some hesitation because of the (to my thinking) unfortunate concepts associated with classical humanism as a life philosophy, I decided to use the term "humanistic astrology."

The general response to my initiative, and to the booklets I subsequently wrote—published with the enlightened co-operation of Ed O'Neal, director of the CSA Press, in Lakemont, Georgia—has been far beyond my expectations. Some of the most progressive-minded astrologers and leaders in the research movement gave me their moral support, and gradually an unceasing stream of applications for membership in ICHA reached my wife and me, warmly and often eloquently testifying to the interest of young people in my ideas and style of presentation, and in the approach to astrology I was promoting. The appearance in paperback editions of my earlier books, *The Astrology of Personality, The Planetarization of Consciousness, The Lunation Cycle, Practice of Astrology,* and my latest work, *The Astrological Houses: The Spectrum of Individual Experience,* has made it possible for the new generations to become acquainted with what I had been writing since 1932, and now a number of humanistic astrologers between the ages of twenty and thirty-five are, according to their own often outstanding abilities, spreading out and adding to what Marc Edmund Jones and I envisioned and formulated.

Michael Meyer is one of the most gifted exponents of the humanistic approach, and his textbook is a remarkable work which I commend highly. Though during the time he wrote this book we met only briefly, as he attended some of my seminars and lectures, he has been able effectively to organize, condense, and formulate the main body of my astrological thinking and other relevant material. He has added original and pertinent ideas to what he learned in books, and, particularly in view of his youth, we can expect that he will play a valuable and important role in fecundating the mind of his generation and of the one now in its teens.

This does not mean, naturally, that I completely agree with every statement and idea in this large volume, which covers the whole field of astrology in its humanistic aspect; but I believe he has performed a very real service to astrology. He has simplified and made clear much that to young students often seemed too abstract and, to older and more matter-of-fact readers, too poetic and "mystical." Michael Meyer's clear, organizing mind and his intellectual generosity and fairness are demonstrated in every page of this book. I warmly thank him for work well done.

DANE RUDHYAR

A HANDBOOK
FOR THE HUMANISTIC
ASTROLOGER

# 1

---

## astrological philosophy;

ASTROLOGY
AS A DISCIPLINE OF MIND

# 1

# THE ORIGIN OF ASTROLOGY

*[Astrology is] man's first attempt to understand the apparent confusion and chaos of his life-experiences by referring them to the ordered pattern of cyclic activity which he discovers in the sky.*

DANE RUDHYAR

## THE EMERGENCE OF ASTROLOGY

Astrology is a functional application of the awareness of the active relationship existing between the microcosm (smaller whole) and the macrocosm (greater whole). At the time when human consciousness was initially emerging from its primordial condition of undifferentiated consciousness, the mind sought to bring order and harmony to the apparent meaninglessness and confusion of human life by consciously regulating human activity with the flow of nature. Man* was in a precarious position; in becoming a self-conscious individual, his contact with nature was severed; his activities could no longer follow the ebb and flow of nature. He had lost his directive instincts and had to maintain a constant fight for survival in a world filled with chaos and fear. To overcome the overwhelming forces of nature, the rudimentary intelligence of the human race had to be implemented and developed.

It was in such conditions that astrology first emerged, from an awareness of seasonal changes in the environment and the way these changes affected man's ability to survive. Gradually it was realized that with the aid of astrological knowledge one could prepare for the future by gathering food and migrating, closely following the patterns

* All references to "man" used here are in the generic meaning of the word; that is, referring to humanity as a whole, not to the sexual biology of a person.

of lower animals, only on a conscious and intellectual level rather than instinctively. Regardless of how uncertain and confused one's own existence may have been, there was always order in the sky. This knowledge gave the much needed psychological and spiritual reassurance for coping with the primitive conditions. Astrology was man's first attempt to bring order within by the realization of the order of the universe.

Later, when human consciousness became more or less free from the fear of the immediate, astrology was used in the establishment of the social state, a system originally set up as a microcosm of the supreme, solar order. However, even though man had reached a state of individual consciousness, at this time astrologers were probably not concerned with the casting of birth-charts, for the tribal or national community was all-important and the individual had, for the most part, no identity or meaning outside of the community in which he was born.

It is difficult to ascertain the degree of exactness and perfection maintained by the early astrologers. We have only our present knowledge of history, psychology, and, of course, science to base our speculations on the nature of prehistoric astrology. We know astrological knowledge was used for more than strictly mundane and political purposes several thousand years ago, possibly, for example, for the invocation of spiritual and transcendental experiences. In addition we know that astrologers of at least as early as 4000 B.C. had a knowledge of celestial cycles *at least* as exact and extensive as that of the modern astrophysicist and scientific astronomer. The Great Pyramid and Stonehenge stand as monuments of a prehistoric technology, based on astrological and other types of knowledge that are today either lost or disregarded, that tapped the source of universal life energy. This energy was not controlled or produced through the destruction of matter, resulting in the chain reaction of pollution which threatens to annihilate all organic life on the earth's surface, but through the understanding of the cyclic nature of the universe and all forms of existence.

This knowledge was eventually lost or veiled, and astrology became, for the most part, a device for everyday success. It remained, however, a very exact instrument—or perhaps its practitioners were simply able to determine things in a very exact manner by some other means. The study of astrology was held in the highest respect by most academic institutions throughout Europe, Asia, and North Africa right up until the dawn of the "Age of Reason"—the eighteenth century, when the "sciences" to which astrology gave birth rationalized that it was invalid.

## THE INDIVIDUALIZATION OF ASTROLOGY

Astrology probably first became individualized around the sixth century B.C. (the time of Buddha, Lao-tzu, and Pythagoras), when a great wave of repolarization took place in man's consciousness, resulting in the transition from a physiological emphasis to a system of psychological values. It was probably around the Mediterranean and India that natal astrology first appeared openly, but it may have been practiced secretly much earlier. The practice of this type of astrology became very popular; the use of astrology by the Greeks and the Romans has been well documented. In the second century A.D., Ptolemy compiled all that was known at the time on natal astrology in his *Tetrabiblos,* and astrologers have closely followed his values and concepts ever since.

It was during the latter part of the Victorian era that astrology started to regain popularity after its decline in the eighteenth century. It met the mass media and became popularized in England through the influence of Alan Leo, and in America by Evangeline Adams and Max Heindel. Even so, the knowledge of Ptolemy was handed down in almost unaltered form, with very little question on the part of contemporary astrologers.

Today an overwhelming, yet steadily decreasing, majority of astrologers and astrological writers continue to base their work on antiquated information and values still tinged with fear and confusion. This type of astrology may have been acceptable and helpful for a humanity living in medieval times, but today's individual needs an astrology able to give meaning and purpose to the apparently meaningless and confused modern way of life. To answer this need, a small movement directed toward the re-examination and reformulation of astrological concepts and values was initiated by Marc Edmund Jones in the 1920s and further elucidated by Dane Rudhyar during the past forty years.

Astrological followers, generally a conservative group, have never encouraged an extensive questioning of traditional concepts; it has taken many years for the new approach to astrological knowledge upon which this book is based to gain extensive recognition. This recent recognition is largely due to the current changes in intellectual atmosphere, which have drawn large numbers of younger persons to search for a new meaning of life through the study of astrology and other occult and esoteric subjects.

# WHAT IS ASTROLOGY FOR?

*What is the purpose of astrology? Before any discussion of astrological technicalities is begun one should answer this question.*

DANE RUDHYAR

## APPROACHING ASTROLOGY
## IN A POSITIVE MANNER

It is vital to recognize what one is seeking in the process of astrological study. True astrology is not a superficial subject, regardless of how it may be promoted by the media. If, however, you are seeking (1) a mental discipline that can make your mind, if you can endure the process of refinement, as sharp as a diamond, (2) a symbolic language that may enable you to understand and interpret—if your mind hasn't become rigid in the process of becoming as sharp as a diamond —the relationship existing between all organic wholes, and (3) an instrument of self-transformation that may be used as a means of actualizing your entire self, of bringing yourself into focus within any existential situation—if this is what you are seeking, you may find the study of the type of astrology presented here a fulfilling experience.

### ASTROLOGY AS A DISCIPLINE OF MIND

Astrology is firstly a discipline of mind, a technique for the development of holistic thinking. The study of the cyclic patterns of astrology places the mind in the habit of constantly perceiving things as wholes rather than as unrelated parts. An understanding of astrology makes the mind aware that what is happening at any given moment is just one point, just one moment of an entire cycle of complex and intricate relationships. It gives one an objective awareness of the unity of all things, the conscious realization that all things are in some way intimately related to everything else.

An outline of the philosophy of astrology naturally includes a statement of the basic concepts of holism. It is out of the scope of this work to give a thorough exposition of the philosophical implications of holism. The interested reader is referred to *Holism and Evolution,* by Jan C. Smuts.

## The Basic Concepts of Holism

1   Holism regards all organic things as wholes, not just assemblages of parts.

2   The whole and its parts mutually and reciprocally influence and change each other.

3   Every whole possesses its own internal order or pattern, as well as being a part of a more extensive pattern.

4   The parts are molded and adjusted by the whole, just as the whole in turn depends on the co-operation of its parts.

5   All wholes are ordered and structured systems in which meaning and purpose are inherent.

6   Evolution is a progressive complexification of parts, giving rise to an entire series of wholes, from the simplest to the most advanced.

7   Holism characterizes the entire process of evolution in an ever-increasing manner. The process is continuous in the sense that the older types of wholes are not discarded, but become starting points for newer, more advanced patterns.

8   Opposites are reconciled and harmonized within the whole.

9   The whole is greater than the sum of its parts. The whole is creative; whenever parts come together to form a whole, something arises that is greater than the parts.

# ASTROLOGY AS A SYMBOLIC LANGUAGE

Astrology is a symbolic language in that it enables one to translate the cyclic interrelationships of all parts of any existential whole. It is the language of the holistic perception of archetypal and evolving patterns. As a symbolic language, astrology correlates everything with everything else, though the procedure of correlation varies depending upon the nature of the wholes being studied. It is a highly sophisticated system, which reduces all functional activities and experiences into a few essential categories. Symbolically, the birth-chart of an individual person is a representation of his archetypal form; it is a mandala of individual selfhood.

Astrology is indeed much like the Glass-Bead Game, as presented by Hermann Hesse in the novel of the same name. Hesse describes the Glass-Bead Game as "a universal language in which all knowledge is reduced to a single principle [which was] built up over several centuries into a universal system and language, in order to express and bring every spiritual and artistic value and concept beneath a common denominator." Hesse was also aware of the all-significance of all things: "I understood in a flash that the language, or at least, in the spirit of the Glass-Bead Game, everything was in actual fact all significant, that each symbol and each combination of symbols led, not hither and thither, not to single examples, experiments and proofs but towards the center." Both astrology and the Glass-Bead Game qualify as systems of universal symbolism, which may be defined as *techniques that apply holistic perception to the interpretation of the dynamic relationship existing between and within all organic wholes for the purpose of revealing a universal or particular truth.*

## ASTROLOGY AS AN INSTRUMENT OF SELF-ACTUALIZATION

The astrological techniques may be used as a tool of self-actualization after a positive relationship with astrology as a discipline of mind and as a system of universal symbolism has been established. Then, after one's mind has been refined and adapted to holistic thought, one may wisely use the astrological knowledge one has acquired as an instrument for the benefit of one's self and others, of integration through active self-actualization. Knowledge implies responsibility. The astrologer who practices this art must assume responsibility for the use of this knowledge. The wise use of astrological knowledge will be discussed more thoroughly later.

# AREAS OF APPLICATION

Astrology may be applied to three general areas:

**1  to the individual,**
**2  to the collective,**
**3  to the occult, or esoteric.**

## ASTROLOGY OF THE INDIVIDUAL

### Natal Astrology

The present work is primarily concerned with this area of astrological application. It involves (1) the casting of a birth-chart, calculated for the first moment of independent existence of a particular individual, and (2) various "symbolic" directions, progressions, and transits, which enable the astrologer to understand the present and future crises through which the individual should realize progress in his or her self-development and integration. Of course, the attitude of the particular astrologer will determine exactly how he will evaluate the significance of the birth-chart and the progressions and transits to the birth-chart.

### Horary Astrology

Horary astrology is a technique based upon the theory that the time a question is asked contains its solution. It involves the casting of a chart for the exact moment a specific question is asked and the examination of the chart (employing a unique and special procedure), which reveals the response to the inquiry. Such an application of astrology is much like the employment of the I Ching for divinatory purposes, in terms of functional operation.

## ASTROLOGY OF THE COLLECTIVE

### Political Astrology

Also called "mundane astrology," political astrology is concerned with the examination and prediction of world events, on the global, the national, and the local levels. It often involves the study of the birth-charts of political leaders and the examination of current planetary configurations.

### Astrology as It Applies to Other Fields

Astrology has also been used for predictive weather analysis and in various other scientific fields, though it may not be called "astrology" by those who use it. In addition, the astrological technique may be used in the study of the natural and social sciences. As a system of universal symbolism, astrology may be applied to anything, the only actual limitation being one's background and creativity.

## OCCULT, OR ESOTERIC, ASTROLOGY

This area of astrological application is not entirely removed from either of the above classifications; in fact, a knowledge of this type of astrology may enhance the astrologer's understanding of astrology in its less abstract applications. It deals with the examination of the nature and origin of the basic principles and symbols used in the astrological technique. The comparative study of astrology in relation to other systems of symbolism and philosophy is an integral part of the study of occult astrology. It is perhaps the most open and unlimited field of astrology and is essentially concerned with the "perfection of man," and it is the "perfection of man" that should be the motivating factor in the study of astrology.

# TWO APPROACHES TO ASTROLOGICAL KNOWLEDGE

*[The two approaches to astrology] refers to a fundamental dualism of attitudes which is found* in every area *of human thinking and activity.*

DANE RUDHYAR

## THE EVENT-ORIENTED APPROACH

The event-oriented approach to astrology is, generally speaking, astrology in its traditional form. Such an approach sees man and his total environment as being constantly subjected to overwhelming external forces. Man is essentially helpless under such conditions and simply at their mercy. It sees the Sun, Moon, and planets as great beings that exert their influence and will upon men, *causing* events to happen. This approach considers the birth-chart of a person as something that must be overcome if one is to be a free, self-determining individual. It divides astrological factors into opposite categories: good—bad, fortunate—unfortunate, and benefic—malefic. Situations and people are seen as separate, unrelated parts. When the event-oriented astrologer approaches his work, he assumes little responsibility for the results his statements may have upon the psychological condition of his clients, concerning himself with the material success of his clients and the prediction of events, rather than the personal integration and self-actualization of those who seek his services.

A person seeking the advice of such an astrologer may be informed to "watch out for accidents; Mars is crossing your Saturn." Naturally, the person is likely to be terrified. And, of course, the astrologer's warnings often become self-fulfilling prophecies. If, and when, they do actually materialize, the astrologer's success is assured: the event-oriented astrologer's greatest asset is his fortunetelling ability.

## THE HUMANISTIC, PERSON-CENTERED APPROACH

The humanistic, person-centered approach to astrology, as its name implies, is an astrological parallel to the "third force" of psychology promoted by Abraham Maslow, Carl Rogers, and many others. This new approach to astrological knowledge and practice has been introduced by Dane Rudhyar in *Person-Centered Astrology,* a collection of six essays first published during 1969–71. The formulation of the humanistic, person-centered approach to astrology represents the culmination of over forty years of extensive research, reinterpretation, and restatement of the ideas and concepts of astrology on the part of Rudhyar, and the beginning of a new era in the history of the ancient study of astrology.

The humanistic approach to astrology sees the person as an independent organic whole consisting of an intricate pattern of interrelated and interacting forces. Rudhyar writes in *Person-Centered Astrology* that this pattern, "formulated at the first moment of independent existence, establishes the individual's life-purpose and its basic relation to all other wholes in the universe. This organic whole —the individual person—is essentially no different from the infinitely greater and vaster organized whole, which we call the universe—the individual is this universal whole, focused at a particular point in space and in terms of the particular need of the exact moment of its emergence into independent existence."

From the humanistic approach, the birth-chart is not something the person has to overcome and is not judged in terms of good or bad. The humanistic, person-centered astrologer sees the birth-chart as a seed pattern, describing what the individual *may* grow to *become,* what he or she is potentially; though, of course, the person may not actually fulfill this potential to its fullest. In other words, the birth-chart describes what *should be* and what *experiences are needed* to bring about the actualization of what is at the moment of birth only a set of potentials.

In practice, the humanistic astrologer studies (perceives) the birth-chart aesthetically rather than ethically, first as a whole and then in terms of its individual factors. Nothing in the birth-chart is seen as good or bad, fortunate or unfortunate; humanistic astrology recognizes no evil planets or bad signs. It considers all astrological factors as having a place in all things; everything is good when in its place in the eternal scheme of things and in relation to everything else. From this approach, the birth-chart is a set of instructions for the actualization of one's potential.

The individual who approaches astrology (and all forms of knowledge) in this manner is concerned with the whole view of the total process rather than with a partial view of an isolated life function. Rudhyar states that this type of astrologer is primarily concerned "with the *fullest possible actualization* of the potentialities inherent in the birth-chart, he considers no significant step ahead can be taken except through some kind of crisis. [It is not the prediction of events that carries the primary importance;] for the basic purpose of studying a birth-chart and discussing it with the person to whom it refers is to help this person to *become more positively, more meaningfully, more creatively, more totally what he potentially is.*"

# OPERATIVE PRINCIPLES

*To understand correctly the words alchemy and astrology, it is necessary to understand and realize the intimate relationship and identity of the Macrocosm and the Microcosm, and their mutual interaction. All powers of the universe are potentially contained in man and his physical body, and all his organs are nothing else but the products and representatives of the powers of Nature.*

PARACELSUS

## WHAT MAKES ASTROLOGY WORK?

The operative principle behind astrology is based upon a connection existing between the life patterns of human beings (or any other organic wholes) and the dynamic pattern of relationship existing within the solar system and symbolized by the cyclic patterns of the planets we see in the sky. The question here is more than merely recognizing the existence of such a connection; we must attempt to understand the nature of the relationship.

## PLANETARY INFLUENCES AS A CAUSAL CONNECTING PRINCIPLE

The theory of planetary influence holds that the Sun, Moon, and planets exert some sort of external influence or force upon human beings and everything else in the solar system less grand than themselves. It is believed that the celestial bodies *make* things happen and *cause* people to feel and react in a certain manner, which may be predicted by the application of the astrological technique. This theory

sees no possible escape from the all-powerful planetary forces and
believes that through astrology men and women may be better
equipped to survive—"forewarned is forearmed."

## SYNCHRONICITY
## AS AN ACAUSAL CONNECTING PRINCIPLE

The synchronistic principle was formulated by C. G. Jung as an
explanation for apparently causally unconnected, though simultane-
ous, events and psychological phenomena and the functional operation of the I Ching and astrology. It contends that parallel phenomena
may be connected by time rather than by cause. As Jung states in the
Appendix of *The Secret of the Golden Flower,* astrological deduc-
tions "are not due to the effects of the constellations, but to our
hypothetical time-characters. In other words, whatever is born or
done at this moment, has the qualities of this moment." Both man
and the solar system are in some way a part of the same system, and
there are no rigid or absolute separations existing between the two.
I see the synchronistic principle (in its most inclusive meaning) as
the primary operative principle of astrology, as an aspect of structuring and formative power, the power that defines the nature of all
things.

# PART ONE

## *Notes*

The opening statement for Chapter 1 is from Rudhyar's *The Practice of Astrology* (Penguin Books, 1970).

A thorough presentation of the emergence of astrology and its early use may be found in *The Astrology of Personality,* by Dane Rudhyar (Doubleday, 1970). An intriguing account of the use of astrology during "pre-pre-historic" times is given in *The View over Atlantis,* by John Michell (Ballantine Books, 1972).

The opening quotes for Chapters 2 and 3 are extracted from Rudhyar's *Person-Centered Astrology* (CSA Press, 1973), which gives a complete introduction to the basic principles of this approach to astrology.

The opening statement for Chapter 4 is from *Paracelsus,* by Franz Hartmann (John W. Lovell, 1891, 1963).

# 2

---

# astrological principles;

## ASTROLOGY
## AS A SYMBOLIC LANGUAGE

# 1

# THE BIRTH-CHART AND ITS IMPLICATIONS

*The birth-chart has to be understood as the archetype or seed-pattern of one's individual being—as the symbolic 'form' of one's individuality, and therefore also of one's destiny, for the two are identical.*

DANE RUDHYAR

## THE BIRTH-CHART AS AN ARCHETYPAL PATTERN
## OF INDIVIDUAL SELFHOOD

A birth-chart is a two-dimensional, graphic representation of a number of select factors in the solar system frozen in time for the exact moment of an individual's initial emergence into existence as an independent entity (his first breath). This image contains, in symbolic form, the archetypal seed pattern of the individual it represents, describing to the astrologer what this individual may potentially become and how he may fulfill this potential. With the aid of a birth-chart, the humanistic astrologer is able to evoke the "celestial name" of the individual, revealing the person's true nature, the "signature" of the self.

In humanistic astrology, a birth-chart is never judged or qualified as "good" or "bad"; rather, it is approached aesthetically. First it is seen and "felt" as a whole, then its individual functional parts are examined and analyzed, summed up, and finally the chart is perceived again as a whole consisting of interactive and interrelated functional processes. Approached in this manner, the birth-chart is in no way considered as something the individual must struggle to overcome if he wishes to achieve true freedom. Instead, it is seen as a formula, a set of instructions, to be lived and actualized to its fullest possible potential. Considered as an answer to the need of the particular time (of the individual's first emergence into the realm of independent being), one's birth-chart is seen as "best" for his particular needs. Being born at any particular moment is no more limiting than being born at any other moment; no birth-chart is any more limiting, in essence, than any other. Birth is the limiting factor; not the time of one's birth, which defines one's individual pattern of selfhood.

To approach a birth-chart holistically and aesthetically is to realize:

**1** A birth-chart is the archetypal pattern of individual selfhood for the person to whom it refers. It is something to be lived and actualized to its fullest possible extent.

**2** No birth-chart, considered as a whole, is either superior or inferior to any other, though one birth-chart may be more or less suited for a particular and limited function or experience.

**3** There are no "good" or "evil" signs, planets, houses, or aspects. All astrological factors are found in all forms of life manifestation, in varying degrees.

## ELEMENTS OF THE BIRTH-CHART

Every birth-chart is composed of the following elements or factors:

**1** The two axes that divide the space surrounding the nativity (birth) into four equal 90° sections of space. However, because this

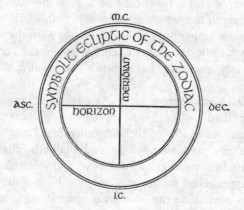

Figure 1

space is distorted when focused at the place of birth, a chart rarely consists of four equal sections of the zodiac. The horizontal axis (see Figure 1), called the horizon, connects the ascendant to its opposite point, the descendant; the vertical axis, the meridian, connects the *medium coeli* (M.C.), popularly known as the midheaven, to the *imum coeli* (I.C.), which is its polar opposite. The horizon symbolizes the points of solar ascension and descension, while the meridian symbolizes the two points of solar culmination. The exact degree of relationship between the horizon-meridian axes and the ecliptic of the zodiac is determined by the casting of a birth-chart for the exact time and place of birth.* The horizon-meridian axes define the basic structure of a birth-chart.

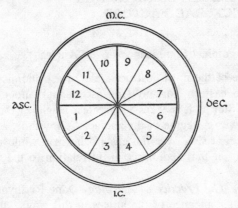

Figure 2

**2** The twelve houses, individually referred to by the order of their position, established by the threefold division of the four quadrants defined by the horizon-meridian (see Figure 2).

**3** The symbolic ecliptic of the zodiac, upon which the twelve signs (of 30° each) are inscribed.

**4** The two "lights" (the Sun and Moon) and the eight planetary bodies, placed within the houses according to their relationship to the zodiac and identified by graphic symbols.

The basic visual impression of the birth-chart is a circle divided into twelve houses (though divisions into four and eight sections are not totally unheard of), with degrees and signs of the zodiac

* Complete instructions for casting a birth-chart are included in Appendix I.

inscribed along the periphery of the circle, describing the boundaries (house cusps) of each house. Within the houses are inscribed the symbols for the two "lights" and the eight planets, with the degrees and signs of the zodiac they occupy. Some astrologers use additional visual indicators: lines may be drawn between planets forming aspects (planetary relationships of an angular nature); also, abstract factors involving planetary syntheses (parts) and planetary orbits (nodes) may be included.

## ASTRONOMICAL SIGNIFICANCE OF STRUCTURAL FACTORS

### The Astronomical Significance of the Angles

This is one of the most abstract areas of astronomical significance. It relates the eastern horizon (the ascendant) and the culminating point of the Sun as it reaches its greatest height in the sky (the medium coeli) with a degree of the zodiac. At any time, a certain degree of the zodiac is rising over the eastern horizon while another degree is culminating at the medium coeli, in relation to the location of the observer.

In his book *The Practice of Astrology* Dane Rudhyar describes the astronomical significance of the angles in this way: "The meridian is the vertical circle which has the polar axis as one of its diameters, and on which the sun is found at noon. In this circle is also found the point overhead (the zenith). The line drawn from this point to the center of the earth is the line of gravity, or plumb-line. The horizon and the meridian are always at a 90° angle to each other. As they are prolonged through space they constitute two celestial planes which divide the entire universe into four quarters. . . . In usual practice each of these four departments of experience (quarters) is divided into three equal 30° sections of space (but not of the zodiac); and thus the twelve houses of the chart are formed." However, the choice of a method by which to divide a chart into twelve houses is one of the most controversial areas in astrology, as we will see later.

## The Astronomical Significance of the Ecliptic

The ecliptic is the apparent annual path of the Sun in the sky. Modern astrologers realize (as did some of their ancient counterparts) that the Sun is relatively stationary in space, while the earth orbits the Sun. But to the observer on earth, the Sun appears to be orbiting the earth, and the perimeter of the plane of this apparent orbit is the ecliptic, upon which the zodiac of signs is symbolically inscribed. One should be careful not to confuse the zodiac of constellations with the zodiac of signs, the latter being a basic astrological frame of reference and a magnetic field surrounding the earth.

## Explanation of the Geocentric and Heliocentric
## Systems of Astronomy

The geocentric (*geo*—earth; *centric*—centered) system of astronomy observes physical phenomena within the solar system (and on a larger scale, within the universe) as they appear from the position of the earthbound observer. This system is almost universally employed by astrologers. The use of this system gives rise to additional astronomical phenomena including the apparent motion of the Sun and retrograde motion (planets appear to have a reverse motion when they reach certain points on the geocentric orbits).†

The heliocentric (*helio*—sun; *centric*—centered) system of astronomy observes physical phenomena within the solar system (and the universe) as they relate to our Sun. It is the only system recognized by most "educated" people and is the system used by "science" teachers in our elementary and high schools to illustrate the nature of the solar system and the universe. This system is, of course, scientifically valid, but it is not entirely adequate for astrological adaptation, because it is not a person-centered system. Natal astrology requires at least an earth-centered system of astronomy. In a very true sense, natal astrology should be "person-centric." A heliocentric system may be adequate for the astrological use of beings living on the Sun, but not for earth beings. There is one area of astrological symbolism that does use heliocentric information: the study of planetary nodes, discussed later in Part Two; however, even this is in reference to the earth, since the geocentric zodiac is used.

† For a discussion of astronomical facts, see Appendix VI.

# 2

# THE AXES OF INDIVIDUAL SELFHOOD AND THE CIRCLE OF HOUSES

*Natal Astrology is the practical application of the "squaring of the circle"—the Conscious Way: TAO. Fourfold T-A-O gives the 12 signs or houses of astrology ($3 \times 4 = 12$).*

DANE RUDHYAR

## THE CYCLIC PROCESS

A great inadequacy of the traditional form of astrology is its failure to regard the houses (as well as other astrological factors) as involving and evolving parts of a whole process. The procedure of traditional texts is simply to list the meaning, key words, and rulerships of the houses (and other astrological factors) as if one house were only loosely related to its precedent and succedent, and almost never considered as a part of a process of unfoldment. Such a presentation of astrological factors naturally leaves gaps in the reader's understanding of the subject matter.

Humanistic astrology, however, holds that the meaning of any individual factor, house, sign, planet, or planetary aspect is inherent in and dependent upon (1) its relation to the nature of the frame of reference (process) as a whole, the frames of reference being the houses, signs, planets, or aspects, and (2) its sequence in this whole process, its relationship to the other individual parts of the same frame of reference. A house, sign, planet, or whatever has meaning and significance only because it is a part of a whole cyclic process.

All things that exist possess an individual cyclic order, as well as being a part of a larger cyclic order, which times its birth, integration, and rebirth. This is the structural pattern of dynamic unfoldment ("from seed to seed"), and it is operative at all levels of activity.

The following description of the cyclic process is a brief statement of the basis of meaning for all astrological factors of a cyclic nature.

## THE BEGINNING

The *beginning* of the cyclic process is a moment of unity and ONENESS, which immediately ceases to be a manifestation of external unity and becomes a process. This process is twofold: involutionary and evolutionary. The involutionary hemicycle succeeds the beginning and involutes *life* into *form* or *matter*. During this phase, life becomes involved with the building of organisms and structures and the continual complexification and differentiation of individual structural patterns. This is the process of the One becoming the Many.

## THE MIDDLE

The *middle* is the point of repolarization, from the complexification and differentiation of structural patterns to the creative release of their contents. This repolarization usually involves some sort of crisis, and often the repolarization is not successfully accomplished. If the transition from the involutionary to the evolutionary hemicycle fails, eventual breakdown and disintegration of the mental functions, if not of the entire organism, may take place. If, on the other hand, the process of repolarization is successful, the following phase will be one of growth in meaning and consciousness.

The axis that extends from the mid-point of the involutionary hemicycle to the mid-point of the evolutionary hemicycle also constitutes a "middle," where the involutionary process of differentiation and organic growth reaches its apex and the evolutionary process of conscious and social expansion reaches its fullest point.

## THE END

The *end* is the moment of in-gathering of the energies and fruits of the just-completed cycle. It is a "seed-moment," when all that has been actualized during the cycle is formulated into a highly condensed form, which will provide the structural patterns for the next cycle.

# THE ANGLES

## HORIZON-MERIDIAN
## AS THE AXES OF INDIVIDUAL SELFHOOD

The axes of the horizon and the meridian define the basic structure of individual selfhood, the "dharma" of the individual and his orientation to his basic life experiences. These axes of individual selfhood provide the basic frame of reference that embraces all the individual's experiences, the focus for his subjective-objective consciousness and his personal-social experiences, and the lens through which his solar energy is released. The axes consist of four points called the *angles:* the ascendant, descendant, M.C., and I.C.

### THE ASCENDANT

The ascendant, the place on the birth-chart where the sun is found at sunrise (popularly referred to as "the rising"), is the point of individual selfhood. It is the symbolic point of individualization, defining (by its sign and degree) the person as a unique, self-conscious individual. It reveals the particular type of activity (sign) that provides the person with the type of experiences he must live through if he is to realize his destiny. The individual's attitude toward himself and his particular quality of self-awareness are also symbolized by the ascendant. The ascendant is the most personal and distinct factor of a birth-chart. It is the symbol of the person's first emergence into independent selfhood; it carries the "seed of the self," and expresses the quality of the time of birth. It presents the individual with basic needs, the need for self-awareness being the most primary. Within the degree of the ascendant is also found the answer to this particular need, the "way through" the experience.

### THE DESCENDANT

As the ascendant's polar opposite (the descendant is always 180° from the ascendant), the descendant is the point where the sun is positioned at sunset. The descendant of a birth-chart is the point of awareness of others, polarizing the ascendant's quality of self-awareness. It defines the individual's approach to interpersonal relationships and to relationships in general. The processes of collecti-

THE AXES OF INDIVIDUAL SELFHOOD 29

vization and socialization are also represented by this point. It reveals the type of activity that provides the individual with the experiences he needs in order to realize the significance of others.

## THE MEDIUM COELI (M.C.)

The medium coeli is the point of social integration and political power, revealing the individual's orientation to social experiences. It symbolizes the type of activity that provides the experiences that should assist the individual in the realization of his social position. The M.C. describes the individual's position in the outer world and the power he has over others (or the power others have over him). Marc Edmund Jones states that the M.C. is "where the individual must give proof of himself as a responsible member of society." But the medium coeli is something more than just a symbol of mundane power and responsibility.

Astrologers generally correlate the M.C. with the cardinal point *south,* because the sun always appears in the south from the perspective of the northern temperate zone. However, this is a basic distortion of the meaning of the medium coeli, which is supposed to be the point where the sun is found when it has reached its greatest height in the sky (around noon). It is on this premise that I correlate the M.C. with *up. Up* has significance in all symbolic languages as being *masculine,* the sky, the father principle, and, most significantly, *spirit power.* When one considers the M.C. in this light, it becomes obvious that it is the point of solar sustainment, describing the individual's spiritual temperament and the quality of his spiritual release. In short, the medium coeli defines the individual's social integration and political power on one level and his spiritual identity on another.

## THE IMUM COELI (I.C.)

The I.C. is the polar opposite of the M.C. It describes the point where the process of growth and differentiation has reached its apex. The individual's personal integration is symbolized here, but this integration is limited to a small and well-defined area of activity. The I.C. is the matrix of personal growth, the psychological womb. Astrologers correlate the cardinal point *north* to the I.C., resulting in the same distortion as assigning south to the M.C. *Down* more clearly symbolizes the nature of the I.C. *Down* symbolizes the *feminine* aspect of nature, the earth, the mother principle; it is the most secure place we know, our *root*. Whatever *down* means is what the I.C. is, and whatever *up* means is what the M.C. is, in terms of astrological symbolism. Astrology correlates symbols, using them to describe other symbols.

## HORIZON-MERIDIAN AS THE AXES OF AWARENESS AND GROWTH

### Horizon as the Axis of Awareness

In the birth-chart the horizon is the horizontal line, which divides the upper and lower hemispheres (see Figure 3). It represents in graphic form the symbolic surface of the earth, with the sky above and the horizon and the earth below. This axis forms the two poles of human awareness: self-awareness and awareness of others.

### Meridian as the Axis of Growth and Power

In the birth-chart the meridian is the vertical line, which divides the eastern from the western hemispheres. This axis defines the two poles of human experience: organic growth and political (or, if transmuted, spiritual) power.

### Organic Oneness of the Horizon-Meridian Axes

When the angles are understood in this manner, one may visualize the horizon as the surface of the earth, separating the earth from the sky, and the meridian as a line extending from the root (the I.C.) to the seed point (point of origin), where the earth meets the sky and the root meets the stem (medium coeli), and, in the case of the actualized man or woman, to the "flower of the spiritual self."

## THE QUADRANTS

The axes of the horizon-meridian divide the astrological chart into four quadrants, or spheres of consciousness and experience (see Figure 3).

The first, or lower-eastern, quadrant, carrying the significance of the ascendant, is the area bounded by the ascendant and the I.C. It signifies intuition (in Jung's terminology) and the discovery of the

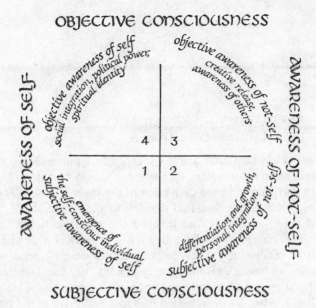

OBJECTIVE CONSCIOUSNESS

AWARENESS OF SELF

objective awareness of self
social integration, political power,
spiritual identity

objective awareness of not-self
creative release,
awareness of others

4  3
1  2

the self-conscious individual
emergence of
subjective awareness of self

differentiation and growth
personal integration
subjective awareness of not-self

AWARENESS OF NOT-SELF

SUBJECTIVE CONSCIOUSNESS

Figure 3

self in the subjective sense. Subjective self-awareness and the area of most-intense organic growth.

The second, or lower-western, quadrant, which carries the significance of the I.C., is the area between the I.C. and the descendant. It symbolizes feelings (in Jung's terminology) and instinctive, spontaneous judgment of one's experiences. Subjective awareness of the not-self. Growth in personal integration.

The third, or upper-western, quadrant, carrying the significance of the descendant, is the area between the descendant and the M.C. It represents sensation (in Jung's terminology) or the objective awareness of the not-self. Creative release through relationships and social participation.

The fourth, or upper-eastern, quadrant, which carries the significance of the M.C., is the area between the medium coeli and the ascendant. It signifies thinking (in Jung's terminology) and the objective awareness of the self and of one's spiritual-social identity.

## NUMEROLOGICAL SIGNIFICANCE OF THE CIRCLE OF HOUSES

It has been said that astrology is applied numerology, since the foundations of astrological symbolism are laid in numerology. This applies particularly to the derivation of the twelve houses. The houses are the result of the threefold division of the quadrants of an astrological chart, a process that involves the multiplication of 4, which symbolizes concrete manifestation (the angles), by 3, symbolizing the three modes of expression and consciousness operative within all forms of manifestation, giving rise to 12, the number of the archetypal houses (and signs). Twelve also carries the value of three; $1 + 2 = 3$. Also, by the addition of 3 to 4 we arrive at the number 7, the symbol of the cyclo-cosmic process. These numbers (3 and 4) are the base upon which astrological symbolism is built. They are the first two numbers, according to some Pythagorean systems of mathematics, and have significance in all systems of philosophy and symbolism as representing the three qualities of expression (the trinity of all religions) and the concrete world.

The threefold division of the quadrants defines the areas within the quadrants where each of the three qualities of expression is dominant. That is, there are twelve houses, three within each quadrant, each one of the qualities being predominant in one house within each quadrant. This brings us once more to the numbers 3 and 4: the twelve houses are divided by the three qualities, each dominating four houses.

## THE THREE QUALITIES OF HOUSE EXPRESSION

### The Angular, or Active, Quality

The houses following the angles (1st, 4th, 7th, and 10th) are referred to as the angular (traditionally), or active, houses. The quality dominant within these areas is of an activating, initiating, and individualizing nature. They set processes into motion and symbolize the primary areas of experience. When a planet is found in one of these houses, it is said to be a factor of motivation; the closer it is to the angle, the more intensely this motivation should be manifest. This quality deals with experiences that *generate energy*.

### The Succedent, or Reactive, Quality

Houses following the active houses (2nd, 5th, 8th, and 11th) are called succedent (traditionally), or reactive. These houses refer to the reaction of the action first expressed in the active houses. They are of a creative significance and represent the expansion, focaliza-tion, and consolidation of the processes initiated by the active houses. This quality deals with experiences that *concentrate form*.

### The Cadent, or Resultant, Quality

The cadent (traditional term), or resultant, houses precede the angles, being the 3rd, 6th, 9th, and 12th houses. These houses are of a universalizing and harmonizing nature, tending to fulfill or disintegrate the processes initiated by the active houses and focused by the reactive houses. This quality deals with experiences that *disperse consciousness*.

## THE CYCLE OF THE TWELVE HOUSES

Once the significance of the horizon-meridian, the hemispheres, the quadrants, and the qualities of house expression are understood, the significance of the twelve houses follows naturally.

The twelve houses symbolize the archetypal areas of individual experience, expression, and circumstance. An interpretation of the twelve houses follows, with their traditional meanings (which should not be overlooked) and humanistic meanings, as well as their qualities of expression, key words, and cyclic meanings. Included also is the meaning of a house when it is found particularly focused or emphasized in a birth-chart. All the meanings given here are necessarily brief and general and should not be rigidly interpreted.

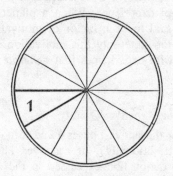

## FIRST HOUSE

*Expression:*   Active/generative
*Process:*      Emergence of self-awareness
*Purpose:*      Conscious selfhood
*Experience:*   Self-consciousness

*Traditional Meaning:*   The personality, the body, the conditions of birth.

*Humanistic Meaning:*   Awareness of self. The most predominant or superficial characteristics projected by the personality. The physical appearance.

*Cyclic Meaning:*   The initial emergence of the individual from the sea of the unconscious. A phase during which the person has little real sense of self, corresponding to the first two years and four months of life.

*In Emphasis:*   Denotes a person who is apparently open and outgoing, though in many ways insecure. If a planet is found in this house, close to the ascendant, its function should be very evident in the personality and physical appearance of the person and should show the way to self-discovery.

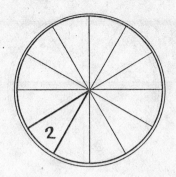

## SECOND HOUSE

*Expression:*   Reactive/concentrative
*Process:*   Identification with substance
*Purpose:*   Definition of self
*Experience:*   Attachment

*Traditional Meaning:* Possessions and one's attitude toward possessions.

*Humanistic Meaning:* Identification of self with substance. The span of most rapid growth of awareness and separatism. Inherent qualities.

*Cyclic Meaning:* Consciousness becomes focused upon substance and matter; the sense of self becomes more defined and the person begins to identify himself with what is "his."

*In Emphasis:* Denotes a person who should be able to focus his attention well upon practical matters or material things.

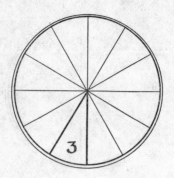

## THIRD HOUSE

*Expression:*   Resultant/dispersive

*Process:*   Relationship with substance

*Purpose:*   To know

*Experience:*   Association

*Traditional Meaning:*   The lower mind, writings, brethren, and short journeys.

*Humanistic Meaning:*   The concrete mind, mental functions, sense impressions, and the associative faculties. Relationship with substance. The initial emergence of the understanding of relationship.

*Cyclic Meaning:*   Focalization of consciousness upon relationships existing between the individual person and his environment. The desire to know the nature of one's environment.

*In Emphasis:*   The person should be concerned with intellectual activities, though too much attention may be given to superficialities.

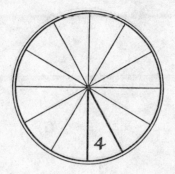

## FOURTH HOUSE

*Expression:*   Active/generative
*Process:*   Personal integration
*Purpose:*   To establish
*Experience:*   Stability

*Traditional Meaning:*   The home, the conditions of home life, security, and the mother.

*Humanistic Meaning:*   Concretization of self. Personal integration within a well-defined and limited area of activity. The parent who represents inner security.

*Cyclic Meaning:*   The person integrates a part of his environment (substance) within himself, thus firmly establishing a base of operation.

*In Emphasis:*   Denotes the type of person who can do well by establishing himself firmly within a defined area of activity, though he is insecure if he must relate outside of that area. If a planet is found on or near the I.C., its function will be deeply involved with the process of personal integration.

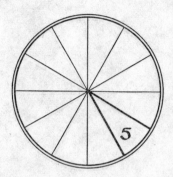

## FIFTH HOUSE

*Expression:*   Reactive/concentrative
*Process:*      Exteriorization of self
*Purpose:*      Self-expression
*Experience:*   Social insecurity

*Traditional Meaning:*  Children, pleasure, speculation, amusement, creativity, and casual relationships.

*Humanistic Meaning:*  The exteriorization and creative release of self. Personal displays and the desire for social relationships.

*Cyclic Meaning:*  The person becomes more secure as he expands his area of activity and his powers of self-expression.

*In Emphasis:*  Denotes the type of person who should seek to express himself in a creative manner in all that he or she does.

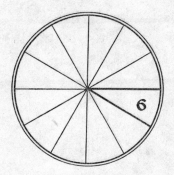

## SIXTH HOUSE

*Expression:*   Resultant/dispersive
*Process:*      Introspection
*Purpose:*      Self-improvement
*Experience:*   Personal conflict

*Traditional Meaning:*   Health, employment, accidents, and service to others.

*Humanistic Meaning:*   Personal inertia and limitations, conflicts resulting from the exteriorization of self. Self-judgment and introspection.

*Cyclic Meaning:*   The person, once secure as an individual, now deals with his particular inadequacies through analytical introspection and critical judgment.

*In Emphasis:*   Attention should be given to matters of self-improvement. There may be a tendency to be intolerant and overly critical of others.

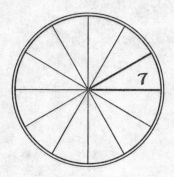

## SEVENTH HOUSE

*Expression:*   Active/generative
*Process:*      Objectification of consciousness
*Purpose:*      To relate
*Experience:*   Social shock

*Traditional Meaning:* Marriage, partnership, contracts, and open enemies.

*Humanistic Meaning:* Human relatedness and interchange. The transition of consciousness from the subjective to the objective realm. Awareness of others and of the social sphere.

*Cyclic Meaning:* The process of introspection takes the individual to the threshold of the objective realm of relationship and participation.

*In Emphasis:* A stress is placed upon social activities and relationships. If a planet is found on or near the descendant, its function should be involved in the realization of the meaning of relationship.

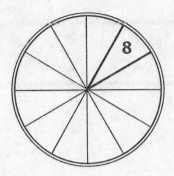

## EIGHTH HOUSE

*Expression:*    Reactive/generative
*Process:*    Expansion of relationship
*Purpose:*    Transcendence of human limitations
*Experience:*    Identification

*Traditional Meaning:*    Death, the occult, legacies, business, and sex.

*Humanistic Meaning:*    The transcendence of human limitations through interpersonal relationships. Identification with something greater than one's self. Expansion of world view and the exchange, regeneration, and transmutation of one's vital energies.

*Cyclic Meaning:*    Self becomes identified with others. Social participation with a limited and defined area.

*In Emphasis:*    Special attention should be placed upon interpersonal relationships.

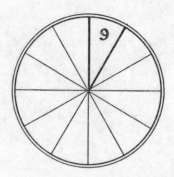

## NINTH HOUSE

*Expression:*    Resultant/dispersive
*Process:*        Expansion of consciousness
*Purpose:*        To understand
*Experience:*    Search for meaning

*Traditional Meaning:*   Philosophy, religion, long journeys, and matters of law.

*Humanistic Meaning:*   The abstract mind and the faculties of recognition and correlation of relationships. The power to understand the meaning of existence.

*Cyclic Meaning:*   The expansion of consciousness. The mind becomes aware of the interplay existing between relationships.

*In Emphasis:*   Denotes the type of person who would do well by focusing his mind on philosophical matters.

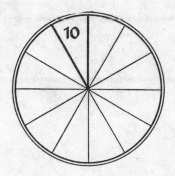

## TENTH HOUSE

*Expression:*   Active/generative

*Process:*   Social participation

*Purpose:*   Collective integration

*Experience:*   Responsibility

*Traditional Meaning:* Position, honor, status, recognition, career, and the father.

*Humanistic Meaning:* Fixation of relationship and one's position and foundation in the outer world. Social participation, political power, and the discovery of one's spiritual identity. The parent who represents the outer world and external security.

*Cyclic Meaning:* Active participation in the outer world. The assumption of responsibility and the realization of one's social and spiritual identity.

*In Emphasis:* Denotes the type of person who could do well by directing his or her energies toward practical, political, and spiritual affairs. If a planet is found on or near the M.C., its function will be involved in the discovery of the individual's social and spiritual identity.

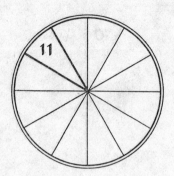

## ELEVENTH HOUSE

*Expression:*   Reactive/concentrative
*Process:*   Fulfillment of one's social position
*Purpose:*   Social expression
*Experience:*   Personal insecurity

*Traditional Meaning:*   Friends, hopes and wishes, social life.

*Humanistic Meaning:*   The exteriorization of one's social position and the influence one's position has upon one's personal life. Progressive politics and social reform. New forms of social expression and relationship.

*Cyclic Meaning:*   The individual has now become a social entity, his social life being all-important, often to the point of abnegation of his own personal identity.

*In Emphasis:*   Denotes the type of person who may find fulfillment through involvement with social or political activities.

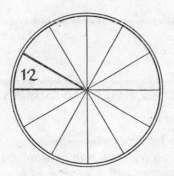

## TWELFTH HOUSE

*Expression:*   Resultant/dispersive
*Process:*       Self-redemption
*Purpose:*       Rebirth
*Experience:*   Personal and social conflicts

*Traditional Meaning:*   Fate, obstacles, confinement, karma, and hidden enemies.

*Humanistic Meaning:*   Conflicts between the individual and society. Social inertia and the limits of the collective-social consciousness. The unconscious, both individual and collective. The process of transformation and rebirth. Accumulated resources, both positive and negative. The inner experiences that bring one to social independence.

*Cyclic Meaning:*   Universalization. Through resolving conflicts of an internal nature, the individual dissolves his relationship with the past cycle, proceeding to the next, carrying with him the seed of the past and his spiritual identity.

*In Emphasis:*   Denotes the type of person whose consciousness is acutely aware of the limitations and inadequacies of the individual and society.

# 3

# THE ZODIAC AND ITS SIGNS

*[One should not] consider the zodiacal signs and the houses of the birth-chart as separate entities with absolute prerogatives and sets of characters, rather as sections of complete cycles (or circles) having meaning only as parts of a whole.*

DANE RUDHYAR

## TWO TYPES OF ZODIACS

It is essential to understand, before exploring the meaning of the signs of the zodiac, the nature of the zodiac itself. The zodiac of signs has nothing to do with the "constellations of the zodiac"; the only thing they hold in common is their names—a great source of confusion. Humanistic astrology uses the zodiac of *signs* as a basic frame of reference because it represents the twelve phases of the cyclic relationship of the sun to the earth. It symbolizes the precession of the seasons and the cycle of organic life on this planet. On the other hand, the zodiac of *constellations* refers to groups of "fixed" stars that have been given names that are the same as the signs of the zodiac.

## SIDEREAL ASTROLOGY AND THE SIDEREAL ZODIAC

There is, however, a relatively small group of vocal, "scientifically oriented" astrologers who claim that the zodiac of constellations (sidereal zodiac) is the only true zodiac for astrological work. This school of astrological thought (sidereal astrology) has been promoted primarily by Cyril Fagan, on the basis of "extensive research into ancient records." He states that about 2,500 years ago the sidereal zodiac coincided with the tropical zodiac (zodiac of signs). The two zodiacs, however, no longer coincide due to the precession of the equinoxes—caused by a twisting motion of the earth's polar axis. Mr. Fagan believes that shortly after the time when the two zodiacs coincided, astrologers made a grave error by adopting the tropical zodiac of signs.

In their astrological practice, sidereal astrologers subtract a certain number of degrees from the positions of the planets and angles given in the reference tables for the tropical zodiac, as ephemerides and tables of houses for the sidereal zodiac are difficult to obtain. Today, the zodiac of signs is about 26° in advance of that generally acknowledged as the sidereal zodiac. But there is dissent among sidereal astrologers as to where the zodiac of constellations begins; this is, of course, further complicated if one realizes that the "fixed" stars are not actually stationary, they just move slowly; meaning that the constellations and the sidereal zodiac itself have changed during the past 2,500 years.

## ZODIAC OF SIGNS, OR THE TROPICAL ZODIAC

The zodiac of signs is, of course, simply the ecliptic divided into twelve sections. This zodiac is called "the tropical zodiac" because it coincides with the seasons, the beginning of the zodiac coinciding with the vernal equinox in the Northern Hemisphere.

## SIGNIFICANCE OF THE ZODIAC

The zodiac of signs is symbolic of the formative powers of the universe, which are focused upon earth and within human beings. The zodiac as a whole has been described as being representative of the macrocosm, the Heavenly Man of which our earth is but a cell. Every sign is representative of an archetypal quality of release of energy as well as the expression of an archetypal human activity.

In *Astrology of the Personality,* Dane Rudhyar refers to the zodiac: "It is an abstraction and a symbol, just as the Holy City with its twelve gates—in Biblical allegory—is an abstraction and a symbol. The zodiac is the Wall that separates all inhabitants of the Earth's surface from the universe. Symbolically, this Wall has twelve gates, twelve signs of the zodiac, twelve channels through which universal energies flow."

The zodiac (as well as the houses and planets) should not be taken to be objects that exist only someplace far off in space. Rather, they are archetypal symbols, which exist everywhere, within us as well as within everything else.

## ZODIAC AS SUBSTANCE

The zodiac consists of four crucial points symbolized by the equinoxes (vernal and autumnal) and the solstices (summer and winter). The equinoxes are the points of the greatest momentum and repolarization, when the days and nights are equal. The solstices are the points of least momentum, when the days and nights are not equal and the sun is found to the extreme north or south, when the "qualities of the polarities of life are to be felt in the purest way. [From this evolves] the meaning of the characterizations of the four crucial periods of the year in terms of the four 'elements': Fire, Earth, Air and Water."

### Collective, Organic, and Cyclic Meaning
### of the Equinoxes and Solstices

From the vernal equinox to the autumnal equinox the day forces are dominant in nature; the days are longer than the nights and the emphasis is on organic growth and differentiation, the process of personalization. From the autumnal equinox to the vernal equinox the night forces are dominant; the nights are longer than the days and the emphasis is on the "in-gathering," collectivizing, and universalizing processes of nature.

*Vernal Equinox (Aries) to Summer Solstice (Cancer).*

This is the period of the most intense organic growth. At the vernal equinox the organic life of the earth repolarizes; the sun enters the Northern Hemisphere, and organic life begins a new cycle of objective manifestation.

*Summer Solstice (Cancer) to Autumnal Equinox (Libra).*

At the summer solstice, the phase of intense organic growth reaches its apex as the day forces overwhelm the night forces, only lasting a moment before the sun enters the return path to equilibrium (equinox).

*Autumnal Equinox (Libra) to Winter Solstice (Capricorn).*

With the autumnal equinox and the harvesting of the fruit of the summer comes the return to latency or organic and objective (above the ground) manifestation. It marks the return to the seed condition and the collective in-gathering of life.

*Winter Solstice (Capricorn) to Vernal Equinox (Aries).*

At the winter solstice, the night forces are at their apex and the seed is left as the hope of future manifestation. At this point the night forces must begin their decline and give way to the day forces and, eventually, to the vernal equinox, when the seed gives birth to the leaf.

## MEANING OF THE ELEMENTS

As explained above, the division of the zodiac by the four cardinal points (equinoxes and solstices) renders an additional group of zodiacal factors: the *elements*. The elements define the *type of substance* being expressed by each sign. That is, every sign expresses the substance manifested in one of the equinoxes or solstices, being either Fire, Earth, Air, or Water.

*Fire.*

The fire element in astrological symbolism represents the principle of animation, vitality, and action. It refers to experiences that are intense, emotional, and individual. The vernal equinox.

*Earth.*

The earth element symbolizes the principle of stability. It refers to the practical, mundane, and collective affairs of life. The winter solstice.

*Air.*

The air element represents the principle of adaptability. It refers to life experiences that involve adaptation and the use of the intellect. It is of a collective nature. The autumnal equinox.

*Water.*

The water element symbolizes the principle of universality. It refers to sensory, emotional, and creative life experiences. The summer solstice.

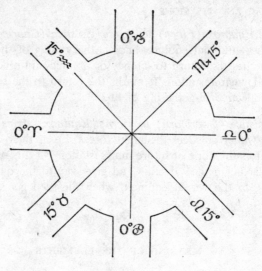

Figure 4

## ZODIAC AS ENERGY

The division of the zodiac by its crucial points results in the definition of the four basic types of cosmic substance, substance being the primary necessity for manifestation. As Rudhyar states in *The Astrology of Personality,* "Energy is not very different from substance. It is substance activated and released, . . . as modern physics has shown most definitely. Thus we can expect the principle of 'energy differentiation' to be similar to that of 'substance differentiation.' Both are based on the principle of polar dualism, of action and reaction. . . . The *energy-zodiac* will thus be eight-fold, while the *substance-zodiac* is four-fold." This division by eight is simply the bisection of the areas defined by the four crucial points, giving us four additional factors, the mid-points between the equinoxes and the solstices (Figure 4). These points refer to the area of maximum dynamic intensity within the span or quadrant of the zodiac defined by two angles.

These points of maximum intensity are the four portals through which cosmic energy flows, the "Four Gates of Avataric Descent." They represent the creative powers of the universe, which are often symbolized by the Bull, the Lion, the Eagle, and the Angel, which are said to guard the four corners of the universe. In basic astrological terms they are: 15° Taurus, 15° Leo, 15° Scorpio, and 15° Aquarius.

## ZODIAC AS FORM

The substance and energy that have been released by the zodiac must be controlled and given *form* in order to be manifest. All *forms of energy* are bound by the Pythagorean axiom "Everything in the universe is divisible by three." All forms of energy involve an action, a reaction, and the interaction between action and reaction. Thus it is only logical for the *form zodiac* to be based on the threefold division of the zodiac. This threefold division gives rise to the *modes* or *qualities of relationship between energy and form.* Each sign carries the meaning of one mode.

*Cardinal, or Initiatory, Mode.*

The cardinal mode is the form of energy expressed at the equinoxes and solstices. It refers to the principle of change and momentum. It represents active and intense life experiences. This mode *generates power.*

*Fixed, or Focal, Mode.*

The fixed mode *concentrates* and focalizes energy, thus symbolizing the principle of definition and structure. It projects the cardinal experience, giving to it depth and meaning. The fifteenth degree of the fixed signs is the point of maximum intensity, where power is found in its most *concentrated form.*

*Mutable, or Common, Mode.*

The mutable mode *distributes* the energy that has been concentrated and released by the fixed mode. It symbolizes the principle of flexibility and adaptation. This mode combines and integrates the cardinal and fixed modes within itself. It distributes the power generated by the cardinal signs and concentrated by the fixed signs.


## ZODIAC AS RELEASE OF POWER

We now return to examine the function of the four points or portals through which *power is released.*

The nature of the power released through these portals depends upon the nature of the energy used. The fixed signs, through which power is concentrated and released, follow the cardinal signs, where power is generated. There are two types of cardinal signs: those which generate equinoctial power (Aries and Libra) and those which generate solstitial power (Cancer and Capricorn).

The points of release may, then, be divided into two basic categories: those dealing with equinoctial power and those dealing with solstitial power.

### 15° Taurus and 15° Scorpio

The fifteenth degrees of the signs Taurus and Scorpio deal with equinoctial power. Equinoctial power is generated by the intense dynamism of the equinoctial signs (Aries and Libra), signs of the maximum speed of solar declination. The fixed signs that follow the equinoctial cardinal signs must arrest the dynamic activity generated by them, limiting it and bringing it into focus, in terms of *purpose* (Taurus) and *identification* (Scorpio).

### 15° Leo and 15° Aquarius

The fifteenth degrees of Leo and Aquarius deal with the solstitial power, which must produce some kind of manifested activity, either personal (Leo) or collective (Aquarius). The release of this type of power will be manifested as a strong outburst of energy toward the focalization of the personality (Leo) or in the form of a society (Aquarius).

The four points of release may also be examined in relation to the hemisphere of the zodiac in which they are found. The fifteenth degrees of Taurus and Leo are part of the day hemisphere. They are involved in the release of "individualizing power." The fifteenth degrees of Scorpio and Aquarius are involved in the release of collectivizing power (night hemisphere), of the expansion of the individual into the collective, or universal, realms.

## CYCLIC FORMULA OF THE FOUR PORTALS*

15° Taurus (the Bull) represents the power released toward the formation of an individual being.

15° Leo (the Lion) symbolizes the power released by the individual being.

* Adapted from *Astrology of Personality*, by Dane Rudhyar.

15° Scorpio (the Eagle) represents the power released toward the formation of the universal being.

15° Aquarius (the Angel) symbolizes the power released by the universal being.

## CYCLIC FORMULA
## OF THE ELEMENTS AND MODES†

At spring equinox:

|  |  |
|---|---|
| Fire power is generated | by Aries |
| then concentrated | through earth—Taurus |
| and distributed | by air—Gemini. |

At summer solstice:

|  |  |
|---|---|
| Water power is generated | by Cancer |
| then concentrated | through fire—Leo |
| and distributed | by earth—Virgo. |

At autumnal equinox:

|  |  |
|---|---|
| Air power is generated | by Libra |
| then concentrated | through water—Scorpio |
| and distributed | by fire—Sagittarius. |

At winter solstice:

|  |  |
|---|---|
| Earth power is generated | by Capricorn |
| then concentrated | through air—Aquarius |
| and distributed | by water—Pisces. |

## THE MEANING OF THE SIGNS OF THE ZODIAC

The twelve signs of the zodiac are arrived at by the same logic that gave us the twelve houses: the division of the circle (the ecliptic) by 4 (the equinoxes and solstices), and the 4 by 3. The signs deal with archetypal forms and energies and should not be mistaken for the houses, which deal with the most individual realms of experience.

† Adapted from *Astrology of Personality*, by Dane Rudhyar.

Aries

## ARIES, the first sign

*Quality:*　　Cardinal/fire
*Principle:*　Will
*Process:*　　Being
*Purpose:*　　Conscious selfhood

*Concrete Meaning:*　Desire, initiative, courage, and impulsiveness.

*Abstract Meaning:*　The process of the formation of self. The concept of self and the primordial structure of the individual.

*Cyclic Meaning:*　The day and night forces are equal. The initial emergence of the individual consciousness from the undifferentiated sea of unconscious. The originating impulse.

*In Emphasis:*　A need to develop one's sense of selfhood, structure, and limits.

*Human Anatomy:*　The head.

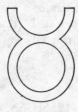

Taurus

## TAURUS, the second sign

*Quality:*　　Fixed/earth
*Principle:*　Self-exertion
*Process:*　　Identification with substance

*Purpose:*    Self-substantiation

*Concrete Meaning:*    Possessiveness and practicality. Inertia and determination.

*Abstract Meaning:*    Self-consciousness through identification of self with substance. Methodical orientation.

*Cyclic Meaning:*    Focalization of Arian impulses, giving to them more depth and meaning. Self establishing itself in a tangible manner.

*15° Taurus:*    Practical release of the power and purpose of personal productivity.

*In Emphasis:*    Purpose and productivity seen as all-important. A need to understand the meaning of what is produced.

*Human Anatomy:*    The neck and ears.

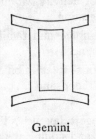

Gemini

## GEMINI, the third sign

*Quality:*    Mutable/air
*Principle:*    Association
*Process:*    Expansion of relationship
*Purpose:*    Personal security

*Concrete Meaning:*    The concrete mind. Changeability, duality, and restlessness. Literary and academic matters.

*Abstract Meaning:*    Mind functioning within the personal sphere. The associative faculties. Creation of systems and techniques. The recognition of concrete relationships.

*Cyclic Meaning:*    Exteriorization of the Arian impulses focalized by Taurus. Expansion of relationship and the formation of personality.

*In Emphasis:*    Constant expansion of one's field of relationship. A need to penetrate the surface of things.

*Human Anatomy:*    The shoulders, arms, hands, and lungs.

Cancer

## CANCER, the fourth sign

*Quality:*    Cardinal/water
*Principle:*    Growth through personal repolarization
*Process:*    Focalization of activity within a limited area
*Purpose:*    Personal integration

*Concrete Meaning:*  The home and family. Receptivity, sensitivity, and feelings. Maternal instincts.

*Abstract Meaning:*  Personal integration within a well-defined area of operation. Concrete selfhood and a concrete basis for the expression of selfhood.

*Cyclic Meaning:*  The longest day meets the shortest night. The apex of the process of growth and complexification. The formation of a firm basis of operation.

*In Emphasis:*  Concerned with the establishment of a firm center of integration; likely to feel insecure when forced to relate on unfamiliar ground. A need for focalized consciousness and assumption of responsibility toward others for conscious participation in a social whole.

*Human Anatomy:*  The chest, breast, and stomach.

## LEO, the fifth sign

*Quality:*    Fixed/fire
*Principle:*    Self-expression
*Process:*    Exteriorization of self
*Purpose:*    Creative release of individual purpose

*Concrete Meaning:*  Self-expression and creativity. Self-confidence, flamboyance, pleasure, and authority. The emotions.

Leo

*Abstract Meaning:* Dramatic exteriorization of the personality as a means of gaining social recognition and increasing self-assurance as a social entity. Social insecurity.

*Cyclic Meaning:* The power to express the self, which has been given concrete foundations through the Cancer span. The person, once secure in his own identity, seeks to expand his field of activity by embracing the social realm, the first step in becoming a "social personage."

*15° Leo:* The creative release of the power and purpose of the individual.

*In Emphasis:* A need to express oneself without assuming an autocratic position.

*Human Anatomy:* The heart and spine.

Virgo

## VIRGO, the sixth sign

*Quality:*     Mutable/earth
*Principle:*   Adjustment through discrimination
*Process:*     Adoption of technique

*Purpose:*   Emotional repolarization

*Concrete Meaning:*   Mental analysis and discrimination. Fastidiousness, detail, and study. Service and health.

*Abstract Meaning:*   Discrimination based upon critical analysis of the outcome of action. Adjustment and judgment of self and life. Personal reorientation, self-criticism, and the process of self-perfection.

*Cyclic Meaning:*   The individual's preparation for participation within a greater whole (Libra) calls for this phase of introspection and purification.

*In Emphasis:*   Identity crises. A need for self-improvement, often under the guidance of a teacher or "guru."

*Human Anatomy:*   The intestines, solar plexus, and spleen.

Libra

## LIBRA, the seventh sign

*Quality:*      Cardinal/air
*Principle:*    Idealism
*Process:*      Human interchange
*Purpose:*      Individual participation within a social whole

*Concrete Meaning:*   Social consciousness and relationships with others. Comparison and evaluation of people and situations. Appreciation of art, beauty, and harmony.

*Abstract Meaning:*   The establishment of a definite set of values, ideals, and "social standards." The objectification of consciousness through association and co-operation with others.

*Cyclic Meaning:*   The day and night forces are once more equal. The emergence of the individual with a greater whole. Social participation.

*In Emphasis:*   Relationship is all-important—a need to perfect relationships with others.

*Human Anatomy:*   The kidneys and liver.

Scorpio

## SCORPIO, the eighth sign

*Quality:* Fixed/water
*Principle:* Sex, in its creative, dynamic aspect
*Process:* Identification with a greater whole
*Purpose:* To become greater; transcendence

*Concrete Meaning:* Sex, will, jealousy, and death. Magic and occultism. Regeneration.

*Abstract Meaning:* Creative tension and the awareness of duality. The urge to merge and become one with others in order to participate together as a greater organic whole.

*Cyclic Meaning:* The process of individuation and creative participation within a greater whole.

*15° Scorpio:* The creative release of the power and purpose of relationship.

*In Emphasis:* There should be a strong urge to become something greater. Sexual or intense relationships may be a way of fulfilling this urge, at least on one level.

*Human Anatomy:* The sex organs.

## SAGITTARIUS, the ninth sign

*Quality:* Mutable/fire
*Principle:* Abstraction
*Process:* Synthesis and universalization
*Purpose:* Expansion and integration of associations

*Concrete Meaning:* Philosophy, religion, inspiration, and idealism. Academic matters and sports.

Sagittarius

*Abstract Meaning:*  The abstract mind. Mind functioning within the social sphere. The recognition of abstract relationships. Social-cultural-religious affairs.

*Cyclic Meaning:*  The individual's identification and absorption within the social whole.

*In Emphasis:*  A need to search constantly for distant contacts, a concern with social-cultural-religious factors. Often willing to sacrifice anything for the sake of the ideal held highest.

*Human Anatomy:*  The thighs and pelvic region.

Capricorn

## CAPRICORN, the tenth sign

*Quality:*      Cardinal/earth
*Principle:*    Social functioning
*Process:*      Acquisition of social position
*Purpose:*      Social integration

*Concrete Meaning:*  Status, ambition, politics, and law. Reliance upon social structures. Stability and the father.

*Abstract Meaning:*  Acquisition of a social position or assumption of spiritual identity. The concrete basis for relationship. The perfection of the social entity.

*Cyclic Meaning:* The individual becomes socially integrated and the state becomes an all-important factor. The longest night meets the shortest day; the in-gathering forces of nature are at their apex.

*In Emphasis:* Focalization of one's activities upon practical, social, and political affairs. If transmuted: assumption of spiritual identity.

*Human Anatomy:* The skeleton and joints.

Aquarius

## AQUARIUS, the eleventh sign

*Quality:* Fixed/air
*Principle:* Social expression
*Process:* Exteriorization of social position
*Purpose:* Response to social need

*Concrete Meaning:* Science, music, and genius. Political movements and revolutions. Humanitarianism, group and collective ideals.

*Abstract Meaning:* The ability to create and express in social or collective terms. Personal insecurity.

*Cyclic Meaning:* The individual is now a complete social entity, though his own sense of individuality has been sacrificed in the process.

*15° Aquarius:* The release of the power and purpose of social need.

*In Emphasis:* A need to be independent of social and cultural support.

*Human Anatomy:* The legs and ankles.

## PISCES, the twelfth sign

*Quality:* Mutable/water
*Principle:* Repolarization
*Process:* Personal and social conflicts
*Purpose:* Self-redemption

Pisces

*Concrete Meaning:* Impressionability and openness. Mysticism, psychicism, devotion, and fanaticism.

*Abstract Meaning:* The unconscious, both individual and collective. The need for sharp, often violent repolarization as an alternative to wholesale disintegration. Threshold phenomena. In a higher sense: compassion and wholeness.

*Cyclic Meaning:* Universalization of experience. Repolarization from social to personal factors; or self-abnegation and disintegration. The return to the primordial condition.

*In Emphasis:* A need to give relevant meaning to one's intensely personal visions and experiences, rather than giving way to irrationalism or fanaticism.

*Human Anatomy:* The feet and lymphatic system.

## THE QUESTION OF MASCULINE AND FEMININE SIGNS

Traditional astrology assigns a gender to each sign, alternating masculine and feminine (positive and negative) beginning with Aries. Thus the fire and air signs are called masculine, while the water and earth signs are called feminine. This classification can be a source of confused misunderstanding if taken to an extreme and applied rigidly. The "masculine" sign Libra (often, though by no means necessarily, a significator of male homosexuality) suggests that a so-called masculine sign does not necessarily represent what may be commonly regarded as "manliness," while the "feminine" signs do not necessarily represent that which is often considered "womanly."

Nevertheless, there is a great deal of validity in this classification. Perhaps it would be more accurate to consider the fire and air signs as "extroverted" and the earth and water signs "introverted." That is, the fire and air signs tend to direct consciousness outward, toward the formation of a positive relationship with external objects, while the earth and water signs tend to direct consciousness inward, toward the formation of a positive relationship with one's self and the confirmation of both externalized and internalized relationships.

# 4

# THE 360 DEGREES
# AND THEIR SYMBOLS

*The Degree is not merely a subdivision of the zodiacal sign, or the whole of the zodiac. It stands, as an astrological element, alone and in a position of supreme (though little understood) significance. The Degree is the most mysterious element in astrology, and indeed the key to all deeper astrological interpretation. . . . In the Degree we witness the operation of the creative with an individual personality or a particular situation. Here meaning stands revealed—for whosoever knows how to read symbols.*

DANE RUDHYAR

## SIGNIFICANCE OF THE DEGREE IN ASTROLOGY

The degree is the most fundamental element of the zodiac and is in a sense an indivisible unit. It is an archetypal symbol of the individual (day) element of being, containing a quality of being of its own. In a very true sense, the degree is the atom of the zodiac; an individual, "indivisible" unit that acts as the container of fantastic power, in spite of its relatively small mass.

## SYMBOLICAL ASTROLOGY

The assignment of symbolic pictures to the degrees of the zodiac, a practice said to go back as far as ancient Egypt, can be an invaluable device for the astrologer conscious of their meaning and limitations. The purpose of such a symbolic series of images is to relate the essence of each degree to the "viewer." The finest set of degree symbols to date was recorded by Marc Edmund Jones, initially in "Symbolical Astrology," a study course issued in 1931, and later revised and published in 1953 under the title *The Sabian Symbols in Astrology.* A reinterpretation of the Sabian Symbols can be found in Rudhyar's *An Astrological Mandala: The Cycle of Transformation and Its 360 Symbolical Phases* (Random House, 1973), to which the reader is referred for a more detailed exposition of this intriguing subject.

## DEGREE SYMBOLS AND THEIR USE

A degree symbol is a poetic reflection of the archetypal quality of activity operative within the degree it symbolizes. It is an image of potential selfhood and the quality of being focused through the degree. The symbols project an image that describes the essence of the degrees and should not be mistaken for the thing they represent or interpreted literally. For instance, the Sabian Symbol for the twenty-seventh degree of Aquarius, "An ancient pottery bowl filled with violets," suggest the nature of that degree. In the case of a person born with the twenty-seventh degree of Aquarius rising, the symbol should represent a very personal quality, a quality that should be apparent within the person with this degree rising. However, the person should not be mistaken for a "violet" simply because of his or her rising symbol any more than one should believe a person to be a *Viola canadensis* simply because her name happens to be Violet.

Degree symbolism may be applied to any point or planetary position in a birth-chart or any other kind of astrological chart. Of course, the manner in which one interprets these meanings must take into consideration not only the type of astrological chart (birth, horary, etc.) but also the nature of the planet, angle, or whatever is occupying the degree. The symbols refer to a quality released at the moment a degree begins; a new degree begins at the moment a whole degree is exceeded. For instance, 20°01′ to 20°59′ Aries is regarded as 21° Aries, while 20°00′ is 20° Aries.*

## SUB-CYCLIC DEGREE CORRESPONDENCE

Another method of determining the meaning of each degree is through the consideration of sub-cyclic correspondence, existing between a lesser whole or cycle (sign or house) and the greater whole

---

* The early Pythagoreans considered anything less than a whole as imperfect and unthinkable. In a sense, astrology is the study of *all beginnings,* the beginning of individual existence as well as the beginning of any of the 360 degrees of the zodiac.

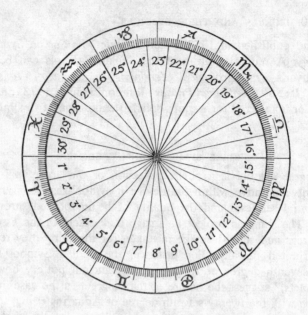

## SUB-CYCLIC CORRESPONDENCE

or cycle (the zodiac or the circle of houses) of which it is a part. This means that each one of the thirty degrees of any sign may be examined by relating the thirty-degree cycle of the sign to the larger cycle of the zodiac. As a result, each degree of any sign may be correlated to twelve specific degrees of the zodiac. For instance, the first degree of any sign corresponds with the first twelve degrees of Aries.

Through the use of this method, one may easily determine how each degree of a particular sign relates to the whole process of the sign itself. In other words, the twenty-fourth degree of Scorpio may be related to the Capricorn (or tenth house) phase of the process represented by the Scorpio.

# 5

# THE PLANETS AND THEIR FUNCTIONS

*The planets are symbolic expressions of functional principles which are found at all levels of functional existence; they refer to nothing in* particular, *but to functions which are found in every organic unit.*

DANE RUDHYAR

## THE PLANETS AND ASTROLOGY

The planets symbolize organic functions found in all forms of life. They represent the higher manifestations or centers of these functions (in relation to a human being, the solar system must be considered as a greater organism), but *not* necessarily the agencies that control and manipulate the functional processes within human beings. The meaning and functional activity of a planet is determined by its relation to the solar system as a whole (geocentrically) as well as its individual characteristics, such as orbit, size, color, etc.

## THE "LIGHTS"

The Sun and the Moon, symbolizing the primary life giving factors of existence, are unique in the geocentric universe by virtue of their light giving and reflecting natures. The Sun, being the fountainhead of life energy within the solar system, represents the purpose of all life sustained by it. The Moon, the symbol of relatedness and actualization of the solar purpose, represents the life experiences of all earth beings. The relationship existing between these two bodies is of special significance, representing the bipolar activity found in all forms of life.* It is from this light that the other planets are symbolically animated; all life within the solar system is dependent upon the Sun.

* For a more detailed explanation of the soli-lunar relationship, refer to Part Three.

## THE PERSONAL PLANETS

The three planets lying within the orbit of the earth are referred to as the personal planets, because the organic functions and the type of consciousness symbolized by them are directed inward, toward the center (Sun) of one's self. The Sun, the innermost "planet," symbolizes the archetypal purpose and form of energy of the individual. Mercury represents the primary differentiation of this primal, archetypal solar energy; while Venus, the first planet within the orbit of the earth, symbolizes all forms of inwardly directed activity or expression. By the traditional system of classification, these planets are said to be "negative," because they tend to complete the processes put into motion by the positive, or social, planets.

## THE SOCIAL PLANETS

The first three planets outside the orbit of the earth are referred to as the social planets, because the organic functions and types of consciousness associated with these planets are directed outwardly, toward the social sphere. Mars, being the first planet outside the earth's orbit, refers to all forms of outwardly directed activity. Jupiter symbolizes expansion, the social sphere and the individual's participation within it. Saturn, the outermost planet by the ancient system, symbolizes the process of focalization, definition, and limitation; it represents the principle of form. Within this scheme, Venus is the polar opposite of Mars, Mercury is paired with Jupiter, and Saturn is polarized by the Sun and the Moon.

## THE COLLECTIVE, OR TRANSCENDENTAL, PLANETS

The three outermost planets of the solar system, Uranus, Neptune, and Pluto, symbolize the process of transformation, reorientation, and refocalization. These planets are referred to as collective, or transcendental, because their functions and the type of consciousness associated with them are so abstract that most human beings are unable to respond to them on a collective, transcendental, or unconscious, level.

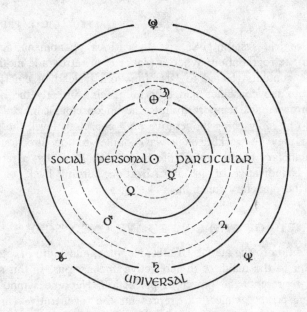

## planets and consciousness

## PLANETS AND CONSCIOUSNESS

A slightly different scheme of planetary classification involves the division of the ten planetary bodies (including the Sun and Moon) into two groups: the intra-Saturnian planets, consisting of all planets from Saturn inward; and the trans-Saturnian planets, Uranus, Neptune, and Pluto. The intra-Saturnian group symbolizes the consciousness of particulars, while the trans-Saturnian group represents the universal realm of consciousness.

## PLANETS AND THE PERSONAL UNCONSCIOUS†

As discussed earlier, in "The Birth-Chart and Its Implications,"

† The personal unconscious may be described as tendencies repressed by the conscious mind, becoming the contents of the unconscious, emerging as complexes, etc. The unconscious is also composed of lost memories, forgotten information, abstract images, and the like. On the other hand, the collective unconscious is quite different. In the words of C. G. Jung, "Just as the human body shows a common anatomy over and above all racial differences, so, too, does the psyche possess a common substratum. I have called the latter the collective unconscious." From Jung's Commentary to *The Secret of the Golden Flower*.

the geocentric system gives rise to various phenomena, including planetary retrogradation. When a planet is in retrograde motion, the "psychic contents related to [its] function, instead of emerging directly into the conscious and thus influencing directly the behavior [are] thrown back temporarily into the unconscious content." In addition to possibly being inoperative on a conscious level, the planet's function may be working in a way counter to the direction of the other planetary functions and life in general. Basically, a retrograde motion is indicative of an internalization, turning back, or repression of the planetary function.

## PLANETS OF THE COLLECTIVE UNCONSCIOUS

In addition to the above, Uranus, Neptune, and Pluto in retrograde may refer to the realm of the collective unconscious. In this scheme, Uranus represents the power of projection, Neptune symbolizes its dissolving power, while Pluto represents the regenerative (manifesting) power of the collective unconscious. When in direct motion, these planets act upon or transform consciousness; when retrograde, they tend to transform the unconscious (both personal and collective).

## STATIONARY PLANETS

When a planet is stationary (having relatively little or no apparent motion due to the repolarization from direct to retrograde motion or vice versa), its symbolic function may be extremely fixed, static, or inert. A stationary planet will also tend to bring its function into sharp focus within the psychological make-up of the individual.

# THE MEANING OF THE PLANETS

Sun

## SUN

*Function:*  Sustainment
*Process:*  Purpose-giving
*Purpose:*  Integration

*Traditional Meaning:*  The source of will, vitality, and personal power. The personality or ego. Qualities of leadership and authority.

*Humanistic Meaning:*  The center and power of self. The person's purpose and direction in life. The principle of self-actualization and centering. The Sun provides the individual with the particular type (sign) of experience needed to discover his "true nature." The person's total self is sustained through the consumption of the type of "fuel" symbolized by the Sun's sign. Life potential is symbolized by the Sun, defined and focused by Saturn.

*Cyclic Meaning:*  The Sun is the fountainhead of all light/life sustained within the solar system.

## MOON

*Function:*  Life provider
*Process:*  Protection and nourishment
*Purpose:*  Growth

*Traditional Meaning:*  Feelings, reactions, and instincts. The body and superficial expressions of the personality. Everyday and practical affairs. The principle of change. The mother.

*Humanistic Meaning:*  The bio-psychic functions and feeling-instinct responses. Adaptation to life experiences and the provision of self

Moon

with nourishment, protection, and assistance. The Moon symbolizes action taken to bring about the actualization of solar purpose through the establishment of relationships and the maintenance of oneself as an individual. The lunar principle enables one to adapt, develop, and mature within the area defined by Saturn.

*Cyclic Meaning:* Mediation of the solar light to earth. The Moon acts as a seventh or synthetic principle, which correlates and links the personal planetary triad (Sun-Mercury-Venus) with the social planetary triad (Mars-Jupiter-Saturn), thus mediating between self and others.

Mercury

## MERCURY

*Function:* Mental
*Process:* Association
*Purpose:* Relatedness

*Traditional Meaning:* The mental functions and thought processes. The ability to perceive and communicate. Academic and intellectual matters.

*Humanistic Meaning:* The principles of interchange, association, and relatedness. Adoption of techniques and the use of knowledge and skill to function in an effective manner. The intellect, reason, and tonal quality of the person.

*Cyclic Meaning:*   The initial differentiation of primal solar energy results in the manifestation of electrical and nervous energy. Mercury is never more than 28° away from the Sun in the zodiac.

*Retrograde:*   The mind may be withdrawn or inverted, perhaps in tune with the universal mind.

Venus

## VENUS

*Function:*   Establishment of values and ideals
*Process:*   Inner meaning
*Purpose:*   Internalization (formation of seed)

*Traditional Meaning:*   Harmony, art, beauty, and affection. The ability to attract others and maintain relationships.

*Humanistic Meaning:*   The centripetal forces active within experience. All attempts to reach the center and partake in communion with one's self and others. Aesthetics and the establishment of a pattern of appreciation and a set of values and ideals. The expression of internal experiences.

*Cyclic Meaning:*   The archetypal seed and generic pattern. Venus is never more than 46° from the Sun in the zodiac.

*Retrograde:*   An emotionally withdrawn, dissatisfied, or reclusive nature. Tendencies toward ascetic life-styles.

## MARS

*Function:*   Outer expression
*Process:*   Emergence
*Purpose:*   Externalization

Mars

*Traditional Meaning:* The principles of energy, force, will, desire, and passion. The manifestation of initiative, assertion, and aggression.

*Humanistic Meaning:* The centrifugal forces active within experience. All forms of outwardly directed activity. How the person begins and maintains things. The desire to be effective and successful as a social entity.

*Cyclic Meaning:* The emergence and germination of the seed and the development of an "ego center."

*Retrograde:* An element of unconscious motivation and an urge to express oneself against the normal direction of life.

Jupiter

## JUPITER

*Function:* Expansion and compensation
*Process:* Assimilation
*Purpose:* To establish a larger frame of reference

*Traditional Meaning:* The principle of expansion, opportunity, success, and prosperity. The great "benefic."

*Humanistic Meaning:* The principle of preservation, increase, and compensation. The process of individual assimilation of the social consciousness. The urge to be a self-sustaining entity consciously participating within the social realm. The establishment of a larger frame of reference and the power to grow through co-operation with experience. *Dharma,* or the individual's "power of right action." The guru, patriarch, or savior image.

*Cyclic Meaning:* The expansion of the individual's realm of activity within the social sphere.

*Retrograde:* A life dedicated to the service of a higher principle; or, social withdrawal.

Saturn

## SATURN

*Function:* Focalization
*Process:* Differentiation
*Purpose:* Individualization

*Traditional Meaning:* The principles of limitation, restriction, and discipline. Sorrow and hardships. The father. The great "malefic."

*Humanistic Meaning:* The principle of form as definition. The process of focalization and differentiation. Personal identity, security, and inertia.

*Cyclic Meaning:* The individual's acquisition of security and identity within both personal and social spheres.

*Retrograde:* Weak defenses against the outer world but great inner strength and endurance. Absence of a father image.

## URANUS

*Function:* To go beyond
*Process:* Revolution
*Purpose:* Transformation

Uranus

*Traditional Meaning:* Change, disruption, and revolution. Instability, eccentricity, and inventiveness.

*Humanistic Meaning:* The power of transformation and the urge to go beyond the area defined by Saturn. Unfocused and uncentered actions. "Threshold" knowledge and experiences. Creative genius.

*Cyclic Meaning:* Revolution and the penetration of Saturnian barriers.

*Retrograde:* The reformation of the unconscious. Internal instability and revolution.

Neptune

## NEPTUNE

*Function:* Destruction of antiquated forms
*Process:* Universalization
*Purpose:* Release of self

*Traditional Meaning:* Impressibility, nebulousness, psychic phenomena, and imagination.

*Humanistic Meaning:* The dissolution of old forms and values established within the Saturnian realm, replacing them with more inclusive and universal systems and values. In its negative manifestation, Neptune represents the urge to escape into a realm of formlessness, irrationality, and meaninglessness.

*Cyclic Meaning:* The destruction and dissolution of antiquated forms.

*Retrograde:* Realization of universal oneness; or, if negative, self-destruction and abnegation.

Pluto

## PLUTO

*Function:* Refocalization
*Process:* Re-examination
*Purpose:* Reformulation

*Traditional Meaning:* Renewal, regeneration, and elimination. Compulsive acts.

*Humanistic Meaning:* Second birth. The establishment of new forms. In a negative manifestation, the establishment of new forms without a positive evolutionary change, as a means of furthering an antiquated interest.

*Cyclic Meaning:* The refocalization and reformulation of values and ideals.

*Retrograde:* An urge to take action against established values.

# THE QUESTION
# OF PLANETARY RULERSHIP

*What is "Venus" but the "Artemisia" which grows in your garden? What is "iron" but "Mars"? That is to say, Venus and Artemisia are both products of the same thing, and Mars and iron are both manifestations of the same cause.*

PARACELSUS

## THE PRINCIPLE OF PLANETARY AFFINITY

Ancient astrologers devised a simple, yet rigid, system for quickly determining the relative strength of any planet in an astrological chart. Part of this system was based on the concept of planetary "rulership," with each planet ruling over one or two signs and houses. It is still believed today that each planet is particularly powerful when occupying certain signs and houses, while weak in others. By this system, the planets were also assigned certain degrees of the zodiac as their positions of exaltation. The signs and houses directly opposing a planet's rule are called its detriment, where it is particularly weak. The degree opposite its place of exaltation is called its "fall." In a position of detriment or fall, a planet is said to be greatly weakened. The table on the opposite page gives the signs and houses ruled by each planet, as well as its positions of detriment, exaltation, and fall.

Many astrologers also regard disposition, house, and chart rulership as relevant to their work. A planet is said to be the dispositor of another when the other is located in a sign or house under its rulership. That is, the planet in disposition is in some way subordinate to its dispositor. The ruler of the sign of a house cusp is referred to as the ruler of that house, being connected with the activities of the

| Planet | Rules Sign/House | Detriment Sign/House | Exalt./Fall |
|--------|------------------|----------------------|-------------|
| Sun | Leo/5th | Aquarius/11th | Aries/Libra |
| Moon | Cancer/4th | Capricorn/10th | Taurus/Scorpio |
| Mercury | Gemini/3rd Virgo/6th | Sagittarius/9th Pisces/12th | Virgo/Pisces |
| Venus | Taurus/2nd Libra/7th | Scorpio/8th Aries/1st | Pisces/Virgo |
| Mars | Aries/1st | Libra/7th | Capricorn/Cancer |
| Jupiter | Sagittarius/9th | Gemini/3rd | Cancer/Capricorn |
| Saturn | Capricorn/10th | Cancer/4th | Libra/Aries |
| Uranus | Aquarius/11th | Leo/5th | Scorpio/Taurus |
| Neptune | Pisces/12th | Virgo/6th | Cancer/Capricorn |
| Pluto | Scorpio/8th | Taurus/2nd | |

house it rules. The planet that rules the sign of the ascendant is often said to be the chart ruler, supposedly serving as the significator of the entire personality.

A complex system of scoring the relative strength and influence of each planet was devised some centuries ago, though it is no longer practiced by most astrologers today. By this technique, each planet is given a certain number of points if it is found in its ruling sign, house, or in exaltation, etc., while a certain number is subtracted if it is found in its fall or its detriment. The total number of points scored by each planet determines its relative influence and strength in the chart.

The great disadvantage of these traditional systems lies in their rigidity. Every sign and every house in some way includes elements of all planets, to various degrees, and all are in some way related. Every relationship is individual; some are co-operative, some are conflicting, and still others are more or less neutral. If a planet occupies a house with which it shares an obvious affinity (such as Moon in the 4th house), the planet's function should flow freely and without obstruction into the matrix of experience. If, on the other hand, a planet is found in a house with a nature greatly contrasting its own, the relationship between the planet's function and experience may be a source of serious conflict.

It is essential to keep in mind that the entire question of any planet's relation to any other chart factor requires the understanding of the chart as a whole, something that cannot be accomplished simply through the use of a rigid system. The traditional system of planetary rulership may to some extent serve one initially as a basic guide to the understanding of planetary affinities, but the serious astrologer should possess sufficient synthetic ability to determine the particular type of affinity (in terms of *meaning* and *quality* rather than *quantity*) existing between any planet and any house, sign, or aspect on the basis of the information given in this volume.

# 7

# PLANETARY ASPECTS:
# THE FORMATION OF
# RELATIONSHIP

*[Aspects] reveal their meaning in terms of the self-actualization
process of individual unfoldment* only *if they are interpreted as
"phases" of several cyclic processes which refer to the organic
functions symbolized by the ten planets.*

DANE RUDHYAR

## INTRODUCTION TO PYTHAGOREAN MATHEMATICS

An understanding of pure number and geometry is particularly
valuable in the study of planetary aspects and orbs.

The Greek sage Pythagoras, the first historical personage to call
himself a "philosopher" (one who is attempting to understand),
taught "numbers are things and divine archetypes." The discovery
of regular polygons, the diatonic scale, the heliocentric nature of the
solar system, and, of course, the Pythagorean theorem are accredited
to this man. Pythagoras traveled throughout most of the then-known
world during the sixth century B.C. and eventually became the high
priest of the temple at Delphi. He later established a unique "university" at Crotona, in southern Italy, where many students received
his teachings on the nature of man and the universe.

Unfortunately, most of the teachings of Pythagoras and his followers have been lost. However, the term "Pythagorean" is still used
today to distinguish pure mathematics from scientific or academic
mathematics.

## THE SIGNIFICANCE OF NUMBERS

The Pythagoreans believed that each number, from one to infinity, had a meaning and nature of its own and held that essence could be found in all things; thus the nature of all things may be described by numbers.

**Monad** (*1*):   According to the Pythagorean system, the monad is the origin of all things, therefore symbolic of the primal state of unity, indivisibility, and essential oneness. Monad is both odd and even, containing the essence of both.

**Dyad** (*2*):   The dyad is the first of an infinite series of even numbers. The dyad, like all even numbers, is related to the principle of *matter* and material evolution—the dyad being symbolic of the initial emergence of life into the form of matter. It divides all things into two realms: good-evil, light-dark, subject-object, internal-external, etc. Its key words are: externalization, separation, tension, and awareness.

**Triad** (*3*):   The triad is the first of an infinite series of odd numbers, thus symbolic of the principle of *spirit* and the process of spiritual evolution. The triad is the principle of reconciliation of opposites through a common element (monad), a process represented in the trinities of all religions. Its key words are: relationship, understanding, growth, and equilibrium.

**Tetrad** (*4*):   The tetrahedron is the first geometric solid or regular polygon, thus the tetrad symbolizes solid power and the emergence of an ordered system of manifestation. The tetrad was held by the Pythagoreans to be the "root of all manifested things." Its key words are: concrete manifestation and actualization of relationship.

**Pentad** (*5*):   The pentad, or five, is the symbol of the individual factor active within creation. It is also representative of Man and the Perfection of Man. Its key words are: individualized activity and expression.

**Hexad** (*6*):   In the Pythagorean system, six is a most unique number. It is one of the very few "perfect" numbers; it is also the only perfect number whose divisors, when multiplied together, result in the number itself. In addition, the hexad is a "triangular" number as well as an "oblong" number.* The hexad represents the product

---

* Six is considered a perfect number because all its divisors add up to six (the number itself). Other perfect numbers are 28, 496, and 8,128. Triangular numbers are numbers that can be "written" in the form of a triangle; as

or result of understanding and wise relatedness. Its key words are: development, time, harmony, and productivity.

**Heptad** (7): Seven is the number of all life and symbolizes the cyclo-cosmic process. It is held to be the most sacred of all numbers by almost every "authority" and is the most difficult to discuss. 3 (the three principles active in all relationship) + 4 (concrete manifestation and organic order) = 7 (the nature of all things).

**Ogdoad** (8): Extreme individualism and intense activity are symbolized by the ogdoad. In geometry it represents 45°, or the point of maximum dynamic activity.

**Ennead** (9): Nine represents limitless power and realization, and the fruit of relationship and understanding in terms of spirit.

**Decad** (10): Ten is symbolic of completion and infinity. It is considered the number of all things, the great archetype of the universe. The first four numbers (1, 2, 3, and 4) are "contained" within the decad, and this in a way gives a clue to why the Pythagoreans considered the "tetractys": ⋰⋰ to be their great secret and held that it revealed the mystery of the universe.

## THE FORMATION OF PLANETARY ASPECTS

Planetary aspects are formed when the cycle of relationship between two or more planets reaches certain points of angular value. These angular relationships, or aspects, are determined by the geometric division of the 360° of the circle, employing the same logic used in the formation of regular polygons. When any aspect is formed between two or more planetary bodies, their functions or centers are linked to or co-operative with one another. In other words, if Venus and Jupiter are found in aspect at the time of birth, a definite relationship is formed between these two planets. The *type of relationship*

---

⋯ ; others are 3, 10, and 15. Oblong numbers are numbers that may be "written" thus: ⋰⋰ ; others include 2, 12, and 20. In addition, triangular numbers are equal to the sum of all successive numbers up to a certain point, while oblongs are the sum of successive even numbers. There are also "square" numbers, which are equal to the sum of successive odd numbers and "written" in this manner: ⋰⋰ ; others are 4 and 16. Gnomons include 3, 5, 7, 9, etc. and are "written": ⋰⋰.

formed is dependent upon the angular value of the aspect involved, while the *quality and expression* of the particular relationship is determined by the degree of inexactness, or orb, of the aspect.

There is no consensus among astrologers regarding the importance of aspects in relation to other factors of the birth-chart. Some believe that aspects are of secondary importance, the planets' positions in terms of house and sign being primary. Others, such as Marc Edmund Jones and the seventeenth-century astrologer-astronomer Kepler, consider planetary aspects to be of the most primary importance, because they compose the most objective of all "major" astrological factors and are not the products of a static, subjective structure.

In any case, planetary aspects serve as important and relevant indicators to a complex area of human activity and personality and as such should neither be lightly treated nor overemphasized in relation to other chart factors.

## THE CYCLIC SIGNIFICANCE OF PLANETARY ASPECTS

Traditional astrology has completely overlooked the importance of the *phase of relationship* of an aspect in determining its meaning. That is, a *waxing* square (a square has an angular value of 90°), formed after the two bodies occupied the same degree of zodiacal space (conjunction), is not the same as a *waning* square, taking place after the opposition (180° aspect) and before the conjunction.

### Aspects and the Waxing Hemisphere

Aspects formed during the waxing phase, from conjunction to opposition (when the faster-moving of the two bodies at birth has already met the slower body at conjunction and is moving away but not yet 180° ahead of the slower planet), are referred to as steps in the development of potentials. This hemisphere is related to the building of organic structures and the process of involution. Feelings-instincts are dominant in relationship, and the mind is subservient to them.

### Aspects and the Waning Hemisphere

Aspects formed in the waning phase, from opposition to conjunction, refer to the release of meaning and significance and the objective actualization of purpose. In this phase, the mind and the evolutionary forces are dominant in relationship.

### The Involutionary or Time-Factor Series of Aspects

This series of aspects is based on the arithmetical progression of the basic unit of the twelvefold zodiac; that is, 0 + 30 + 30 + 30 + 30 + 30 + 30. This process involves six steps, producing seven aspects: conjunction, semisextile, sextile, square, trine, quincunx, and opposition. Each step represents a further stage in the process of differentiation and complexification of the energy released at the beginning of the cycle in terms of interfunctional relationship.

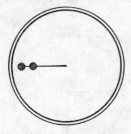

Conjunction

**The conjunction,** which has an angular value of 0°, symbolizes the beginning of a new cycle of relationship and the release of a new set or pattern of potentials.

Semisextile

**The semisextile,** having an angular value of 30°, is the preparation for the sextile, or the establishment of a focal center. It represents the initial emergence of self-awareness (ego).

Sextile

**The sextile,** with an angular value of 60°, represents the focalization of relationship through which potential creativity may become manifest. The establishment of external relationships. Adolescence.

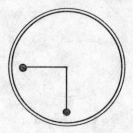

Square

**The square,** having an angular value of 90°, represents crucial repolarization or the crisis of reorientation.

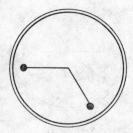

Trine

**The trine,** with an angular value of 120°, represents the resolution of relationships in a harmonious manner.

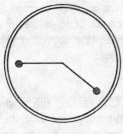

Quincunx

**The quincunx,** having an angular value of 150°, brings relationship into a clear focus.

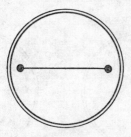

Opposition

**The opposition,** with an angular value of 180°, is the final aspect or step in this series. It represents the objective manifestation or actualization of purpose if integration has been maintained throughout the entire cycle, or the realization of failure and eventual disintegration if integration has not been successfully maintained.

### The Evolutionary or Space-Factor Series of Aspects

The evolutionary series of aspects is based upon the division of the circle, or zodiacal space, by 2, 3, 4, 5, 6, 7, 8, 9, and 12; or essentially by 2, 3, 5, and 7.

**Division by two** refers to the process of exteriorization and concrete manifestation. Aspects derived through divisions by two are regarded as "evil," "afflicting," and "unfortunate" by traditional astrologers. This negative attitude is no doubt a result of the dualistic concept of nature so dominant in our Western culture.

The basic key word for aspects derived from divisions by two is *exteriorization of awareness*. The initial division of zodiacal space by two results in the opposition aspect, which symbolizes direct consciousness and participation.

**Division by four.** The division of the *opposition* by two produces the square aspect, which symbolizes a further stage of exteriorization and the actualization of relationship. This aspect, having a numerical value of four, is the first aspect of solid, three-dimensional (concrete) manifestation. The square aspect also represents a condition in which the results of confrontations have either taken definite form or have resulted in a clear-cut crisis necessitating a definite action.

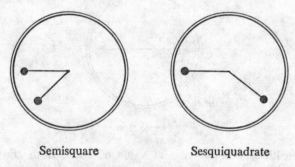

Semisquare                        Sesquiquadrate

**Division by eight.** A further division by two results in the semisquare (45°) and the sesquiquadrate (135°), aspects that refer to the points of maximum dynamic interfunctional activity.

**Division by three** refers to all modes of expression and activity having duality or polarity as a base. Aspects derived from this division symbolize the harmonious factor in relationships, by which polarity is transcended through understanding. The key words for divisions by three are: growth and harmony through understanding.

The initial division of zodiacal space by three produces the trine aspect, which refers to growth in understanding and the expansion of horizons. This aspect, and others based on the threefold division of the circle, are considered to be "good," "harmonious," and "fortunate" by traditional astrologers.

**Division by six** produces the sextile aspect, an aspect of ambiguous and significant origin, 3 × 2. This aspect refers to productive relationships and the exteriorization (2) or practical application of understanding (3).

Novile

**Division by nine** produces the novile aspect of 40°, geometrically equal to one third of the trine. This seldom-used aspect symbolizes the process of subjective growth (as in the nine months of gestation and the forty days of Christ in the desert).

**Division by twelve** results in the semisextile and the quincunx aspects, representing the most intimate form of interfunctional relationship.

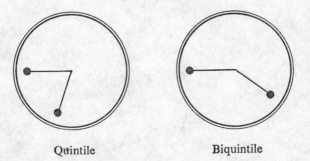

Quintile                    Biquintile

**Division by five** produces the infrequently used (by traditional astrologers) series of quintile aspects. These aspects, the quintile (72°) and the biquintile (144°), refer to the expression of talent and the creative mind.

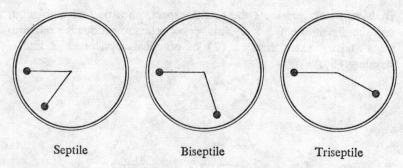

| Septile | Biseptile | Triseptile |

**Division by seven** produces the first "irrational" aspect and a series almost never used by traditional astrologers. The septile series, consisting of the septile (51°25'), the biseptile (102°50'), and the triseptile (154°15'), refer to "fate," compulsive acts, and the unpredictable elements of life.

# THE MEANING OF PLANETARY ASPECTS

## THE PRIMARY ASPECTS

The following aspects are regarded as primary, because they symbolize the types of relationships individuals are able to respond to objectively and thus hold in common with one another.

Conjunction

## CONJUNCTION

*Angular Value:*     0°
*Numerical Value:*   1
*Process:*           Touching
*Form:*              A point, or tangent

Tangent

*Traditional Meaning:* Coming together, unification, intensification, and general strengthening.

*Humanistic Meaning:* The beginning of a new cycle of interfunctional relationship. The release of a new idea or a new set of potentials. Unity in functional operation.

*Cyclic Meaning:* Beginning. Unity. The seed.

Opposition

## OPPOSITION

*Angular Value:*       180°
*Numerical Value:*     2
*Process:*             Awareness
*Form:*                A line

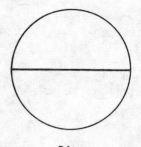

Line

*Traditional Meaning:*   "Bad," conflicting, tension, the pulling apart or separation of the one.

*Humanistic Meaning:*   Objectification of awareness. The crisis involved in the repolarization of one's consciousness. Objective actualization of purpose or the realization of failure and eventual disintegration. Confrontations resulting from the externalization of one's conscious awareness. The culmination of any experience and the conscious facing of existence and relationship.

*Cyclic Meaning:*   Repolarization and the apex of a cycle.

Trine

## TRINE

*Angular Value:*     120°
*Numerical Value:*   3
*Process:*           Understanding
*Form:*              A triangle

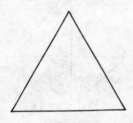

Triangle

*Traditional Meaning:*  "Good," helpful, easy, harmonious.

*Humanistic Meaning:*  The harmonious blending or synthesizing of energies. The transcendence of polarity through understanding. The expansion of one's horizons and consciousness. Perseverance, growth, and the growth process. Inherent abilities or gifts.

*Cyclic Meaning:*  Expansion of activity.

*Waxing Trine:*  Expansion of the concrete mind and the growth of practical knowledge. The use of knowledge and abilities to establish one's self within one's environment.

*Waning Trine:*  Expansion and refinement of the abstract mind. Growth in universal understanding. The use of one's understanding and abilities as a creative and social release.

Square

## SQUARE

*Angular Value:*      90°
*Numerical Value:*    4
*Process:*            Construction
*Form:*               A tetrahedron

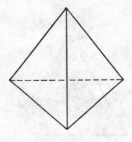

Tetrahedron

*Traditional Meaning:*  "Bad," difficult, stressful, and afflicting.

*Humanistic Meaning:*  The exteriorization and actualization of relationship. The giving of concrete form. Crisis and the need to take clear-cut action. Confrontations and their results. Creative tension. Solid power.

*Cyclic Meaning:*  The concrete manifestation of interfunctional relationship.

*Waxing Square:*  Crises encountered in the process of instinctive, body-building self-exteriorization. Establishment of a concrete basis for action and operation. Ego-building activity.

*Waning Square:*  Crises in the development of new forms and the release of the contents of such forms. The preliminary building of a new foundation from which a new cycle of activity may begin.

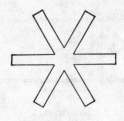

Sextile

## SEXTILE

*Angular Value:*     60°
*Numerical Value:*   6
*Process:*           Production
*Form:*              An octahedron

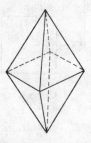

Octahedron

*Traditional Meaning:*  "Good," like a weak trine.

*Humanistic Meaning:*  The practical application of understanding. The products of relationships. Development of techniques and skills.

*Cyclic Meaning:*  Exteriorization or constructive application of understanding and experience.

*Waxing Sextile:*  Instinctive development and spontaneous growth.

*Waning Sextile:*  Productive use of new forms of consciousness.

Semisquare

## SEMISQUARE

*Angular Value:*     45°
*Numerical Value:*   8
*Process:*           Activity
*Form:*              A cube

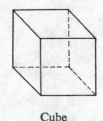

Cube

*Traditional Meaning:*    "Bad," difficult, like a weak square.

*Humanistic Meaning:*    Intense interfunctional activity. Release of meaning and individual expression. Exteriorization of the square.

*Cyclic Meaning:*    Point of maximum interfunctional activity.

*Waxing Semisquare:*    Interfunctional awareness.

*Waning Semisquare:*    Creative release of self through interchange.

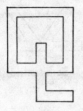

Sesquiquadrate

## SESQUIQUADRATE

*Angular Value:*      135°
*Numerical Value:*    3:8
*Process:*            Creative activity
*Form:*               A cube

*Traditional Meaning:*  Difficult, stressful.

*Humanistic Meaning:*  The conscious need and desire to take action.

*Cyclic Meaning:*  Point of maximum interfunctional activity.

*Waxing Sesquiquadrate:*  The apex of willful activity. The urge to express oneself through action.

*Waning Sesquiquadrate:*  Crisis in relationship. The urge to express one's self through relationship or within the social sphere.

## MEANING OF THE INTIMATE ASPECTS

The two aspects given here are based upon the twelvefold division of zodiacal space. These aspects are more refined and complex than the primary aspects, thus manifesting less tangible evidence of their operation and making a definition of their meanings difficult.

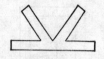

Semisextile

## SEMISEXTILE

*Angular Value:*      30°
*Numerical Value:*    12
*Nature:*             Intimate
*Form:*               An icosahedron

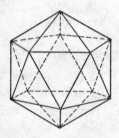

Icosahedron

*Traditional Meaning:*   Slightly good, weak.

*Humanistic Meaning:*   The most intimate linking of centers or forms of interfunctional relatedness.

*Cyclic Meaning:*   Emergence.

*Waxing Semisextile:*   Emergence of a center of conscious awareness.

*Waning Semisextile:*   Emergence of new forms.

Quincunx

## QUINCUNX

*Angular Value:*      150°
*Numerical Value:*    3:5
*Nature:*             Clarification
*Form:*               An icosahedron

*Traditional Meaning:*  Slightly difficult, weak.

*Humanistic Meaning:*  The bringing of relationship into clearer focus. The maturity of relationship.

*Cyclic Meaning:*  Bringing consciousness into a focused state.

*Waxing Quincunx:*  Clarification of one's concept of self.

*Waning Quincunx:*  Clarification of one's concept of others.


## MEANING OF THE ABSTRACT ASPECTS

Divisions of the circle by 5, 7, and 9 produce the most abstract and subtle set of aspects. Although it has been said that only more sensitive individuals are able to respond to the higher vibrations of these aspects, they, as well as the intimate aspects, actually represent a more complex and subtle order of interfunctional (geometric) relationship. In order to actualize and/or be conscious of such subtle relationships, the formation of a positive relationship to experience within the cubic (semisquare, sesquiquadrate) realm may be seen as a prerequisite.

Quintile

## QUINTILE

*Angular Value:*      72°
*Numerical Value:*    5
*Process:*            Creative transformation
*Form:*               A dodecahedron

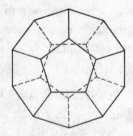

Dodecahedron

*Meaning:*   The individual element active within life and experience. The externalization (expression) of true individuality. An extremely individualistic manner of relating to existence. Talent or natural abilities.

## BIQUINTILE

*Angular Value:*   144°
*Process:*         Externalization of individuality.

Septile

## SEPTILE

*Angular Value:*    51°25′
*Numerical Value:*  7
*Process:*       Occult direction
*Form:*         Two interlaced tetrahedra

Interlaced Tetrahedra

*Meaning:* The unexpected or unpredictable elements in life. Narrow destiny and fixed goals or patterns. The planetary functions may be involved with compulsive or inexplicable actions directed by collective needs, occult powers, and/or one's own destiny. Such actions may lead to personal sacrifice, a symbolic life, social ostracism, and to fulfillment of personal destiny.

## BISEPTILE

*Angular Value:*   102°50′
*Process:*          Exteriorization of septile (destiny).


## TRISEPTILE

*Angular Value:*   154°15′
*Process:*          Co-operation with a collective need or cosmic
                    force.


## NOVILE

*Angular Value:*     40°
*Numerical Value:*   9
*Process:*           Subjective growth
*Meaning:* Subjective or unmanifested growth. Nourishment and gestation.

### Significance of the Superconjunction

When any planet is found within 0°17′ (in terms of the zodiac) of the Sun, a *cazimi* conjunction is formed, because the planet is symbolically contained within the Sun's corona. The planet in cazimi will be greatly intensified in its functional operation within the personality of the individual.


## IMPORTANCE OF VISUALIZING ASPECTS

Colored lines should be drawn between aspecting planets, preferably within an area specially provided for this purpose in the center of the chart. This enables one to actually see the aspects and the patterns and configurations formed by them. It is also advisable, especially in the case of highly aspected charts, to repeat this procedure three times—making one chart with all the aspects formed at the time of birth, another with just the primary aspects, and a third showing only the intimate and abstract aspects.

# 8

# PLANETARY ORBS:
# THE QUALITY OF RELATIONSHIP

*Orbs [or] spheres of planetary effectiveness in astrology are a matter of prime importance in delineation. In the nativity it is the permissible deviation from exactness of the aspects of the planets at birth, or a determination of the quality of pertinence to be accepted in what essentially is a spatial judgment.*

MARC EDMUND JONES

## THE PRINCIPLE OF PLANETARY ORBS

The meaning of any planetary aspect is determined by the degree of inexactness (deviation of angular relationship from the exact value) of the particular aspect as well as by the nature of the aspect itself. Technically, orbs designate the number of degrees more or less than the exact angular value necessary for two planets to form a perfect aspect. For instance, if Venus occupies the tenth degree of Cancer while Jupiter is positioned on the thirteenth degree of Scorpio, one would say that a trine aspect is formed between these two bodies with an orb of three degrees.

There are no objective criteria for determining optimum and maximum planetary orbs. Consequently there is no generally accepted practice in the application of orbs, though there is wide agreement that the closer the orb is, the more intense and active the relationship may be. If we apply a basic law of physics to the function of orbs, we could say that the "influence" of an aspect with a two-degree orb is the square (mathematically) of the "influence" of the same aspect with a three-degree orb, and in turn the three-degree orb is the square of the same aspect with an orb of four degrees, and so on. This concept, though it is no doubt basically true, fails to reveal how a two-degree aspect differs from a three-degree aspect other than in the intensity of "influence." However, as we will see later, the application of Pythagorean mathematics to planetary orbs offers an insight into their meaning.


## THE QUESTION OF ORB ALLOWANCE

In the past, astrologers have been inclined to allow a relatively large degree of deviation on the most commonly used aspects. The general trend today, however, is toward a general reduction of orb allowance. The tabulation given below gives the maximum orbs recommended by most recent astrological writers.

The reader will notice that the orbs are given under three headings. The first column gives maximum orbs under "normal" or "average" conditions. The second column of figures is recommended for aspects between the intra-Venusian planets (Sun, Mercury, and Venus) and the trans-Saturnian planets (Uranus, Neptune, and Pluto). Tighter orbs are used here, because the three intra-Venusian planets move more rapidly and are always close to one another, thus frequently forming small aspects; the trans-Saturnian planets are, relatively, very slow in motion. These planets remain in aspect to one another for longer periods of time (and for this reason should be considered as relating to collective rather than individual factors). The third listing is recommended for aspects involving either the Sun or the Moon, with the exception of solar aspects with Venus or Mercury.

The table on the opposite page is meant to serve simply as a guideline for the application of orb allowances; it is frequently advisable to improvise in the application of orb allowance, such as when two planets are found in relatively close conjunction (about four or five degrees in most cases). In such a situation it may be wise to consider the two bodies as an operative unit, using the mid-point of the conjunction to determine aspects. For instance, suppose Mars is found in the twenty-fifth degree of Aries and Jupiter is in the twenty-second degree of the same sign: the mid-point between the two would be 24° Aries and may be used to calculate aspects from these two planets acting as an operative unit.

| aspect | normal orb | intra-Venusian or trans-Saturnian | solar or lunar |
|--------|-----------|-----------------------------------|----------------|
| Conjunction | 8° | 4–6° | 10° |
| Opposition | 8° | 6–8° | 10° |
| Trine | 6° | 4° | 8° |
| Square | 5° | 4° | 7° |
| Sextile | 3° | 2° | 4° |
| Semisquare | 2° | 1° | 3° |
| Sesquiquadrate | 2° | 1° | 3° |
| Semisextile | 1° | 1° | 1½° |
| Quincunx | 1° | 1° | 1½° |
| Quintile | 1½° | 1° | 2° |
| Septile | 1½° | 1° | 2° |
| Novile | 1° | 1° | 2° |
| Biquintile | 2° | 1° | 2° |
| Bi & triseptile | 2° | 1° | 2° |

## THE MEANING OF PLANETARY ORBS

The influence of orbs in determining the quality of an aspect has been of no significant interest to traditional astrologers, who differentiate only loose aspects from tightly orbed aspects, and then only in terms of intensity of influence. The pioneer work in the field of the meaning of planetary orbs was carried out by Marc Edmund Jones some forty years ago in the study course "Pythagorean Astrology."

Generally, in addition to determining the *quality* of an aspect, examination of the degree of inexactness also gives an insight into the extent to which the factor of individual freedom and activity is functional in the relationship symbolized by the aspect itself; the wider the orb, the greater the potential for individual expression and activity. Another way of expressing this concept is through the proposition that aspects with relatively tight orbs operate in a somewhat unconscious or compulsive manner, being to some extent beyond the conscious control or manipulation of the individual. In such instances the aspect *operates through the personality.* Looser orbs operate in a more conscious manner, allowing the individual with some degree of self-knowledge to use the relationship symbolized by the aspect as a facet of self-expression and in a self-determined manner. In this way the individual *expresses himself through the aspect*.

The degree of orb determines the particular quality of an aspect in terms of number; that is, whether the aspect has a one-degree orb, a two-degree orb, and so on.* The orb indicates the manner in which the aspect (functional relationship) should become manifest, the form or appearance it could adopt or assume to actualize its function of relationship.

### ONE-DEGREE ASPECT

*Quality of Form:*    Emphasis
*Numerical Value:*    1
*Value of Orb:*       0°01'–1°

The one-degree aspect brings its particular functional relationship into manifestation in the purest and most impersonal manner possible. The particular functional relationship will make a deep impression upon the personality and the personal unconscious.

### TWO-DEGREE ASPECT

*Quality of Form:*    Intensity
*Numerical Value:*    2
*Value of Orb:*       1°01'–2°

The two-degree aspect is the first in a series of values that constitutes a deviation from the essential nature of the aspect itself. It carries the essential quality of the opposition and tends to manifest itself through the process of exteriorization of conscious awareness.

### THREE-DEGREE ASPECT

*Quality of Form:*    Expansive
*Numerical Value:*    3
*Value of Orb:*       2°01'–3°

* The value of the orb is always the next higher degree if it is any fraction above an exact degree; an orb of 1°01' is considered to be a 2° orb.

The three-degree aspect carries the essential quality of the trine, tending to become manifest through growth and expansion of understanding, co-operation, and consciousness.

## FOUR-DEGREE ASPECT

*Quality of Form:* Concrete
*Numerical Value:* 4
*Value of Orb:* 3°01′–4°

The four-degree aspect, carrying the essential quality of the square, tends to manifest its functional relationship in a concrete or constructive manner, acting as an agency for the establishment and actualization of self.

## FIVE-DEGREE ASPECT

*Quality of Form:* Expressive
*Numerical Value:* 5
*Value of Orb:* 4°01′–5°

The five-degree aspect carries the essential quality of the quintile and may become manifest through the expression of individual selfhood or creativity.

## SIX-DEGREE ASPECT

*Quality of Form:* Productive
*Numerical Value:* 6
*Value of Orb:* 5°01′–6°

The six-degree aspect, carrying the essential quality of the sextile, should manifest itself through the productive application of practical knowledge, skills, and techniques.

## SEVEN-DEGREE ASPECT

*Quality of Form:* Inclusive
*Numerical Value:* 7
*Value of Orb:* 6°01′–7°

The seven-degree aspect, which carries the essential quality of the septile, indicates the possibility of a co-operative relationship existing between self and the world (cosmos) in terms of activity and experience, which may manifest the functional relationship in an unusual, unique, or unpredictable manner.

## EIGHT-DEGREE ASPECT

*Quality of Form:*    Reactive
*Numerical Value:*    8
*Value of Orb:*       7°01′–8°

The eight-degree aspect, which carries the essential quality of the semisquare, indicates the possibility of objective response and activity, which should manifest the functional relationship in an intense and individualistic manner.

## NINE-DEGREE ASPECT

*Quality of Form:*    Actualizing
*Numerical Value:*    9
*Value of Orb:*       8°01′–9°

The nine-degree aspect, carrying the essential quality of the novile, indicates the possibility that the functional relationship may manifest itself (after a period of gestation) as a facet of realization of purpose and actualization of self.

## TEN-DEGREE ASPECT

*Quality of Form:*    Perfection
*Numerical Value:*    10
*Value of Orb:*       9°01′–10°

The ten-degree aspect is symbolic of completion and perfection.

## THE MEANING OF APPLYING
## AND SEPARATING ASPECTS

An applying aspect is one that has an angular value less than exact, moving toward its exact angular value. A separating aspect has an angular value greater than the exact angular value, thus moving out of aspect. An applying aspect generally indicates a situation in which energy and momentum are increasing and preparing for a culmination of activity and a release of meaning and energy. On the other hand, separating aspects tend to indicate a condition in which the intensity generated during the preculmination phase is released in a more or less orderly and significant manner.

To determine whether an aspect is in its applying phase or its separating phase, simply check to see if the faster-moving planet (at the time of birth) is moving along a course that leads toward the exact angular value of the aspect (applying) or out of aspect (separating).

# 9

# PLANETARY MID-POINTS:
# THE RELEASE OF RELATIONSHIP

*All things consist of three.*
*Establish the triangle and two thirds of the problem is solved.*

PYTHAGORAS OF SAMOS

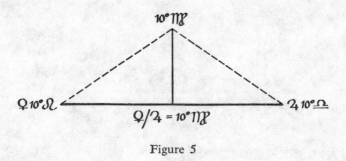

Figure 5

## FORMATION OF PLANETARY MID-POINTS

The point in space exactly midway between any two planets is a planetary mid-point (see Figure 5). The degree and particularly the house of the mid-point symbolize the point where the particular relationship represented by the two bodies involved should be released in the most dynamic and focused manner.

## SIGNIFICANCE OF PLANETARY MID-POINTS

Numerologically a mid-point divides the angular distance between two planets (or structural factors) by two, resulting in a third factor, the mid-point. A mid-point may be thought of as the external manifestation of the interfunctional relationship existing between two bodies. On the other hand, the point directly opposing the mid-point (inverse mid-point) symbolizes the internalized or personal significance of the particular interrelationship symbolized by the two planets.

## MID-POINT OF TWO PLANETS IN ASPECT

A planetary mid-point is particularly significant when the two planets involved are in aspect with one another. In such cases it represents the point where the function and quality of the relationship expressed should be most obvious and operative in terms of external manifestation. The inverse mid-point, also significant, symbolizes the point in zodiacal space where the function and quality of the relationship will be most sensitive in an internal, intimate, or personal sense (see Figure 6).

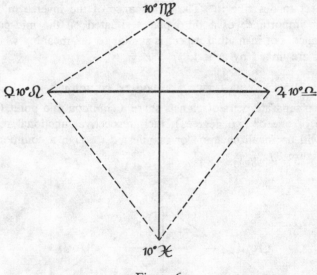

Figure 6

If another planet happens to be situated on or near (one or two degrees distant) the degree of either a mid-point or an inverse mid-point, that planet's function should be intimately involved in this process (see Figure 7).

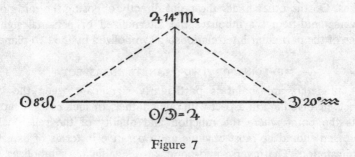

Figure 7

## MID-POINT OF TWO PLANETS NOT IN ASPECT

The mid-point of two planetary bodies that are not in aspect to one another acts as a focal point for the functional relationship active between the two bodies even though the relationship does not form an aspect to describe it.* The significance of the inverse mid-point and the importance of a third planet situated on the mid-point of two planets not in mutual aspect is similar to the meaning when two planets are linked by aspect.

## WHEN TWO MID-POINTS COINCIDE

If two separate pairs of planets share a common mid-point (within an orb of one or two degrees), their respective functional relationships will be focalized upon or manifested through a common facet (see Figure 8).

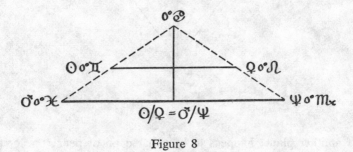

Figure 8

* The direct employment of mid-points will be discussed in greater detail in Part Three.

## THE APPLICATION OF MID-POINTS
## TO OTHER FACTORS

Mid-points may be calculated for a great many chart factors (planets, angles, nodes, etc.). In fact, their application is almost inexhaustible. The study of mid-points is a valuable and significant part of the astrological technique which has, unfortunately, been considerably overlooked (except by a number of scientific astrologers) until recently.

It is important to be aware that excessive use of any chart factor, including mid-points, may distract one's attention from the other, equally important chart factors, resulting in a distorted view of the birth-chart as a whole. Therefore, selectivity is recommended—there are forty-five planetary mid-points alone, not including inverse mid-points. For general use, only the more significant mid-points (such as mid-points between planets in mutual aspect, coinciding mid-points, and the mid-points of planets of opposing polarity) need be considered.

# 10

# PLANETARY NODES AND PARTS:
# THE SYNTHESIS OF RELATIONSHIP

*The more unusual or remote astronomical events or the more cosmic or abstract the relationship between celestial bodies, the deeper or more transcendent the characteristics which they represent in the personality and the life-experiences of human-beings.*

DANE RUDHYAR

## ORBITAL ASTROLOGY

Orbital astrology, which is very much a part of natal astrology, involves the consideration of *entire* planetary orbits and the phenomena created by these orbits when they are related to the ecliptic. In orbital astrology the position of a planet on its orbit refers to its point of *focused release,* while the entire orbit defines the *realm of the planet.* Examination of a planet's orbit reveals four significant points: the two points where a planet contacts its nodes and the points at which it reaches maximum northern latitude and maximum southern latitude.

## THE CONCEPT OF THE NODAL AXIS

The points where the plane of a planet's orbit intersects the plane of the ecliptic are referred to as nodes (see Figure 9). The nodes, being one in process but different in function, actually compose an axis—a nodal axis. The north node is the point where the planet intersects the ecliptic as it is moving in a celestial northerly direction, while the south node is the point where the orbit intersects the ecliptic as it is moving southward.

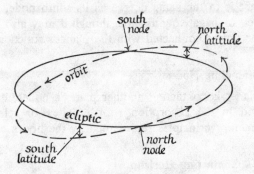

Figure 9

The heliocentric system is ordinarily used for the determination of nodes (with the exception of the Moon, as it is a natural geocentric satellite) primarily for the following reasons: (1) orbital astrology deals with the orbits of the planets (including the earth) as components of a whole (solar) system, and (2) the basic polarity of the nodal axis is lost when nodes are determined by the geocentric system.

### MEANING OF THE NORTH NODE

The north node of a planet refers to the spiritual power of that planet's function. It is the point of intake of life energies for the growth and building of the bio-psychic organisms connected with the planetary function. It symbolizes direction.

When a planet is in the same degree as its north node, it is said to be "powerful," perhaps even destructive and compulsive, as the planetary function represented becomes highly focalized within the consciousness of the individual.

### MEANING OF THE SOUTH NODE

The south node refers to the emotional power of the planet's function. It is the point of release of waste contents, which must be disposed of to prevent poisoning of the system—and seed. The south node represents spontaneous action and the root of the planetary function, as well as habitual patterns associated with the planet. When a planet is in the same degree as its south node, its function may be wasted or negatively applied, though it may also be a source of great inner power connected with the planet's function.

### Planets Contacting Nodes

When a planet is contacting another planet's nodes, it should become involved in the absorption (north node) or release (south node) of planetary principles represented by the nodes contacted.

### Nodal Axis Contacting Horizon

When a planet's nodes are contacting the horizon of a birth-chart, the individual to whom it refers should display the qualities of that planet or may act as an agency for the release of the planet's symbol.

### Position of the Planetary Nodes

Unlike lunar nodes (positions for which may be found in astrological ephemerides), planetary nodes are rather static in terms of the zodiac, though very meaningful in terms of house placement. A table for the longitudes of the planetary nodes is included in Appendix VI. The information is given for the north node in each case; the south node is always its polar opposite.

## THE CONCEPT OF CELESTIAL LATITUDE

The celestial latitude of a planet is determined by the distance the planet is north or south of the ecliptic (see Figure 9). A planet is at 0° north latitude when it is at its north node and moving northward; it is 0° south latitude when at its south node and moving southward. A table of maximum planetary latitudes appears in Appendix VI (the exact latitude for the planets may be found in most ephemerides).

### THE MEANING OF A PLANET AT ITS MAXIMUM LATITUDE

A planet's maximum southern latitude symbolizes its point of repolarization in terms of personal growth, while the point of maximum northern latitude represents the point of inner repolarization in terms of consciousness.

**The Meaning of the North Latitude.** When a planet is in the northern hemisphere of its latitude cycle, its function is operating in its personalizing aspect, dealing with the intake of spiritual power and resulting in the organic growth of the organism.

**The Meaning of the South Latitude.** A planet in its southern latitude is operative in its social aspect, involving the release of self and the expansion of consciousness.

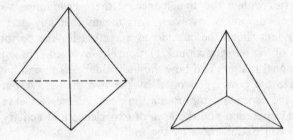

Figure 10

## ARABIAN ASTROLOGY

The use of abstract points formulated by the synthesis of any two planets with any other chart factor is said to be of Arabian origin. These abstract points are called planetary parts.

The fact that any two planets (or, for that matter, any two points) of an astrological chart may be synthesized with the ascendant (or any angle, house cusp, etc.) will make it obvious to the reader that Arabian astrology, the study of *sensitive points,* is almost boundless. The present discussion presents the basic concept of planetary parts; the examination and application of the most primary of these parts will be treated later in the text.

The principle behind the concept of planetary parts is that the relationship between any two points or planets may be focused through the ascendant, or any other angle, and projected to create a new point symbolizing the concrete operation of the interfunctional relation as it refers to selfhood or identity. If an angle other than the ascendant is used, the part will carry or symbolize the significance of that angle's meaning in relation to the interfunctional activity symbolized by the two cosynthesizing factors (planets). The significance of the formative principle behind planetary parts may be symbolized by the tetrahedron (see Figure 10), in which the synthesis of the three points of a triad project their meaning as a whole (the whole is greater than the sum of the parts) to an entirely new dimension, forming a fourth point.

## PLANETARY PARTS AND THE ANGLES

When the relationship between two planets is focused through the "lens" of the ascendant, a planetary part is formed. Such a part naturally carries with it the significance of the ascendant as well as the two planets or points involved. This means that any part involving the ascendant should be considered a symbol for the personal manifestation of the interfunctional relationship involved. These parts deal with personal matters and how the individual person can best express and utilize the power generated by the two planets. A part derived through the ascendant represents the point of greatest ease of interfunctional operation and the area of experience and activity in which this ease will be felt most by the individual.

### Inverse Parts

The point opposing a part derived through the ascendant is referred to as an *inverse part* and carries the significance of the descendant. Inverse parts symbolize the release points of creative expression for planetary functions through the blending of (opposite) natures.

### Parts and the Meridian

Parts involving the M.C. as a third factor refer to the point where the planetary relationship involved manifests itself in terms of spiritual power or expression. They represent the point of interfunctional spiritual integration.

Parts involving the I.C. as a third factor refer to the point where the planetary relationship manifests itself in terms of personal growth. They represent the point of personal integration of a relationship.

## PARTS CONTACTING PLANETS AND POINTS

When a part is found in the same degree or very near (in conjunction with) a planet or point of a birth-chart, that planet or point will be deeply involved with the process symbolized by the part. The opposition is the only other aspect that should be used when considering planetary parts, because in a sense parts are aspects in themselves.

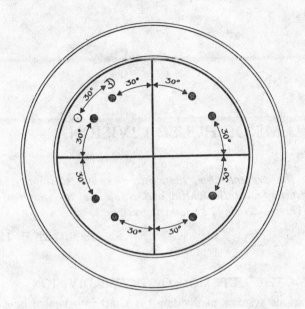

FORMATION OF THE EIGHT PARTS
OF THE SUN AND MOON

## FORMULA FOR CALCULATING PLANETARY PARTS

The formula used for the calculation of planetary parts is a simple one: planet longitude* + ascendant longitude − planet longitude. For instance, the part of fortune, the most popular part, is calculated by adding Moon to ascendant and subtracting Sun from the sum.

## ASCENDANTS OF THE PLANETS

Planetary ascendants, which symbolize the manner in which a planet's function is distributed through or manifested within the personality, may be calculated by the formula: ascendant + planet − Sun.

---

* The planetary position added to the ascendant is normally considered a dominant factor in the meaning of the part.

# 11

# SYSTEMS OF HOUSE DIVISION

*Up to the present time, there has been no unanimity, even amongst the most thoughtful and careful, as to which of the many [house-division] systems is best.*

MARGARET E. HONE

## THE QUESTION OF HOUSE DIVISION

The various systems of dividing the chart into twelve houses and the choice of a system to use is probably one of the most confusing and controversial areas of astrological opinion. This chapter will hopefully shed some light on the subject and perhaps offer some valuable alternatives to the situation.

## HOUSE-DIVISION SYSTEMS

There are today two major systems of house division: the equal house system and the quadrant house system.

### EQUAL HOUSE SYSTEM

This is the system used by "ancient" astrologers, before the employment of the meridian. It was held in great disfavor during recent centuries because of its simplicity and is at the present time experiencing a revival, due largely to the efforts of Margaret E. Hone, Carl Payne Tobey, and others.

The equal house system employs the logic of numerology by dividing the 360° of the ecliptic into twelve equal houses of 30°, beginning with the degree on the ascendant. In other words, the ascendant establishes the first house cusp, the second house cusp is 30° from the first house cusp, while the third house cusp is 30° from the second, and so on (see Figure 11).

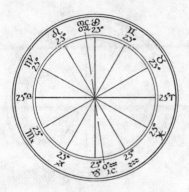

Figure 11

This house-division system is unique on the basis of its pure simplicity, which makes it quite attractive for both numerological and practical reasons. However, there is one important disadvantage to this system: the horizon and meridian are almost never perpendicular when one casts a chart by this system. That is, the tenth-house cusp almost never coincides with the M.C.

Nevertheless, this system is valuable, because the entire chart carries the significance of the *ascendant;* that is, the houses divided by this system refer their meaning directly to the ascendant. I suggest using it as a *part* of a whole process of house examination, a process that will be discussed in detail later on in this chapter.

QUADRANT HOUSE SYSTEMS

The quadrant house systems (of which there are many) are based upon the division of the 360° of the ecliptic into twelve equal sections of *space* or *time*. The major variations in the three or four quadrant systems now in use are (1) whether they divide space or time, and (2) in the case of the former, what space they divide.

The astrologers who developed these systems were highly trained mathematicians, and one needs to be fairly familiar with mathematics to grasp the principle behind these systems. The explanations given here will be necessarily brief and nontechnical.

The quadrant systems most used today, in the order of their popularity, are the Placidus system, the Regiomontanus system, and the Campanus system.*

* House cusps calculated for identical times, but by different house-division systems, are given in Figures 11–15.

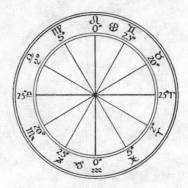

Figure 12

**Placidus System.** This system (see Figure 12) was developed by the monk Placidus early in the eighteenth century. It was a complete departure from all other systems before its time, because it arrived at the degree of the house cusps by dividing the *time* needed for the sun to cover the space between the quadrants. Because of the time-based nature of this system, it was initially violently opposed by astrologers. It gained popular favor only because until about twenty years ago no other tables of houses were available.

To my mind, this system is of dubious worth for natal astrological work, because I consider the birth-chart a *space* factor. It is, symbolically speaking, time frozen in space; the employment of a time-based house-division system is, as I see it, incongruent.

Figure 13

**Regiomontanus System.** This is a *space* system (see Figure 13) developed in the fifteenth century and very popular until 1800. It determines the cusps of the twelve houses by the equal division of the space along the celestial equator into twelve equal parts, relating them to the ecliptic. This system is still in use on the European continent.

Figure 14

**Campanus System.** This is another *space* system (see Figure 14), developed during the thirteenth century. It determines the house cusps by dividing the space along the *prime vertical*† into twelve equal parts and relating them to the ecliptic. This system is not widely used today, though many may find it the most philosophically acceptable of all the quadrant systems. It seems to be the most logical approach to the future development of a three-dimensional birthchart or "birth-sphere." In the contemporary two-dimensional chart, however, the Campanus system often tends to produce exaggerated house proportions. Nevertheless I find it quite meaningful and use it in my own work with success.

### Inequality of Houses

The use of a quadrant house system implies, with the exception of a birth on the equator, unequal houses, particularly in the case of births at extreme northern or southern latitudes. The larger the span of a house (the more degrees within it), the greater or broader the importance the experiences represented by the house play in the individual's life, the smaller houses having a lesser, or perhaps more condensed, importance.

† Which "links" the zenith and the nadir.

### Significance of Intercepted Signs

The use of a quadrant-based house system also gives rise to the phenomenon of *intercepted signs*. A sign becomes intercepted when one house is so large that it surrounds an entire sign (see third and ninth houses of Figures 12 and 13, and second and eighth houses of Figure 14). When a sign is intercepted, its importance is said to be withdrawn or turned inward. Intercepted signs always appear in polar opposites, as do house cusps.

## ALTERNATE SYSTEMS OF QUADRANT DIVISION

Those who find the equal house system and the three major quadrant systems given in the preceding sections inadequate for their astrological work may find one of the following systems of "quadrant division" more satisfactory. These include the Porphyry system of quadrant division, bisection of quadrants, and no division at all.

### THE PORPHYRY SYSTEM

This is the oldest system (3rd century A.D.) dividing the ecliptic into twelve sections while still *representing the horizon-meridian as perpendicular axes*. It determines the house cusps by dividing the space of the quadrants into three equal sections along the ecliptic. In other words, it divides the number of degrees within a quadrant by three, resulting in the number of degrees to be contained within each house of that quadrant (and its opposing quadrant). Using the same time and place as we used to illustrate the other house-division systems, in Figures 11–14, the reader will note that there are 83° within the upper eastern and lower western quadrants and 97° within the upper western and lower eastern quadrants. Dividing 83° by 3 gives 27°40' within each house (Figure 15) of the upper eastern and lower western quadrants. The houses within the upper western and lower eastern quadrants contain 32°20'.

This system is unique and significant, because it combines the best of two systems. Visually it represents the horizon-meridian—the primary structuring factor of the birth-chart, symbolic of the person's unique selfhood—as perpendicular axes within the birth-chart, and it divides the area defined by the quadrants *logically*, into three equal sections of the zodiac. This is an excellent system of house division,

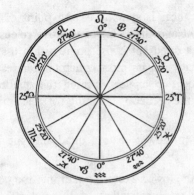

Figure 15

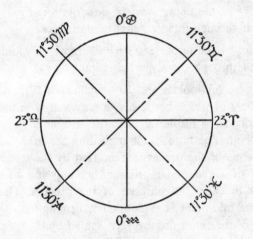

Figure 16

yet today it is virtually out of use. The Porphyry System is mentioned in only a very few astrological books, which may be responsible for its unpopularity.

BISECTION OF QUADRANTS

The idea of bisecting the quadrants is relatively new to modern astrological thought. As the term implies, the quadrants are divided into two equal parts, the line of division being the mid-point between the two angles that define the quadrant (Figure 16). This mid-point is of great significance; it symbolizes the point of greatest intensity within the quadrant and the point of creative release of its meaning. The mid-point of a quadrant is the point within that quadrant where its process is operative in its most concrete manifestation of purpose (symbolized by the two angles defining the quadrant). Below, the reader will find the general meaning of the mid-point of each quadrant:

(1) Mid-point of the lower eastern quadrant: the point of the dramatic emergence of self-awareness.

(2) Mid-point of the lower western quadrant: the point of emergence of the personality and realization of the not-self in the subjective sense.

(3) Mid-point of the upper western quadrant: the point of creative release of self through interpersonal relationships.

(4) Mid-point of the upper eastern quadrant: the point of creative release of self through social participation.

Because these mid-points are very significant, their use is encouraged, regardless of which house-division system is in use.

This practice is of further significance in that it gives meaning to each biquadrant. The biquadrant preceding the mid-point is involutionary, in terms of the process symbolized by the quadrant; that is, the first half of a quadrant represents building and complexification of structures to carry the purpose of the process. The biquadrant succeeding the mid-point is evolutionary, dealing with the release of the meaning of the entire process represented by the quadrant.

It is advisable to use this system along with a system of quadrant trisection, though the reader who finds all systems of house division unacceptable may find quadrant bisection the only acceptable system for his astrological work.


## No Division at All

The simple division of the chart by its quadrants, without houses or quadrant mid-points, is not totally unheard of and may be the only alternate available to one who finds all house-division systems as well as mid-points unacceptable.

## AN ALTERNATE SYSTEM OF HOUSE ANALYSIS

For a greater insight and understanding of the houses and quadrants of a birth-chart, the following procedure is suggested.

The planets (as well as, if one wishes, planetary parts and nodes) are charted by a quadrant house system, with the quadrant mid-points clearly marked. Attention should be given to the following: (1) what, if any, planets are on or near the quadrants' mid-points, and (2) which planets fall into which biquadrants.

The planets are then charted by the equal house system, notice being taken of any inconsistencies of the planets' placement within the houses; that is, if any planets fall into different houses when the equal house system is used.

### SIGNIFICANCE OF PLANETS ON THE QUADRANT MID-POINTS

If a planet is found on the mid-point of a quadrant, this planet's function will be involved in the release and concretization of the purpose of the process symbolized by that quadrant. That is to say, if, for instance, Mercury is found on the mid-point of the upper western quadrant, the individual's mind and associative perception should be involved in the creative release of self through relationships. In a similar case, if the mid-point between two planets is found at the mid-point of a quadrant, the concrete manifestation and release of the meaning of their relationship should be involved in the release and concretization of the purpose of that respective quadrant.

### SIGNIFICANCE OF A PLANET IN A BIQUADRANT

When a planet is found in the first half of a quadrant, that planet's function will be involved in the involutionary process of that biquadrant. For instance, if a planet is in the first half of the lower eastern quadrant, its function will take part in the process of developing and structuring the subject sense of self-awareness. If a planet is found in the second half of a quadrant, its function should assist the person in releasing and expanding the purpose of the quadrant.

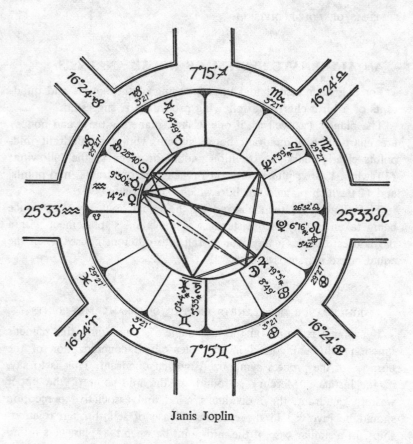

Janis Joplin

Using the chart of Janis Joplin to exemplify this, the reader will
notice that her Mars, the planet most connected with her career, is
in the first half of the upper eastern quadrant. Janis was able to penetrate the social sphere of rock, and climb to the top of the pile (Mars
in the tenth house) by virtue of her outgoing and sexual personality.
This does not imply she was not talented; she was indeed (Venus
biquintile Moon), but a rock star needs more than just talent to get
to the top; and in Janis' case the added something was dynamic and
hypnotic sexuality. The message (release) of her songs was of the
pain and sorrow (Sun, Mercury, and Venus in the twelfth house)
that follow an ill-fated romance (Mars septile Venus).

### Changes in Planet/House Relationships

If, by charting the planets by the equal house system, any planets are found to occupy different houses from those occupied by the quadrant system of your choice, a basic conflict in the personal integration of the experiences of the two houses involved is indicated. The conflict is a personal one, due to the nature of the equal house system, which carries the significance of the ascendant through the entire series of twelve houses. In the chart of Janis Joplin, Mars is found in the tenth house by the Porphyry system but in the eleventh house by the equal house system. This situation denotes a conflict in the personal integration of her social and professional position, and the result it had upon herself and her relationship with others, particularly "professional" (eleventh house) relations. This particular conflict may be illustrated by her initial breakup with Big Brother and the Holding Company, which preceded continual difficulties with musicians and a continual search for a new band.

# PART TWO

## *Notes*

The opening statements from Chapters 1, 7, and 10 are from *Person-Centered Astrology*, by Dane Rudhyar (CSA Press, 1973). Those from Chapters 2 and 4 are extracted from Rudhyar's *The Astrology of Personality* (Doubleday, 1970).

Other opening quotes are from the following sources: Chapter 3: *The Practice of Astrology*, by Dane Rudhyar (Penguin Books, 1970); Chapter 5: *An Astrological Study of Psychological Complexes*, by Dane Rudhyar (Servire N.V., 1969); Chapter 6: *Tetragranum*, by Paracelsus; Chapter 8: *Scope of Astrological Prediction*, by Marc Edmund Jones (Sabian Publishing Society, 1969); Chapter 11: *The Modern Text-Book of Astrology*, by Margaret E. Hone (Fowler, 1968).

A thorough explanation of the cyclic process and many other philosophical concepts and formulations which should provide the student of astrology with inspiration and broaden his or her understanding of astrology may be found in Rudhyar's *The Planetarization of Consciousness* (Harper & Row, 1972).

The concept of the involving and evolving series of aspects was first presented by Rudhyar in the essay "Form in Astrological Space and Time," included in *Person-Centered Astrology*.

A more detailed explanation of the houses may be found in Rudhyar's *The Astrological Houses* (Doubleday, 1972) or in *Tools of Astrology: HOUSES* by Dona Marie Lorenz (Eomega Press, 1973).

# 3

## technique and procedure of astrological interpretation;

### ASTROLOGY AS AN INSTRUMENT OF SELF-ACTUALIZATION

# 1

# THE PROCESS
# OF ASTROLOGICAL INTERPRETATION

*The astrologer who casts a chart and attempts to solve the problems of his clients is using power, power born of the knowledge of structural patterns of nature as it unfolds through cyclic time. What he does is to relate the client's individual being to his evolving structure of human-nature and universal nature; and relationships always release power, the power to build or the power to destroy. If the astrologer thinks he merely gives bits of information and then is through with the whole thing, he is greatly mistaken. He has established a relationship.*

DANE RUDHYAR

From the humanistic approach the real worth and value of natal astrology is in its ability, when used by an astrologer well versed in the symbolic language of astrology, to act as an instrument of self-actualization and eventual self-transcendence, rather than as a means of predicting events or analyzing character. The humanistic astrologer should see the birth-chart as an archetypal pattern of individual selfhood, a set of instructions to be fulfilled and actualized, transcending all labels expressing value judgments. From this approach, the planets, signs, houses, and aspects are never considered good or bad, fortunate or unfortunate; they simply *are*. The purpose of humanistic astrology and the process of astrological interpretation are to help individual persons in discovering the particular experiences they must live through so that they may fulfill their potential as whole persons. Whether these experiences are conventionally regarded as good or bad is incidental; total actualization and transcendence of self is, in the end, all that really matters.

This is not to say that all other approaches to astrology are worthless. It is particularly in the realm of natal astrology that the humanistic approach surpasses the previous attempts of astrologers to understand the meaning of individual existence—and it is, indeed, the only approach to natal astrology that really makes sense. When we are dealing with individuals and attempting to assist them in actualizing themselves through the process of astrological interpretation, our primary concern is with the individual—not events, not collective factors, not external social pressures, but the individual person. Events, collective factors, and social pressures are meaningful only to the consciousness that perceives and experiences them. Any approach to natal astrology (and any process of astrological interpretation) that is not essentially person-centered and does not see the person as the center of his own universe is not actually natal astrology at all, because it is dealing primarily with collective, social, or other factors.

This, of course, indicates a total change in the meaning and purpose of astrological practice directed toward translating the personal mandala, or birth-chart. Not only must traditional attitudes associated with astrology be evolved, but so must the traditional way of practicing astrology and the traditional relationship existing between the astrologer and his or her "clients." The importance of understanding the person as an individual and forming a warm and positive relationship with him is paramount. The astrologer should see a person as a dynamic, unique, and whole person, not as just a collection of standardized and interchangeable parts. Astrology is a universal language utilizing a vast and rich array of symbols, symbols having no particular significance in themselves but revealing their meaning only when applied to particular individuals and specific situations. Any astrological factor appearing in any birth-chart may mean any number of things, isolated from the whole birth-chart and the whole person represented by the birth-chart. It is only when these symbols are applied to a particular individual involved in a specific situation and with a specific background that the symbolic factors reveal their significance as they relate to the individual at that time.

The traditional one-time, one-hour astrological sessions, as well as the traditional "cookbook" type of textbook and interpretation, are obviously inadequate in this approach; the humanistic astrologer should understand the person as a whole, vital, creative being. The primary function of the humanistic astrologer is to help those who seek his or her services in fulfilling their individual potential in the fullest possible manner.

## THE ACT OF ASTROLOGICAL INTERPRETATION

When the moment comes for the actual act of interpretation, the astrologer's mind should be free from prejudices and preconceptions regarding the birth-chart and the person to whom it refers. When interpreting a birth-chart, the astrologer is acting as a mediator, placing himself between the person and the universe. He should be as clear and distortion free as a finely ground lens. In addition to a sufficient understanding of the birth-chart of the person whom he is about to counsel, one should have a real understanding of the person himself. This usually calls for at least one preliminary session. The astrologer should feel comfortable within the situation and should do all he can to help the person feel comfortable and secure, as well as help him understand the true nature of astrology and the significance of what is about to take place. As the session(s) proceed, and personal understanding and responsibility grow, the astrologer should have a concept of what the person needs at that moment to further the actualization of himself as a whole individual.* Whether the person's chart reveals a "charming personality" or an "aggressive nature" is secondary; the assistance of the person in the process of becoming more of who and what he truly is, at that moment and in the future, is the primary consideration of the humanistic astrologer.

## HOW TO USE THE ASTROLOGICAL FRAMES OF REFERENCE

A birth-chart represents what one was born for—the meaning of one's individual existence. When seen as a set of instructions to be fulfilled and actualized, the birth-chart reveals the best way for the person to approach life experiences, how he should fulfill his destiny and actualize his wholeness as an individual. From this approach the

* This calls for a *time analysis* of the birth-chart, a procedure discussed in Part Four.

*horizon-meridian* represents the basic factor of the person's individuality. The *angles* are symbolic of the most individual and unique qualities of the person, and the twelve *houses* derived from them represent his fields of individual experience. The *zodiac* and the twelve *signs* represent the collective factor of human nature and the manner in which it is manifest within the individual. A *planet* always represents the same life function, regardless of its position in terms of houses and signs. *A planet in a house* reveals the best way for the individual to approach all matters and experiences represented by that house. The function symbolized by the planet should manifest itself in its most focused manner within the realms of experience represented by the house. More than one planet in a house means that the experiences of that house should be rich, varied, and complex. *A planet in a sign* represents the type of energy and activity the planetary function should use as a means of propelling it through the experiences symbolized by its house. *The sign on a house cusp* reveals the type of human activity that should be associated with the actualization of the potential experience symbolized by the particular house. *The sign on a house cusp and the planet in a house* reveal the manner in which the experiences of the house should be met in order to actualize their potential meaning in the fullest possible manner. *Planetary aspects* reveal the type of relationship existing between two or more life functions (planets) working together, while their *orbs* symbolize the quality of the relationship.

## THE PROCEDURE OF ASTROLOGICAL INTERPRETATION

The procedure of astrological interpretation given in the following pages involves first the consideration of the birth-chart as a whole, then the identification of its focal points and the examination of its many factors; and, lastly, a reconsideration of the chart as a whole. This system is meant to serve as a guideline; it is not intended for rigid adherence in actual practice. Every individual and situation is unique, and for this reason a differential approach is valuable; that is, a special method and procedure should be devised in order to meet the special needs of each person.

The meanings given within the next several chapters are condensed and should be understood as essential and inclusive rather than fixed or exclusive. The beginner may find it difficult to simultaneously assimilate all of the information and techniques given here—for instance, a thorough understanding of the significance of a dyadic relationship is essential for the understanding of a synthetic point produced by that relationship.

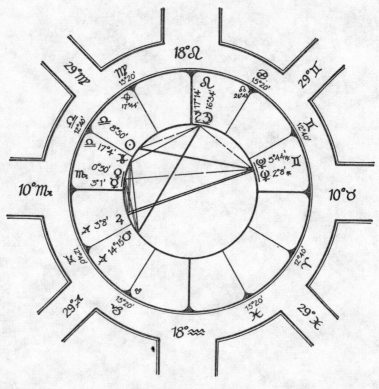

Marc Edmund Jones

# 2

# WHOLE PLANETARY PATTERNS

*The planetary types have been developed as a means for quick and accurate preliminary classification. They are a guide to horoscope interpretation because, in the first place, they have the broadest possible orientation, and in the second, they facilitate the recognition of focal determinators with which, under proper circumstances, the interpretation of the horoscope begins.*

MARC EDMUND JONES

## RECOGNITION OF GESTALT CONFIGURATION

The first phase of astrological interpretation involves the examination of the birth-chart according to its over-all, or whole, planetary pattern: its gestalt configuration. This means classifying the chart by its particular *form;* or, by the first characteristic that strikes the viewer. Before looking to see which planets occupy what spaces, one will first notice if all planets fall into one tight group, in one half of the chart, and so on. This is the initial procedure of astrological interpretation because it considers the pattern or form of the whole chart and provides the astrologer with a starting point, a direction, and a frame of reference for the whole of his interpretation.

Each of the nine planetary patterns or chart shapes given here represents a certain temperamental quality and a particular approach to life experiences. Above all, the whole planetary pattern symbolizes the internal pattern of the individual person; the consideration of the planets' positions within this pattern reveals what life potentials are focused through which activities and life experiences.

This method of "whole-view" was pioneered by Marc Edmund Jones, and first introduced by him in *Guide to Horoscope Interpretation,* published in 1941; it was recently re-examined by Rudhyar in

*Person-Centered Astrology.* The types given here differ somewhat from those given by Jones, the primary deviation being the inclusion of a category for "non-harmonic," or *asymmetric,* formations.

## HEMISPHERIC PATTERN

This pattern is typified by a chart with all planets (parts, nodes, and other abstract points are not included when considering planetary patterns) found within approximately 180°, leaving half of the chart empty while the other half is full. Ideally there should be no empty houses within the occupied half (though this is unusual), and never more than two.

The hemispheric pattern is basically dualistic in principle, and in some instances it may be difficult to determine to what extent compensation is acting as a motivating force within the personality. Any situation such as this, which involves a clear-cut dualism, is almost bound to involve compensation to some degree. Initially, one may feel the individual's attention could be drawn and held almost exclusively by the activities symbolized by the full hemisphere, with the empty hemisphere's life experiences being of relative unimportance. This is not always true; the empty space may provide the person with a feeling and need to explore the unknown. Another way of viewing this situation is considering the occupied hemisphere as representative of the individual's goals and ideals, his obvious potential, with the empty hemisphere symbolic of pure potential and the life experiences that must be integrated and brought together within the individual's personality.

The mid-point of the two extreme planets of such a pattern is significant insomuch as it represents the center of gravity or the point of focalized purpose. It is interesting to note that the birth-chart of Alice A. Bailey, the theosophical writer and organizer of the "Arcane School," illustrates a "typical" hemispheric pattern, except that the center of gravity is exactly conjunct the south lunar node. An example of a more unusual hemispheric pattern is provided by the birth-chart of Marc Edmund Jones. Here we find the center of gravity conjunct the part of fortune. The two extreme planets are also of significance in themselves, for they act as structuring agents, defining the boundaries or limits of the person's tangible and conscious energies.

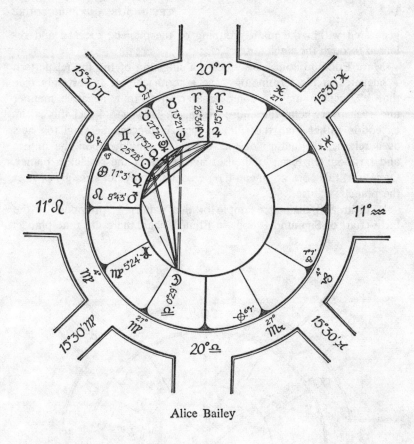

Alice Bailey

## FUNNEL, OR WEDGE, PATTERN

This pattern is also based on the principle of twofold division, though it is more distinct in both form and function than the hemispheric pattern. It is made up of a primary group of nine planets with one "singleton" planet, ideally opposing the main group's center of gravity. The primary group should occupy no more than 180°, with no more than one empty house within the grouping, and preferably none. Two planets in conjunction may also act as a singleton.

The pattern is called a wedge or a funnel because its mode of operation is quite similar to that of a wedge or a funnel; power is generated within the main grouping of the planets, focused and released through the singleton.

Marc Edmund Jones describes the singleton of the funnel pattern ("bucket," in his terminology) as a toothache. It is certainly true that a singleton may in some cases operate in a negative manner and even overwhelm the entire organism. However, I feel this is the exception rather than the rule; in most instances, the singleton acts as a release, the nature of this release depending upon the nature and position (in terms of house, sign, etc.) of the singleton planet. Of course, this does not mean the personality may not strongly project the planet's nature.

A clear and defined example of this pattern is provided by the birth-chart of Sigmund Freud. In Freud's chart there are nine planets

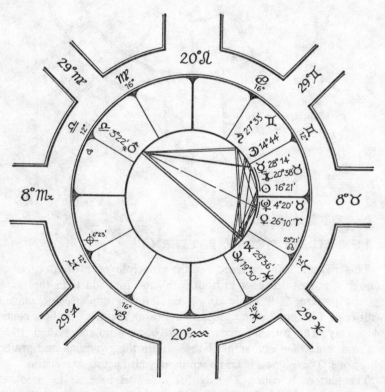

Sigmund Freud

within a tight group occupying the western hemisphere. Mars retrograde is in focus, being isolated from the main group and located in the eleventh house (professional associations).


## SEE-SAW FORMATION

The see-saw formation is an example of operative dualism in its most distinct form. It is formed by two planetary groups, separated by at least two empty houses on each end and with no more than one empty house within each group. There should be at least one opposition, and the closer the "central" bodies are to opposition, the more intense the situation symbolized by this formation should be.

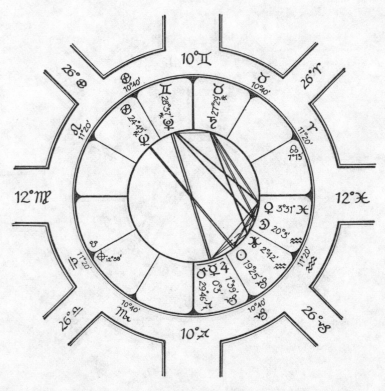

Richard M. Nixon

A typical example of this pattern may be found in the birth-chart of Richard M. Nixon. Here we find two tight groups separated by the horizon. The see-saw pattern represents a personality that acts after the consideration of opposing views and is always aware of contrasting or antagonistic possibilities. Nixon's method of operation has been the close consideration of what effect his actions will have upon others (particularly upon any kind of opposing faction), placing him in a better position to respond to criticism and opposition. A person with this temperament is constantly aware of conflict, an awareness that may be put to selfish use by manipulating the dynamic forces operative within the field of dualism. An additional point of interest concerning Nixon's chart is the retrograde motion of all three planets

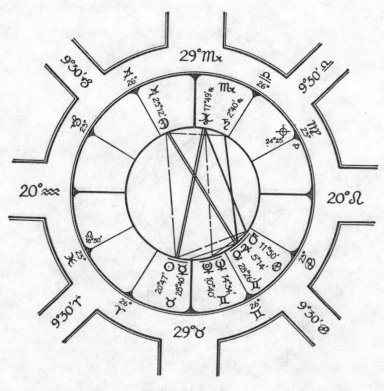

J. Krishnamurti

above the horizon, suggesting a personality that is forceful and uncompromising in the area of relationships and social participation, possibly as a compensation for some deeply rooted feeling of insecurity.

Another example of the see-saw formation is provided by the birthchart of the Indian philosopher J. Krishnamurti, with Saturn, Uranus, and Moon above the horizon, and with the mid-point of this group exactly conjunct the M.C. In Krishnamurti's instance, the basic awareness of conflict symbolized by the see-saw pattern has been utilized in a more positive manner than in the case of President Nixon. Through his early awareness of conflict, Krishnamurti was able to formulate a unique philosophy concerning the nature of conflict itself.

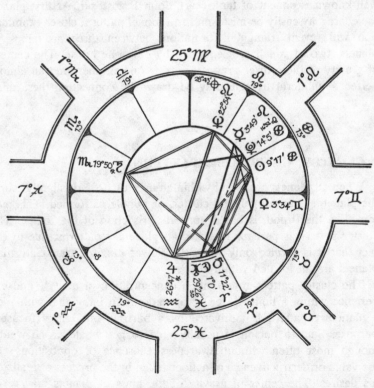

John Brzostoski

## TRIPOD PATTERN

This pattern is formed by the placement of all planets within three distinct groups. Ideally, the center of gravity of each group should be in a trine aspect to the center of gravity of the other two groups, though this is not always the case.

Essentially this pattern carries the significance of *three,* symbolizing a person for whom growth through understanding should be emphasized. The tripod pattern represents a temperament that can potentially transcend duality through the synthesis, or blending, of opposites.

An excellent example of such a planetary pattern is found in the birth-chart of the curator of the Staten Island Tibetan Museum and well-known exponent of tantric art, John Brzostoski. At first glance the chart may easily be mistaken for a funnel pattern; closer examination will reveal triangular formations between three groupings of planets, two of which are separated by only one house. The centers of gravity of these three groups are trine one another, and an almost perfect equilateral triangle may be drawn by connecting these midpoints.

## CLUSTER, OR BUNDLE, PATTERN

When all planets are found within an area of 120° or slightly more, the planetary pattern called a cluster, or bundle, is formed. This pattern, like the tripod, is based upon the trisection of the zodiac. The cluster pattern is perhaps rarest of all planetary patterns, due to the fact that it is formed only when the slower moving, trans-Saturnian planets are all located within 120°.

The cluster pattern represents a concentration of activity and experience within a limited area of operation. An individual with such a planetary pattern is motivated by a narrow, but highly focused, purpose. Such a person is usually able to get whatever he wants, though most often without awareness (absence of oppositions) of the value or destructiveness of actions taken in the process of realizing his desires. The center of gravity of the mass of planets may serve as an indicator for the nature of the individual's motivation.

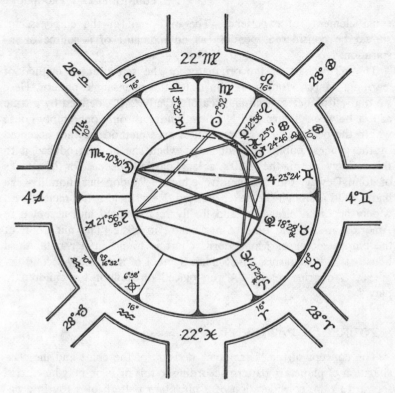

Maria Montessori

## OPEN-ANGLE PATTERN

This pattern is also based on the trisection of the circle and is, in a sense, the opposite of the cluster pattern. It is formed when all planets are within 240°, or two thirds of the zodiac, with 120° empty. The occupied area may be slightly more or less than 240°, and there should be no more than one empty house. The planets should be, ideally, evenly distributed within the area.

The open-angle pattern suggests a type of personality with an inherent quality of openness to the transcendent elements of life. This may mean a spiritual or mystic temperament as well as an ability or urge to transcend the conventional element within any situation. Activities should be well balanced and open to the wider, transpersonal elements of experience. The mid-point of the empty sector should be considered, possibly as an indicator of a source of inspiration.

The birth-chart of the originator of the self-initiated method of learning, Maria Montessori, illustrates the open-angle pattern. Here we find all planets within an area of exactly 240°, defined by a trine aspect between Saturn and Neptune, and with only one empty house within the occupied area. Dr. Montessori's method was not accepted by the general public and educators when she first introduced it to this country, during the 1920's, at least partially because of the attacks of John Dewey, the "progressive educator," upon her morality—she had a child although she never married. Nevertheless, her method was widely accepted elsewhere and finally reintroduced and accepted in America around the time of her death, in 1952. The mid-point of the empty sector of Montessori's chart is found in her natal third house at 22° Aquarius. The Sabian Symbol of the twenty-second degree of Aquarius reads: "A rug placed on a floor for children to play."

## FOURFOLD PATTERNS

The concept of the "harmonic" division of the chart and the classification of planetary pattern according to this division may be carried forward to the consideration of a planetary pattern of a fourfold nature. Such a pattern is formed by the division of all planetary bodies into four distinct groups and is characterized by at least one clearly defined T square (a configuration formed by two opposing planets with a third squaring both opposing bodies). The type of temperament represented by such a planetary pattern is really no different, though more focalized, from the type of temperament symbolized by the T square.* The fourfold pattern is formed by four groups of planets, ideally spaced at 90° intervals, thus projecting the image of a cross.

## STAR PATTERNS

Rarely does one find a five- or a six-pointed star, or the suggestion of four or five points of a six-pointed star in a birth-chart. However, one may come across one now and again, as well as a chart with six alternating full/empty houses.

* See Chapter 4.

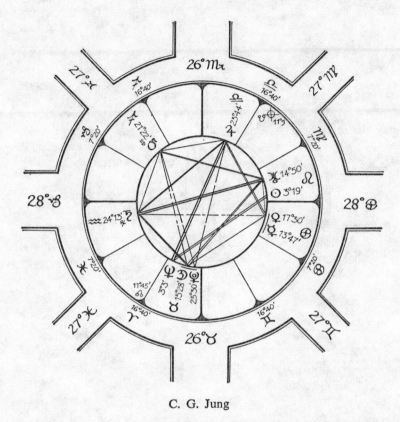

C. G. Jung

The birth-chart of C. G. Jung is what may be considered a five-pointed star. It is formed by the significant conjunction of the Moon and Pluto, which form quincunxes with Jupiter and Mars; Jupiter, in turn, is trining Saturn, Saturn opposing Uranus, while Uranus is linked by a trine to Mars. It is, of course, geometrically an imperfect five-pointed star, though certainly indicative of a *potentially* well-integrated and creative personality with a gift of synthesis and an individualistic temperament.

## ASYMMETRIC, OR NON-HARMONIC, PATTERNS

Frequently one finds a chart that defies classification, often because it contains qualities of two patterns. Such charts may be considered asymmetric or non-harmonic, because this formation is not based upon a symmetric division of the circle.

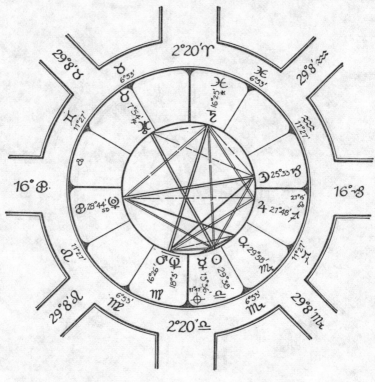

Bobby Seale

The asymmetric pattern denotes a unique and highly individual approach to all life experiences and a personality with a very special "destiny" or an eccentric, non-conforming nature. Such a person is likely to have his own special way of approaching life and his own unique manner of relating to situations and others. This is not to say that there is not a unique quality in all individuals; persons with asymmetric patterns are simply more likely to manifest their uniqueness overtly.

An example of an asymmetric pattern is illustrated by the birthchart of the Chairman of the Black Panther Party, Bobby Seale. Here there is a main body of seven planets, occupying four houses within less than 130°. The three remaining planets are located in three of the six remaining houses. There are numerous squares and oppositions and at least two clearly defined T squares. This unusual situation is indicative of a unique individual with a very special destiny to fulfill.

# 3

# FOCAL POINTS

*Determinators of focal emphasis in the horoscope indicate the special gifts of self-expression through which each individual is equipped to meet the issues of any internal inharmony or any challenge to his well-being. Personality has its weapons, in one way of putting it, or its creative tools in a perhaps happier way of describing the matter.*

MARC EDMUND JONES

## THE CONCEPT OF FOCAL POINTS

After perceiving a chart as a whole by considering its planetary pattern, the next logical step in astrological interpretation is the determination of focal points or emphasized areas and factors. When any astrological factor is heavily emphasized, it should be considered as a focal point. Such points should be regarded as symbolic of a primary manifestation of personality, an area of great personal strength and creativity, or an indicator of overdeveloped activity. This is one area of interpretation in which prudence is especially called for, and one should be careful not to put too much importance on these factors.

## HEMISPHERIC EMPHASIS

When all planets are found in one hemisphere, it is considered to be in emphasis.

### EASTERN-HEMISPHERIC EMPHASIS

Self-fixation. Focalization of energies upon self and self-directed and determined activities. The individual should be able to maintain a great deal of control over his life patterns. However, he may find himself easily bound to a situation of his own making.

### WESTERN-HEMISPHERIC EMPHASIS

Dependency upon others. The individual's attention should be turned to affairs that may not directly affect his situation, or activities detached from a self-centered principle. Such a person has much less control over his destiny and life patterns than does one with eastern-hemispheric emphasis, making it more difficult for him or her to effect internal change, though he may be less affected by external situations. He may be described as a product of his time and culture and may need to give attention to a weak sense of identity, which may be compensated by an overemphasized need or search for personal meaning.

### UPPER-HEMISPHERIC EMPHASIS

Object oriented. Emphasis is placed upon the individual's desire to understand the meaning and significance of all life experiences. The social-collective activities should be given attention, and the individual may find it difficult not to relate to people and situations from a very "object"-ive perspective.

### LOWER-HEMISPHERIC EMPHASIS

Subject oriented. The individual's attention may be placed upon the personal realm of activity. Such a person may find little freedom within relationships and may approach situations from a subjective perspective.

### SINGLETON PLANET IN HEMISPHERE

When only one planet is found within a hemisphere, regardless of planetary pattern a great deal of attention should be placed upon that planet's functional principle and its hemisphere. The operative principle here is functional compensation, the isolated planet overwhelming and/or channeling, hopefully, power generated by the remaining planets.

## STELLIUM

When several planets are found in one sign or house, the experiences symbolized by that house or the activities represented by the sign should be highly focused within the individual's personality. A

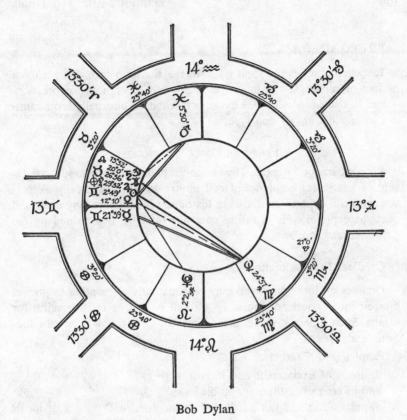

Bob Dylan

grouping of four or more planetary bodies within one sign or house is called a stellium. This situation indicates that the particular area of life defined by the focused area will be complex, confusing, and possibly overwhelming. In any case, the individual's consciousness should greatly benefit from the experiences of the area emphasized by the presence of the stellium.

In the birth-chart of Bob Dylan, we find a stellium in the twelfth house, with five planets within less than 20°. Venus is on the ascendant (effeminate appearance) and forming a close biseptile aspect to Neptune retrograde, which is singleton in the western hemisphere. The planetary pattern is asymmetric. It should be obvious to anyone familiar with Dylan's works that he is sensitive and aware of the personal and social conflicts of life and the need for self-redemption and rebirth—truly a man of startling and prophetic insight.

## PREPONDERANCE

Preponderance is the term given to the situation formed by a mass of five or more planets in one element, mode, or house expression. There is also preponderance by aspect, when an unusually large number of aspects are of one type.

Preponderance by mode (five or more planets in one mode) represents a particular emphasis placed upon one form of energy. A person with this type of emphasis in his or her birth-chart may meet and react to experience in a rather constant manner, determined by the preponderant mode.

### Cardinal Preponderance

Denotes an individual who may be constantly attempting to project himself into experience, possibly without regard or consideration for others. Such a person can express himself well through external situations and issues.

Emphasized Characteristics:

- desirous of excitement and intense activity
- ambitious rather than adaptable
- opportunistic and not particularly concerned with values or ideals
- situations and issues are placed over individuals.

### Fixed Preponderance

Refers to a type of person with fixed, or even rigid, ideals and goals, concerned with the definition and perfection of function in its purest form. Such a person may be able to achieve whatever he or she desires, often through the sheer force of determination. There may be a concern with the karmic circumstances surrounding any situation or action (its consequences and outcome).

Emphasized Characteristics:

- strong-willed and resistant to external influences
- concerned with the value of an act or situation
- values and ideals are placed over individuals and situations
- uncompromising.

## Mutable Preponderance

Such an individual is adaptable and practical rather than idealistic or exploitive, fitting easily into most situations. There is a possibility of much personal freedom, though the person may be incapable of decisive or self-directed action.

Emphasized Characteristics:

· devotional rather than idealistic or ambitious
· personal and sentimental
· superficial, indecisive, and weak-willed
· concerned with people and relationships rather than ideals and personal ambitions.

### PREPONDERANCE BY ELEMENT

When five or more planets are found in one element, it is considered a preponderance.

## Preponderance by Fire

Refers to the type of person who puts all of himself into whatever he does. There should be an intense degree of vitality, concentration, and effort put into experience.

Emphasized Characteristics:

· intensely emotional
· individualistic
· active
· self-expressive.

## Preponderance by Earth

Denotes the type of person who is involved in the mundane, immediate, and practical affairs of life. Stable and concerned with physical well-being rather than spiritual attainment.

Emphasized Characteristics:

· responsible, though rigid
· methodical and detail-conscious
· "down to earth"
· concerned with manifested realities.

### Preponderance by Air

Refers to a person who may be involved in the formation of ideals and values through the use of intellect. Such a person, however, needs to ground his ideas in reality and put them to practical use.

Emphasized Characteristics:

· intellectual
· superficial
· compulsive
· adaptive.

### Preponderance by Water

Such a person should have an urge to achieve universal harmony and at-one-ment. The person, in the desire to reach universality, often becomes deeply involved with creativity, sensuality, and emotionality.

Emphasized Characteristics:

· sensitive
· concerned with universal concepts
· penetrative
· flowing.

## PREPONDERANCE BY HOUSE EXPRESSION

When five or more planets are found in one mode of house expression, it is considered a preponderance.

### Active Preponderance

Refers to an individual who may be constantly involved in the initiation of new experiences and activities. Such a person has unusual personal resources and vitality, though he may be too busy looking for new activities to deeply penetrate anything.

Emphasized Characteristics:

· individualistic
· dominant
· intense.

### Reactive Preponderance

Denotes a person who should be concerned with giving meaning and significance to his or her experiences. To a person with reactive preponderance, it is not the initial action that is important, but the effect and reception of the act. However, this type of person may need to experience and take direct action in his life.

Emphasized Characteristics:
- concerned with expansion, focalization, and consolidation
- able to learn from experience.


### Resultant Preponderance

Denotes a person who may be able to foresee the final outcome of a particular situation or action. Such a person is often concerned with the entire process surrounding an act, rather than just the isolated act and reaction to the initial act. This type of person, however, may become so involved in analyzing actions and reactions that he may forget how to make things happen himself.

Emphasized Characteristics:
- harmonious
- perceptive
- impressionable.


#### PREPONDERANCE BY ASPECT

When one aspect is found to be about 50 per cent more numerous than the next most numerous, it is considered to be preponderant.


### Preponderance by Conjunction

Represents an individual who should be deeply involved with the idea of mutual or group effort and the release of new ideas.

Emphasized Characteristics:
- integrated, though possibly isolated
- concerned with new forms of expression
- complex.

### Preponderance by Opposition

Refers to an individual with an acute awareness of the duality of life. Such a person may be conscious of the extreme tension operative within his or her own being and may try to channel it in a creative direction.

Emphasized Characteristics:

- aware
- extreme
- fulfillment oriented
- creative.

### Preponderance by Trine

A person with preponderance by trine may be able to get things easily, having a brilliant, but superficial, knowledge of things. Such a person should try to penetrate the surface of life, directing his creative faculties and his ability to bring things together toward the formulation of a firm body of wisdom.

Emphasized Characteristics:

- gifted
- concerned with bringing things together or keeping them as they are.

### Preponderance by Square

This type of person may be in a continual state of crisis. Clear-cut action may seem the only way of resolving such a situation. There may be a need for much constructive action here, to bring about external manifestation of inner purpose.

Emphasized Characteristics:

- needs to externalize
- aware of tension and conflict
- concerned with giving definition and form to things.

### Preponderance by Sextile

Denotes the type of individual who may be interested in the practical application of understanding and knowledge. The person should be productive and constantly developing new potentials.

Emphasized Characteristics:
* attention to detail
* intimate
* able to synthesize.

## NEGATIVE DYNAMICS

When a chart has no planets in one of the elements, modes, or qualities of house expression, or complete absence of one of the five major aspects, the missing factor is considered negatively preponderant. The interpretation of negative preponderance is particularly delicate and does not necessarily mean something is lacking in the personality of the individual; rather, the missing factor *may* not need the person's attention in order for him or her to grow and actualize. The below are simply general descriptions, which may apply in many external instances.

### NEGATIVE PREPONDERANCE BY MODE

### Absence of Cardinal Signs

Denotes an individual who may have great control over the outcome of any situation in which he becomes involved. Such a person does not need to become attached to a situation or ideal in order to realize the meaning of personal existence.

### Absence of Fixed Signs

The individual may be free to seek new areas of self-expression and freely exchange and examine contrasting ideals and values without inner conflict. Such a person, however, may need to develop structure and the sense of order needed to define and give meaning to his own life experiences.

### Absence of Mutable Signs

Refers to a person with a highly developed sense of individuality who may remain essentially unchanged through an experience. Such a person should enter interpersonal relationships without seeking to define his identity through others. There is a need for flexibility and co-operation.

## NEGATIVE PREPONDERANCE BY ELEMENT

### Absence of Fire Signs

Such a person needs to experience life more actively and more vitally. Self-expression, both emotional and creative, may be difficult, or, to compensate, the person may try to force self-expression.

### Absence of Earth Signs

Refers to a person who may be lacking in responsibility and stability, though he or she should have a deep and penetrating insight into life that transcends the mundane realm. There may be a compulsive urge toward neatness and detail as a compensative trait.

### Absence of Air Signs

Such a person may need to learn adaptability and the use of the mental functions in a creative manner. As compensation, one with an absence of air signs may strive to be "intellectual."

### Absence of Water Signs

Denotes an individual who may be unable to penetrate the surface of situations or experiences. Life, to such a person, may be unfulfilling and meaningless. There is a need to understand the unity of life and to universalize one's own consciousness.

## NEGATIVE PREPONDERANCE BY HOUSE EXPRESSION

### Absence of Planets in the Active Houses

A person with an absence of planets in the active houses may find it difficult to initiate and carry through new undertakings. Such a person needs to center himself and may compensate for this by the development of some special quality or ability.

### Absence of Planets in the Reactive Houses

Refers to the person who needs to learn from experience and focalize his energies adequately in order to bring about desired reactions.

## Absence of Planets in the Resultive Houses

Such a person needs to see the entire cycle of cause and effect that surrounds any act or situation. He or she should use this perception as an instrument of self-awareness.

NEGATIVE PREPONDERANCE BY ASPECT

## Absence of Conjunctions

The individual with no conjunctions may have scattered or poorly integrated energies. He or she may be free from dependent relationships, possibly isolated from others. Such an individual needs to learn how to bring his energies together.

## Absence of Oppositions

Denotes the type of person who is completely responsible for the maintenance of his own internal equilibrium. This may place him in great control of his own destiny, or may lead to the eventual disintegration of personality. Such a person needs to learn how to maintain an objective life perspective.

## Absence of Trines

Refers to a person who may be wasteful and careless of energy. Such a person needs to learn how to preserve and bring things together.

## Absence of Squares

Denotes an individual who has total responsibility for the application of his energies in order to bring about the actualization of any goal or purpose he may set for himself. This type of person needs to learn to exert a great deal of effort for prolonged periods.

## Absence of Sextiles

Refers to a person who may be overly concerned with petty matters and small details. The person may need to learn how to maintain interpersonal relationships and other forms of productive activity.

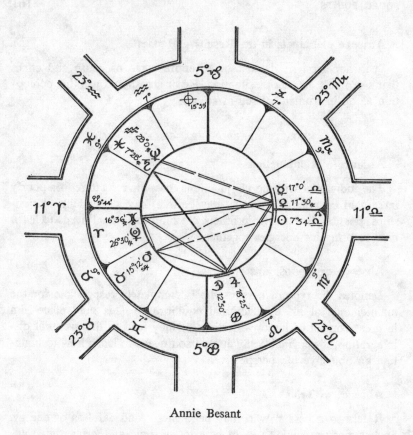

Annie Besant

## RETROGRADATION

### PREPONDERANCE BY RETROGRADATION

Formed when five or more planets are found in retrograde, preponderance by retrogradation indicates an awareness and expression of one's inner nature. Such a person's life pattern may be in direct conflict with convention, and there may be a desire to remake the world in the image of one's own likeness.

The birth-chart of Annie Besant, political agitator, freethinker, and theosophist, is an example of preponderance by retrogradation. There is also preponderance by cardinal signs (seven), by square (seven), and by active-house expression (six). Uranus is on the ascendant, and Sun is near the descendant. The chart has an asymmetric pattern.

All planets in the eastern hemisphere are retrograde. Besant's personality always seemed to manifest itself against the normal grain. She was active in women's liberation and published a book on birth control when it was almost unheard of and certainly "immoral." Later she became involved in political expression (cardinal preponderance) and the theosophical movement. She had intensity and self-reliance, which enabled her to carry anything she initiated to its ultimate conclusion and in some instances (perhaps her promotion of J. Krishnamurti being among them) past their logical conclusion.

### All Planets East Retrograde

When all planets in the eastern hemisphere are found in retrogradation, there may be a peculiar type of self-centeredness or self-reliance. Such a person is very involved with and attached to his or her own personal opinions and ideals, though not likely to force such beliefs upon others. There is a need to learn openness.

### All Planets West Retrograde

Refers to a person who may be concerned with the inner or personal significance of relationships. The individual may find it uneasy to achieve satisfaction and fulfillment through relationships, however.

### All Upper Planets Retrograde

Such a person may find little fulfillment in social life, while seeking to project himself into social activities and searching for personal meaning through identification with the social sphere.

### All Lower Planets Retrograde

Refers to an individual who may have little desire to become involved in domestic situations and may feel uneasy within a tight family situation. Such a person identifies himself as a solitary being, though he may feel that all men have a common "root" source.

## FOCAL PLANETS

When a planet appears to be outstanding or in focal emphasis, its function is manifested in a clear (if not dominant) manner by the personality. The individual's quality of self-expression and response to life experiences will reflect the principle and process symbolized by this planet. More than one focal planet (there are often many) in a chart symbolizes a more complex personality and mode of operation. More than plain, cold intellectual analysis is needed; here the astrologer should feel the chart as a whole and sense its focal centers as well as examine them.

### Singleton as Focal Planet

A singleton planet is always a focal planet. This does not alter its role as a release of energy or an object of distraction.

### Angular Planet

A planet standing alone on or near an angle is focal, and its functional principle should be integrated with the meaning of the particular angle. If a mass of planets happens to be situated on or near an angle, the angle itself will be focalized. Traditionally, a planet located on or near the M.C. is called *elevated;* a planet on or near the ascendant and in the first house is called *rising*.

### Location

A planet is naturally more focal when heavily aspected or placed in a sign or house with which it has an affinity. If a planet is placed in a sign or house of "opposing" nature, however, such as Saturn in the fourth house, the planet may also be highly focalized because of the unbalanced situation created.

Unaspected planets* are also very significant, because the function of the planet has no direct channel, or relationship, for its activity and must operate through other, less suitable or unconscious channels.

### Leading Planet

The first planet to cross the ascendant after birth is the leading planet. Its function is focused and leads the individual to new forms of experience of a personal significance.

* It may be advisable to use only the primary aspects here.

## Cutting Planet

The first counterclockwise planet from the ascendant of the main planetary group in a chart with a hemispheric, cluster, or open-angle pattern is called the cutting planet and is focal.

## Planets Contacting Abstract Points

A planet should be considered focal if it is contacting its own north or south node or its point of maximum latitude.

## Trigger

The trigger indicates a point of tension within a heavily squared chart and the channel through which this tension may be released and used by the process of creativity and self-actualization. It is formed by a focal planet and the body that happens to be squaring it with the closest orb. If the square is applying (closing), the release of power should be directed toward the self-centering process; if the square is separating, the release should be diffusive and directed toward the actualization of objectives rather than actualization of the self. An example of a trigger is Moon square Venus in the chart of Annie Besant.

# 4

# PLANETARY FORMATIONS

*Whenever parts conspire to form a whole, there something arises which is more than the parts.*

JAN C. SMUTS

## THE PRINCIPLE OF PLANETARY FORMATIONS

The next logical step in the process of interpretation is the consideration of important planetary configurations. When three or more planets are linked together by aspects, forming a three-or-more-sided formation, a special quality, purpose, and emphasis come into being. There are many possible variations of planetary formation (not to be confused with "planetary patterns"), some obvious in principle and operation, others less recognizable and more abstract in significance and principle, but all representing a special synthetic quality of relationship.

The first type of formations presented here are "greater" formations, which are composed of larger aspects, meaning that "lesser" and "minor" formations may be built within their structural framework.

### GREATER TRIANGLES

The T Square and the Grand Trine are composed of no fewer than three planets, at least one of which acts as a release for the dynamic energy built up within the formation.

#### THE T SQUARE

A T Square is formed by at least three planets, two in opposition and a third at or near their mid-point, squaring both ends of the op-

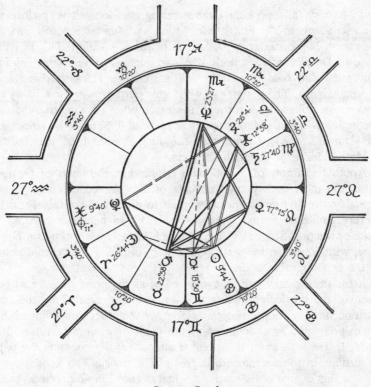

George Sand

position. The third planet, at the apex, acts as a release for the externalization of the special type of awareness symbolized by the opposition. The manner in which this awareness should be manifested and utilized may be determined by the nature and position of this body.

When found in a birth-chart, it is representative of a special need to take dynamic action, a situation brought about by the formation's principle of cross relationship. An individual with this formation in his or her chart may feel a great necessity to bring a certain type of situation into being, and frustration may be the result if the person is unable to bring it into concrete form.

An example of a T Square is found in the birth-chart of Annie Besant. Here there is a triple conjunction, involving the Sun, Venus, and Mercury, all opposing Uranus retrograde, located very close to the ascendant, in the first house. Moon and Jupiter are conjunct in the fourth house, squaring both ends of the opposition. This is symbolic of Dr. Besant's intensely dynamic personality and her deep involvement and commitment to political change (Uranus rising and cardinal signs). The manner in which this purpose was most likely to have been utilized was through the assumption of a matriarchal or protective position (Moon-Jupiter at apex of T Square in Cancer, in the fourth house); Besant was the first President of the Indian ("Mother India") National Congress.

Another example of a T Square is found in the chart of George Sand, the most widely read novelist of the nineteenth century and probably the first emancipated woman to enter the exclusively male literary circles of the early-romantic period. In her chart we find a close opposition between a third-house Mars and a ninth-house Neptune, with Venus in the sixth house, Leo, directing on the mid-point of the two opposing bodies.

If the third planet can be conceived of as the point of external release of the particular quality of awareness represented by the opposition, the point opposing this planet, or the other mid-point of the opposition, may be thought of as the point of awareness turned inward. In Besant's chart this point is almost exactly conjunct the part of fortune, in the seventeenth degree of Capricorn. The Sabian symbol for this degree aptly reads: "A mature but long-repressed young woman is bathing surreptitiously in the nude and finding a release in spirit."

### THE GRAND TRINE

A Grand Trine is formed by three or more planets situated at intervals of 120°, all in trine aspect to one another. If one draws lines connecting these planets, a triangle will appear.

In the Grand Trine, planets are linked to one another for some special purpose symbolized by the quality of the element involved, and particular sensitivity and emphasis are placed upon that elemental quality. If more than one element is involved, a complex and possibly conflicting nature is indicated. Often the Grand Trine is representative of a superficial, confused, or disoriented personality. The mind may be overly abstract or distant, in a dreamlike condition. The Grand Trine may also be indicative of an exceptionally gifted and sensitive personality.

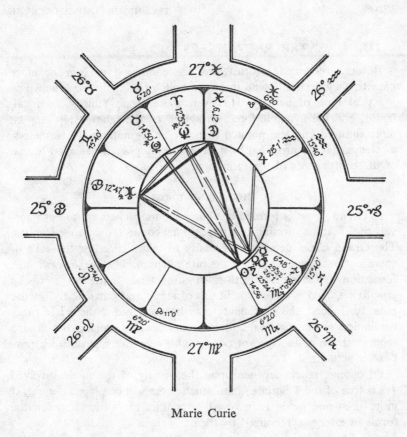

Marie Curie

The birth-chart of Marie Curie illustrates an example of a Grand Trine in water. The planetary pattern suggests an open nature, and we find no fewer than five planets in the fifth house, four of which are in the zodiacal sign of Scorpio. The Grand Trine is composed of a Sun-Saturn-Mars-Venus conjunction in Scorpio, which forms trines to the Moon in the ninth house, Pisces, and to Uranus retrograde, Cancer, in the twelfth house. The planet forming the closest square (if there are no squares, another aspect may be used, preferably a semisquare, sesquiquadrate, or opposition) to one of the components of the Grand Trine generally acts as a release. In the case of Marie Curie, an exact opposition between Sun and Pluto retrograde acts in this capacity.

## THE GREATER RECTANGLES

Because rectangular formations are composed of four or more planets, they generally tend to be symbolic of a highly constructive or practical type of activity. However, there is no "third," or focal, factor, and the dynamic forces produced by the relationship may be more diffused and less pointed than triadic formations. Nevertheless, a release may be provided by a trigger or by planets aspected to one of the components of the formation.

### THE GRAND CROSS

A Grand Cross is formed by four or more planets spaced at intervals of 90°, thus forming two oppositions connected by four squares. The Grand Cross denotes a necessity to take action for the sake of some concrete and seemingly definite purpose. The person with this formation in his or her birth-chart often leads a life of "symbolic crucifixion," living under conditions of stress and particularly intense polarity. Indeed, the personality may be polarized if there is no reconciliation of the two axes of awareness. The Grand Cross is also representative of the type of person who does not rest until his purpose is actualized.

Of course, much depends upon the quality of the mode involved (as is true of the T Square), and much stress will be placed upon it. If more than one mode is involved, a conflict may arise between the forms of energy symbolized by them.

### Grand Cross or T Square in the Cardinal Mode

Denotes a critical, impersonal, dominant individual who is primarily concerned with the vital issues of personal existence. A person with a Grand Cross or T Square in the cardinal mode should be constantly searching for new things to do and to put his or her vast energies into.

### Grand Cross or T Square in the Fixed Mode

Refers to a person concerned with the structure and meaning of individual existence. Attention should be given to abstractions, values, and ideals. The individual with a Fixed Cross or T Square in his or her birth-chart needs to use restraint when dealing with others, rather than being extremely determined or rigid.

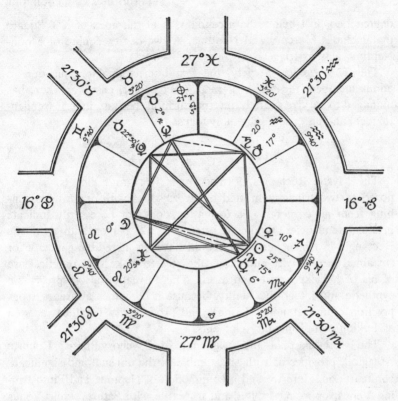

Theosophical Society

### Grand Cross or T Square in Mutable Mode

Characterizes an individual who should be concerned with people and personal or intimate relationships rather than with criticism, ideals, and values. A person with a Mutable Cross or T Square needs to be an individual rather than a follower of the leader and trends of the times.

An example of a well-defined Fixed Cross is found in the chart of the Theosophical Society (founded 1875). The cross involves no less than eight planets, and nine of the ten planetary bodies are located in fixed signs. All aspects are either squares or oppositions, with the exception of a biseptile between Jupiter and Moon and a biquintile between Saturn-Mars and Neptune. The planetary pattern is a well-defined fourfold. The Moon, in the first house, and the first degree Leo, just below the ascendant, is at the apex of a T Square that includes Mercury and Neptune. A two-degree square of Moon-Neptune acts as trigger.

The Theosophical Society, the first international organization to admit members regardless of race, creed, color, caste, and sex, has managed to survive years of internal turmoil, because its transcendental ideal and purpose is incredibly focused.

### THE MYSTIC RECTANGLE

The Mystic Rectangle, formed by at least four planets, is composed of two trines connected by two sextiles with oppositions running from all corners. This formation does not necessarily indicate mystical tendencies, though it often does. A person with a Mystic Rectangle in his or her chart should have an incredible capacity for sustained productivity and should be able to make very practical use of his or her experience and assets. This formation also represents a synthetic and integrative ability, because it combines awareness (opposition), understanding (trine), and productivity (sextile), as well as linking complementary elements.

The birth-chart of the originator of Psychosynthesis, Roberto Assagioli, provides us with an example of the unusual and significant configuration. Here we find a conjunction of Neptune and Pluto trining Venus, opposing Jupiter and in sextile with Saturn, while Venus is also opposing Saturn and in sextile aspect with Jupiter. In addition, one will notice a Mutable Cross, a Cardinal-Fixed T Square and numerous other formations and points of significance. All this denotes a most unique, creative, and sensitive personality. It is no wonder that Dr. Assagioli was able to synthesize and develop some of today's most significant and remarkable psychological techniques and theories.

## LESSER PLANETARY FORMATIONS

Lesser planetary formations may be divided into two groups: triangles, or triads; and rectangles, or tetrads. The lesser triangles are formed in the same manner as the T Square, while the lesser rectangles are formed by the geometric division of an area.

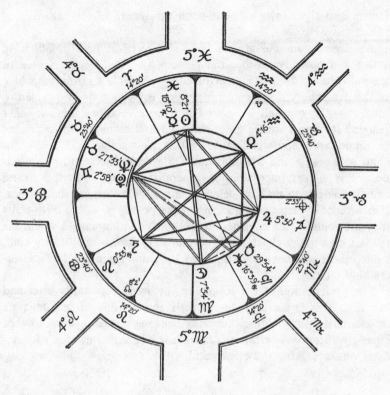

Roberto Assagioli

### LESSER TRIANGLES

There are at least nine formations in this group. The formulative principle here is the same as in the case of the T Square, three or more planets being involved, with at least one at the mid-point of an aspect formed by at least two other bodies. In some of these formations the third body is found at inverse mid-point. The planet at the apex of the formation (mid-point), of course, acts as an agency for the synthesis and externalization (mid-point) or internalization (inverse mid-point) of the functional principles symbolized by the first two planets. The exact nature of the process and the manner in which it should be utilized by the individual depend not only upon the houses and signs involved, but upon the nature of the aspects and planets as well.

All these formations are symbolic of a certain type of relationship active and operative within the personality and life experiences of the individual. The functions involved may be isolated from the whole of the personality if the entire formation is isolated or unaspected to other planets; or, well integrated if it is in relationship with other planets. It often requires great skill and understanding to determine the importance and significance of these formations within a birth-chart as a whole and the individual's life experiences and potentialities. It is almost impossible to generalize in their description and equally difficult to make a definite statement concerning their operation without a deep understanding of the person in whose birth-chart they are found. This consideration is further compounded when one realizes that many charts have no planetary formations of any kind, while others will have several, often built upon one another and incredibly interrelated.

The presentation of the formations below is necessarily brief and essential. This is partially due to their abstract and often intangible or indescribable qualities, but also because this is a new area of chart significance. For this reason one is advised to use such formations with a careful and open mind.

### Sextile/Trine/Sextile

This formation is composed of two planets in trine aspect with a third at their mid-point forming sextiles to both ends of the trine. It is representative of the practical and productive application of one's natural abilities and sensitivities. The planet at the apex acts as a release through which the relationship is manifest in an external and concrete form. An illustration of a sextile/trine/sextile formation is found in the birth-chart of Lewis Carroll, author of *Through the Looking-Glass and What Alice Found There*. The planetary pattern is a funnel, with Saturn retrograde in the ninth house, Virgo, and in focal emphasis, no doubt a significator of Carroll's unusual symbolic and abstract mathematical mind. The Moon and Pluto form a six-degree trine, defining the area of the funnel's main grouping, with the Sun at their exact mid-point, giving rise to the formation discussed here.

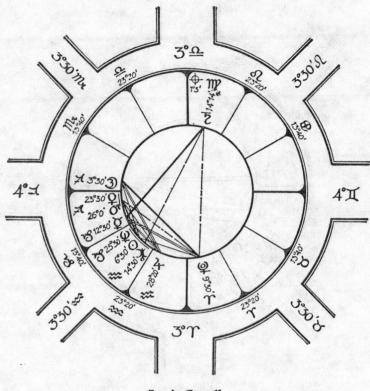

Lewis Carroll

### Semisquare/Square/Semisquare

This formation is composed of two planets in square aspect with a third at their mid-point, forming semisquares to both ends of the square. It is representative of intense interfunctional activity and focalization for the purpose of external self-expression and actualization of one's goals. Such a formation is found in the birth-chart (on page 176) of the well-known "foodist" Adelle Davis. Here we find a Fire-Water T Square, with Uranus and Neptune opposed on the horizon (several years ago she wrote a book on LSD, under a pseudonym), with a close conjunction of Mars and Jupiter at the apex in the third house, contacting the south lunar node. The Semisquare/ Square/Semisquare formation is significantly hooked up with this T

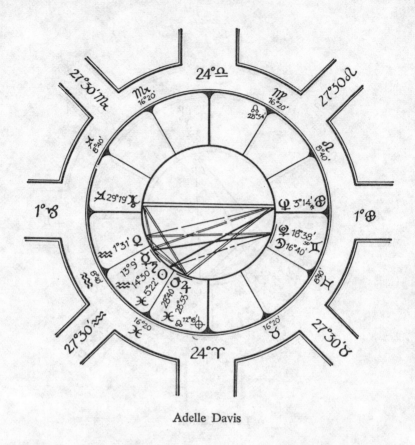

Adelle Davis

Square, with a conjunction of Mercury and Saturn at the mid-point of the Uranus-Mars with Mercury square, integrating the lesser triad with the T Square.

### Sesquiquadrate/Square/Sesquiquadrate

This is the inverse of the Semisquare/Square/Semisquare formation. It is composed of two planets in square with a third at their inverse mid-point. This formation is representative of an intense interfunctional activity and focalization for the purpose of actualizing one's self, and it is symbolic of a need to express one's internal awareness of self externally, within the social sphere. An example of this formation is found in the birth-chart of Timothy Leary. Here we find

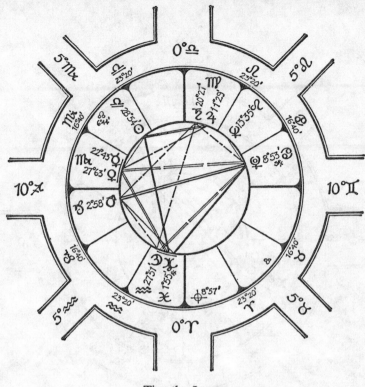

Timothy Leary

an open-angle pattern defined by a loose trine between Uranus and Pluto, with the center of gravity of the empty space coinciding with the mid-point of the lower-western quadrant and within two degrees of the south lunar node. The formation discussed here is formed by a square between a Mercury-Venus conjunction and the Moon (forming a seven-degree conjunction with Uranus) with Pluto retrograde at the inverse mid-point, forming sesquiquadrates to both ends of the square and opposing a first-house Mars.

### Semisextile/Sextile/Semisextile

This formation is composed of two planets in sextile aspect with a third at their mid-point forming semisextiles to both ends of the

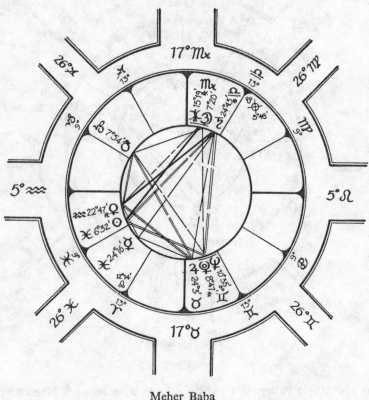

Meher Baba

sextile. It is representative of a highly intimate and abstract linking of centers for the release and expression of a very sensitive facet of personality.

### Quincunx/Sextile/Quincunx

The Quincunx/Sextile/Quincunx formation, better known as the "Finger of God," is the inverse of the above formation. It is composed of two planets in sextile with a third planet at inverse mid-point, forming quincunxes to both ends of the sextile. It is representative of a highly intimate linking of centers and symbolic of an internal or spiritual sensitivity. An example of this formation is found in the birth-chart of the "silent mystic," Meher Baba. The planetary

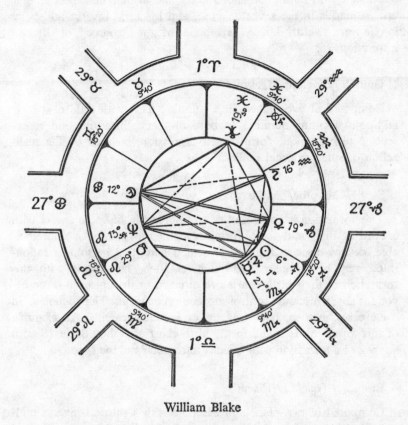

William Blake

pattern is asymmetric. Venus is retrograde and rising (symbolic of an ascetic life). Mars and the Moon are in sextile with a close conjunction of Neptune, with Pluto retrograde at the apex of the formation. Another is formed between the Sun, Jupiter, and Saturn.

### Biquintile/Quintile/Biquintile

This formation is composed of two planets in quintile aspect with a third at inverse mid-point. It is representative of interfunctional activity and focalization for the purpose of bringing a highly individual and unique form of self-expression into being, inspired by an internal realization. Such a formation is found in the birth-chart of the mystic, prophet, and artist William Blake. Here we find a Sagittarius

Sun in the fifth house conjunct Jupiter and in quintile aspect to Saturn, Aquarius in the seventh house, and Moon at inverse mid-point in Cancer, twelfth house (symbolic of the "source" of Blake's inspiration).

### Quintile/Biquintile/Quintile

Composed of two planets in biquintile aspect with a third at their mid-point forming quintiles to both of them, this formation represents a highly unique form of self-expression, inspired by the realization of some external reality.

### Septile/Biseptile/Septile

This formation is composed of two planets in biseptile aspect with a third at their mid-point, forming septiles to them. An unpredictable, destiny-directed life is represented here, and personal relationships may be complex and intense. Often, individuals with this formation in their birth-charts are directed or driven, by a force beyond their conscious control or comprehension. This denotes, in some cases, sudden, fateful events or karmic incidents. An example of this formation is found in the birth-chart of Bobby Seale (Saturn at apex of a formation with Uranus retrograde and the Moon).

### Biseptile/Triseptile/Biseptile

Composed of two planets in triseptile with a third at inverse mid-point, this formation represents internal or spiritual experiences and events. An example of it is found in the chart of Lewis Carroll, with Saturn retrograde at the apex of a formation with Pluto and a conjunction of Venus and Mars.

#### LESSER TETRADIC FORMATIONS

A lesser tetradic formation is basically two or more triadic formations built upon one another. Generally, these formations are representative of an integrated or synthesizing nature with the ability to function well in crises.

There are several formations in this group; some of the most significant are:

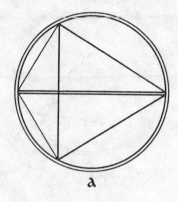

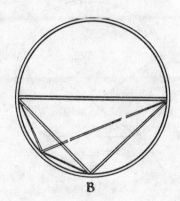

a

B

**a**   the Kite, composed of a Grand Trine with a planet at the mid-point of one of the trines;

**b**   a T Square with a planet at the mid-point or inverse mid-points of one of its squares;

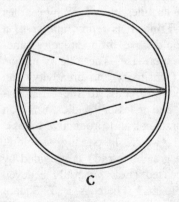

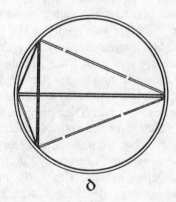

C

d

**c**   a Finger of God with a planet at the mid-point of its sextile;

**d**   a Sesquiquadrant/Square/Sesquiquadrant triangle with a planet at the mid-point of the square;

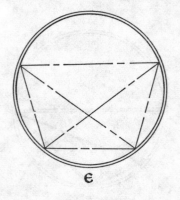

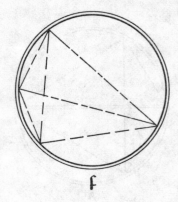

e    a Biquintile/Quintile/Biquintile formation with a planet at the mid-point of one of its biquintiles;

f    a Triseptile/Biseptile/Biseptile formation with a planet at the mid-point of one its biseptiles.

These formations rarely appear in birth-charts.

*The Kite:* This is perhaps the most commonly seen of the lesser tetradic formations. It is extremely significant, because it is composed of a Grand Trine with an opposition running from one of its points to a planet at the mid-point of one of its sides, thus forming sextiles to the other two points of the Grand Trine. It is representative of a highly integrated personality that should have little difficulty functioning well within any situation or experience. The Kite is unique because it combines a Grand Trine (sensitivity and creativity), an opposition (which gives direction and awareness to the often disoriented Grand Trine temperament), and a lesser triadic formation (which gives the entire formation a practical and productive focus).

Another example of a lesser tetrad (which, in passing, shouldn't be considered necessarily inferior to a greater tetrad) is provided by the chart of Karl Krafft, the man accused (now generally believed wrongfully) of being "Hitler's astrologer." There is a T Square formed by an opposition between Venus and Saturn with the Moon at the apex. A Sesquiquadrant/Square/Sesquiquadrant formation, composed by the Saturn-Moon side of the T Square with the Sun at inverse mid-point, completing the formation with a semisquare to Venus. The entire formation projects the image of an elongated

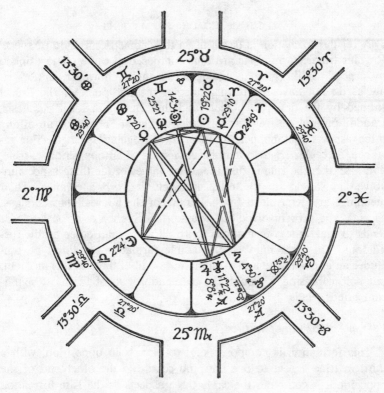

Karl Krafft

tetrahedron. Krafft was said to have cast and statistically studied over sixty thousand birth-charts during his lifetime and was one of the originators of a scientific and statistical form of astrology: Cosmobiology. Despite his open admiration of the Third Reich, Krafft was among the many astrologers imprisoned during World War II and forced to produce propaganda. Eventually he defied his captors; he died shortly before the fall of the Third Reich.

## MINOR PLANETARY FORMATIONS

Minor planetary formations are the type of planetary configurations most frequently found in astrological charts. They may be divided into two sets of dichotomous categories: regular and irregular; triadic and tetradic.

### REGULAR TRIADIC FORMATIONS

A regular formation is based upon the geometric division of space. Regular triadic formations are thus composed of three planets linked by aspect. Unlike greater and lesser triangles, however, minor triangles do not have the third planet at the mid-point of the aspect formed by the first two planets and thus have less focal emphasis. In addition, unlike irregular formations, they are not made up of any three aspects that happen to form an "irregular" triangle. For instance, a regular triangle may be composed of an opposition, a trine, and a sextile; the rule is that the exact values of the three aspects involved must add up to 360°, not including orb allowance. Their meanings are determined by the nature of the houses, planets, signs, aspects, and orbs involved. Of course, the absence of a focal release tends to make these formations more diffusive than other triadic formations. The large number of possible formations of this type precludes an enumeration and examination of all of them at this moment, but before passing, I would like to mention two of the most significant minor triads.

#### Opposition/Trine/Sextile

This formation is composed of two planets in opposition, with a third in trine aspect to one end and sextile to the other end of the opposition. It combines the same three aspects as the Kite formation and is in a sense half of a Kite. It is representative of the synthetic and harmonious blending of awareness, sensitivity, and creativity with technique and productivity, potentially acting as a great asset to the person with it in his or her birth-chart. An example may be found in the birth-chart of the actress Sarah Bernhardt. Here we find an opposition between a conjunction of Sun and Mercury in the fifth house and a triple conjunction of Moon, Jupiter, and Uranus in the eleventh house. The formation is completed by Saturn on the M.C., forming a trine to Sun and Mercury and a sextile to the Moon-Jupiter-Uranus conjunction.

#### Triseptile/Biseptile/Septile

This formation is composed of two planets in triseptile aspect with a third planet forming a septile to one end and a biseptile to the other end of the triseptile. It is interesting that this formation is com-

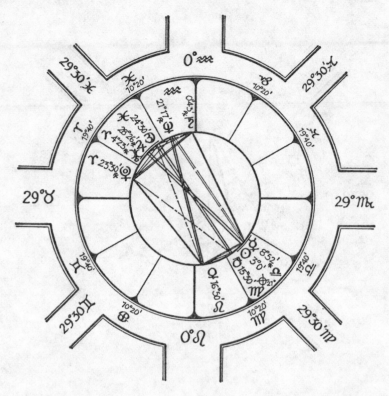

Sarah Bernhardt

monly found in the birth-charts of persons who lead unusual, fateful, or symbolic lives. An example of this formation is found in the birth-chart of Isadora Duncan (on page 186). It is formed by a triseptile between Mars (very near the I.C.) in Cancer and Jupiter retrograde in the tenth house, Aquarius. This formation is completed by an otherwise unaspected Saturn in the twelfth house, Pisces, forming a septile to Jupiter and a biseptile to Mars. There are also a waning septile between the Sun and Moon and a biseptile between Uranus and Mercury, which are not a part of this formation. Isadora Duncan, who was one of the most significant figures in the liberation of the dance, led a very unusual and fateful life. Other examples of this formation may be found in the birth-charts of Timothy Leary and William Blake.

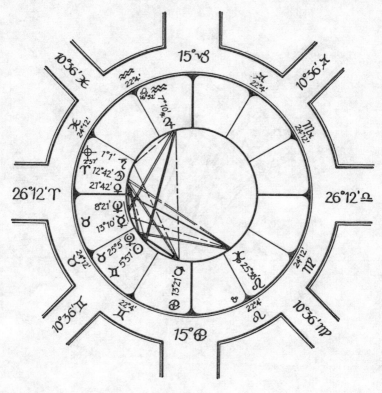

Isadora Duncan

### REGULAR TETRADIC FORMATIONS

These formations are based upon the same principle as the regular triads, only they are composed of four or more planets. There are several such formations possible, and all generally represent a practical and functional blending and externalization of the activities and principles involved. Of course, much depends upon the nature of the factors. An example of such a formation is found in the birth-chart of George Gurdjieff. Here we find what may be called a Trine/Square/Trine/Semisquare formation, composed of a trine between Sun and Pluto, a square between Pluto and Uranus, another trine between Uranus and a Venus-Jupiter conjunction, and finally a semisquare running from this conjunction and the Sun. Gurdjieff was an

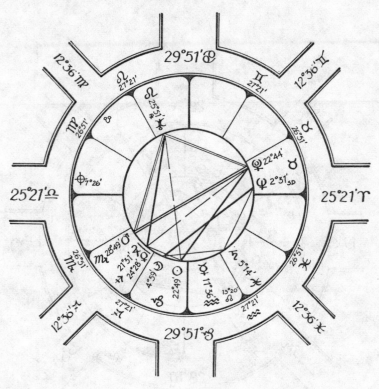

George Gurdjieff

inventive genius, which enabled him not only to exercise great control over practical and mundane affairs, but also to formulate a highly complex, metaphysical philosophy.

### Irregular Formations

Irregular formations are composed of random aspects and are not based on the geometric division of space. An example of an irregular formation would be two planets in trine aspect with a third forming a septile to one end of the trine and a quintile to the other. The manner in which these formations harmonize (triadic) or externalize (rectangular) the functions involved depends upon the nature of the planets, houses, signs, and aspects.

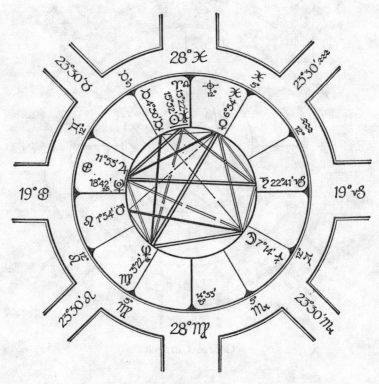

Baba Ram Dass

## MULTIPLANETARY FORMATIONS

Occasionally, five or more planetary bodies are linked together by aspect and encircle the entire birth-chart. Such formations often produce quite interesting visuals, some of which suggest a three-dimensional quality. Generally, one may say that these formations are representative of a potentially highly integrated and unique personality. A person with this type of formation in his or her birth-chart may be one who is able to bring many varied and diverse elements of personality into a focused and operative synthesis within any specific area of experience and activity.

A pentagon type of formation is found in the birth-chart of Baba

Ram Dass. Here we find Neptune retrograde in Virgo, and in the second house, squaring the Moon in the fifth house, which in turn semi-squares Saturn. Saturn then forms a T Square with an opposition to a Jupiter-Pluto conjunction with the Sun at the apex with one degree of Uranus, in the tenth house, Aries, while Jupiter-Pluto semisquares Neptune. The planetary pattern appears to be a tripod, though it may be considered as asymmetric. There are no planets in the air element. Baba Ram Dass, formerly known as Dr. Richard Alpert, was a coworker of Timothy Leary, involved in the LSD research that took place at Harvard (Uranus conjunct Sun and north lunar node). Subsequently, Alpert, Leary, and a third researcher, Dr. Ralph Metzner, were expelled from the faculty. During 1967 Alpert began a study of Ashtanga yoga in the Himalayas, adopted the name Baba Ram Dass, and returned to the West, where he became affiliated with the Lama Foundation.

The same type of pentagon may be seen in the chart of John Brzostoski.

One should avoid overstressing the importance of these formations and those given earlier in the chapter. The manner in which such patterns may manifest themselves, and to what extent, are very difficult to ascertain; any formation may be indicative of a well-integrated, highly creative individual as well as a superficial, ego-centered personality with a sense of superiority over others. This is not to say that one should ignore the more complex and abstract planetary formations, though one should know and understand the person whose chart is being interpreted, considering these formations carefully, as related to the needs of the person.

## PERFECT FORMATIONS

There are four arrangements that could be regarded as "perfect" formations, because the planets involved are spaced at regular and equal intervals throughout the 360° of the zodiac. However, one may never see any of these formations, and for this reason they might be regarded as archetypes that are not necessarily actualized. In other words, these formations represent perfect forms, even though they may never occur within the framework of astronomy.

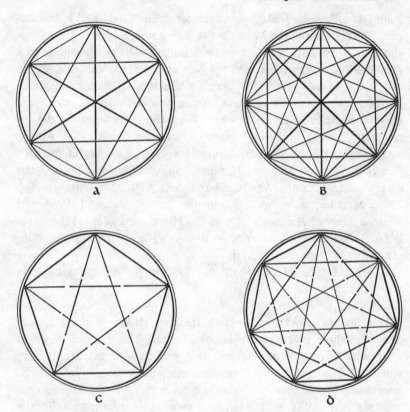

The perfect formations are:

**a**  The Grand Sextile, formed by a series of six sextiles
**b**  The Grand Semisquare, formed by a series of eight semisquares
**c**  The Grand Quintile, formed by a series of five quintiles
**d**  The Grand Septile, formed by a series of seven septiles.

# 5

# THE LUNATION CYCLE:
# THE ARCHETYPAL CYCLE
# OF RELATIONSHIP

*The relationship of the sun to the moon refers to the very essence of life. . . .*

DANE RUDHYAR

## THE SOLI-LUNAR RELATIONSHIP

The Sun's relationship with the Moon is ever-changing in appearance though of a structurally ordered and cyclic nature. The "primitive" mind was no doubt quick to correlate changes in the appearance of the Moon to natural rhythmic cycles operative on a less grand scale, particularly to the female menstrual cycle. What this type of mentality probably didn't understand, however, is that the Moon does not change, it is the soli-lunar relationship that changes; the Moon simply *reflects* the changing relationship.

What we will be considering in this chapter is the significance of the lunation cycle in natal astrology and what the soli-lunar relationship symbolizes in human personality. The lunation cycle deals with the very substance of the personality itself; it symbolizes how the life process is operative within the person and how he or she brings about the actualization of the archetypal purpose symbolized by the house and degree of the Sun in the birth-chart.

Occultly speaking, human evolution on this planet is not yet advanced enough (with a few exceptions) to assimilate directly the life forces of the Sun. This necessitates a lunar principle to mediate the solar light forces to the earth. It is in this context that the Sun can be understood as being symbolic of the root energy and source of the

basic archetypal purpose of the human being, with the Moon symbolic of relatedness and the fulfillment and actualization of this solar
purpose, and provider of assimilatable nourishment.


## THE ARCHETYPAL CYCLE OF RELATIONSHIP

Relationship (an integral component of existence) is dynamic and
cyclic by nature; life implies relationship, and relationship means
change. In astrological terms any cycle of relationship begins with a
conjunction, culminates at the opposition, and ends, only to begin
again, at the next conjunction. The following conjunction, however,
never takes place at the same point as the precedent. The soli-lunar
relationship is *archetypal,* because it deals with the bipolar *life process* operative in all existence and is the most apparent of all cyclic
celestial phenomena.

The cyclic process is operative within all relationship—the *phase,*
not just the *position* of relationship, should be considered when the
astrologer studies a birth-chart. In other words, the entire cycle of relationship existing between two planetary bodies is significant, not
just their angular relationship.


## THE TWO HEMICYCLES

The reader will recall earlier in the text the formula of the cyclic
process outlined and applied to the houses, signs, and aspects. Here
the cyclic process will be described as it is active and operative within
the realm of bipolar relationships (symbolized by the pairing of
planets), for which the lunation cycle serves as an archetype.

Every cycle contains two distinct hemicycles; in astrological terms,
a *waxing* hemicycle (from conjunction to opposition) and a *waning*
hemicycle (from opposition to conjunction), each having a distinct
process and function.


### THE WAXING HEMICYCLE

In terms of the soli-lunar relationship, the waxing hemicycle covers
the span from New Moon (conjunction) to Full Moon (opposition).
*Process:*  Spontaneous, instinctual growth and action.
*Function:*  Building and development of organic structures.

### THE WANING HEMICYCLE

From Full Moon to New Moon, when the Moon's light is decreasing.

*Process:*  Release of and conscious growth in meaning and self-hood.

*Function:*  Release of the meaning and significance contained within the structures built during the waxing hemicycle and its synthesis into the basic personality of the individual.

## THE FOUR QUADRICYCLES

The two hemicycles may be divided into four quadricycles, giving us two additional points of reference. The mid-point of each quadricycle may be seen as the point of maximum intensity within that quadricycle.

### New Moon to First Quarter

*Position:*  Moon 0° to 90° ahead of Sun in terms of the zodiac.

*Process:*  Instinctual and unconscious activity; subjectivity—little differentiation between internal and external realms.

*Function:*  The search for a definite sense of self.

*Mid-point:*  Crisis in relationship brings about a clash between the old forms left over from the precedent cycle and new forms to be developed.

### First Quarter to Full Moon

*Position:*  Moon 90° to 180° ahead of Sun.

*Process:*  Development of structures for the future use of the "builder" and the attainment of status and authority within a group through the employment of such structures.

*Function:*  The building of a firm basis for personality.

*Mid-point:*  The apex of willful activity and the urge for self-expression.

### Full Moon to Third Quarter

*Position:*  Moon 180° to 90° behind Sun in terms of the zodiac.

*Process:*  Gradual release of meaning and significance; growth and expansion of consciousness.

*Function:* Repolarization. If the waxing hemicyclic experience was integrated into the personality in a positive manner, the relationship will bear its fruit. If the experiences of the waxing hemicycle were not successfully integrated, relationship may break down and disintegrate during the waning hemicycle, leaving the person in a state of alienation.

*Mid-point:* Crisis in relationship. Objective participation within a greater whole, or a sense of defeat and an attempt to lose oneself through identification with some highly organized social movement as an escape from creative participation.

### Third Quarter to New Moon

*Position:* Moon 90° to 0° behind Sun.

*Process:* Breaking down of old images. Completion and assimilation of experience.

*Function:* The challenge of old and antiquated forms and social structures. Re-formation of social-collective ideals and formation of seed.

*Mid-point:* Crisis in repolarization and personal sacrifice. Focalization on the new birth or new beginning and the sowing of the seed.

## THE EIGHT SOLI-LUNAR TYPES

A framework may now be devised that will enable one to understand the basic manner in which the individual's personal, social, and cultural relationships are polarized and manifested. The determination of how the soli-lunar relationship at the time of birth fits into this structure (which is organic, whole, and cyclic by nature) should offer significant insight into the person's purpose of living (Sun-Moon).

## NEW-MOON TYPE

Moon 0° to 45° ahead of Sun.

*Key Word:* **Emergence.**

*Temperament:* Subjective and impulsive; responds to relationship instinctively.

*Process:* Projection of one's personal ideals and concepts (which may be somewhat confused) upon the outer world.

*Examples:* Freud, Marx, LBJ, Nixon.

## CRESCENT-MOON TYPE

Moon 45° to 90° ahead of Sun.

*Key Word:* **Assertion.**

*Temperament:* Confident in one's self and having the need to make an impression upon the outer world.

*Process:* Challenge of old forms left over from the former cycle. Repolarization from personal emphasis to individual concern.

*Examples:* JFK, Bobby Seale, Maria Montessori.

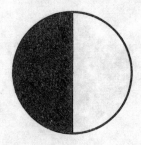

## FIRST-QUARTER TYPE

Moon 90° to 135° ahead of Sun.

*Key Word:* **Action.**

*Temperament:* Strong-willed. Ego emphasis or ego-building activities predominant. If negative: exploitive and ruthless.

*Process:* Crisis in action. Building of structures to serve the person in the actualization of his objectives and purposes. A need for direct action and a feeling of urgency.

*Examples:* Stalin, Alice Bailey, John Lennon.

## GIBBOUS-MOON TYPE

Moon 135° to 180° ahead of Sun.

*Key Word:* **Expression.**

*Temperament:* Mental and associative. Questioning and searching for some kind of revelation or illumination.

*Process:* Introspection. Personal growth and a need to contribute to society or culture in a creative manner.

*Examples:* Janis Joplin, FDR, Jakob Boehme.

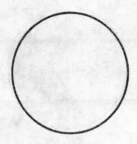

## FULL-MOON TYPE

Moon 180° to 135° behind Sun.

*Key Word:* **Fulfillment.**

*Temperament:* Open and full. Theoretically objective and fulfillment oriented. Functionally objective, rather than instinctive.

*Process:* Fulfillment of relationship. If negative, separation and divorce from reality and disintegration of personality. The fulfillment urge may become distorted and may result in a desire to withdraw from all but the most "ideal" or "absolute" relationship.

*Examples:* Rudolf Steiner, J. Krishnamurti.

## DISSEMINATING TYPE

Moon 135° to 90° behind Sun.

*Key Word:* **Synthesis.**

*Temperament:* Assimilative, evaluative, and innovative.

*Process:* Dissemination of what one has learned or experienced. The need to impress and inspire others and release new ideas.

*Examples:* Meher Baba, Baba Ram Dass, Hitler.

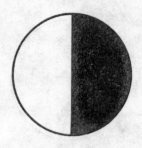

## THIRD-QUARTER TYPE

Moon 90° to 45° behind Sun.

*Key Word:* **Reorientation.**

*Temperament:* Future oriented and inventive. May lack flexibility and may be forceful with issues.

*Process:* The embodiment of personal ideals and philosophy into an organized system or institution. The application of universal principles to practical and historical affairs.

*Examples:* Lenin, Trotsky, Marc Edmund Jones, Henry Steele Olcott, Annie Besant.

## BALSAMIC-MOON TYPE

Moon less than 45° behind Sun.

*Key Word:* **Release.**

*Temperament:* Future oriented, yet aware of the past and its influence upon the future. A feeling of "destiny" and the will to sacrifice one's self for the well-being and future growth of humanity.

*Process:* The release of seed ideas and the assistance of the future growth of a greater whole. The imparting of visions of the future to humanity.

*Examples:* Thomas Paine, Kant, Dane Rudhyar, Bob Dylan.

## SUB-CYCLIC CORRESPONDENCE

Each phase of the soli-lunar relationship may be seen as a smaller cycle within the greater cycle of the entire lunation cycle. In other words, a 226° Disseminating Moon is not the same as a 269° Disseminating Moon, and this distinction may be determined by superimposing the great cycle of the soli-lunar relationship with its eight types upon the individual 45° cycle of each of its eight types. For instance, the 226° Disseminating Moon refers to the initial, or New Moon, phase of the disseminating process, while the 269° Disseminating Moon refers to the closing, or balsamic, phase of the same process. Within this context each 45° phase is divided by eight, with each sub-cyclic phase occupying 5°37′30″.

## PLANETARY PLACEMENT WITHIN THE STRUCTURE OF THE LUNATION CYCLE

The manner in which the planets are placed in reference to the framework provided by the lunation cycle carries significance.

*Planets Contained Within the Span Covered by the Lunation Cycle.* Planets found within the space covered by the Moon after its conjunction with the Sun are considered the contents inherent at birth. The functions of these planets may be considered developed at birth due to antecedent causes.

*Planets Contained Outside the Span of the Lunation Cycle.* If the Moon is waxing, these planets represent powers and faculties that are not yet fully developed, or the faculties upon which the individual should place particular stress and that he or she should attempt to develop.

*Planets Contacted After Full Moon.* These planets, in the case where the Moon is waning at the time of birth, will be involved in the creative release of the personality and the creative contribution of the individual to a greater whole.

*Participants in the Dawn.* As the lunation cycle draws to a close, these planets are found between the Sun and the Moon. They are symbolic seeds and may represent the special message of the person.

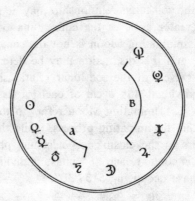

a) Planets contacted          b) Planets outside the
   by the Moon                   span of the lunation
                                 cycle

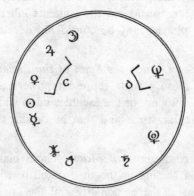

c) Participants in            d) Planet contacted
   the dawn                      after Full Moon

## SOLI-LUNAR-HORIZON ARRANGEMENT

The outline below of soli-lunar-horizon arrangements is quite useful in the interpretation of a birth-chart.

$$\frac{\text{☽}}{\text{☉}}$$

*Moon above, Sun below the horizon*

Denotes a person who should strive to give individual meaning to collective-social ideals and values.
EXAMPLES: Meher Baba, Bobby Seale, Oscar Wilde.

$$\frac{\text{☉}}{\text{☽}}$$

*Sun above, Moon below the horizon*

This type of person strives to give social and collective meaning to his own personal values and ideals.
EXAMPLES: Alice Bailey, Annie Besant, Baba Ram Dass, Timothy Leary.

$$\underline{\text{☉ - ☽}}$$

*Sun and Moon above the horizon*

The individual energies should be focused upon social-collective-cultural activities or political and spiritual values and ideals.
EXAMPLES: Bob Dylan, C. G. Jung, Maria Montessori.

$$\overline{\text{☉ - ☽}}$$

*Sun and Moon below the horizon*

Denotes a person concerned with the fulfillment and actualization of his or her own ideals, plans, and interests.
EXAMPLES: John Lennon, Richard Nixon, Stalin.

## THE TRIAD OF PERSONALITY PROJECTION

The Sun, Moon, and ascendant are symbols of personality, when considered as an operative whole. Within this context the Sun is the significator of self as it relates and is operative within the archetypal (and in a sense collective) field of experience. It has collective and archetypal meaning, because the Sun's apparent position on the ecliptic represents the individual's relationship to the social whole—the yearly solar cycle. In other words, the Sun's position is determined by what part (day) of the year the person was born in. By the same logic, the natal Moon represents the person's characteristic way of manifesting self within the personal realm of experience, being representative of the part of the month during which birth occurred. Finally, the ascendant, the most individual and particular of the three personalizing facets of self, represents the moment of birth in terms of the daily motion or rotation of the earth. When these three principles or facets of personalizing force are synthesized, they emerge as an integrated and operative whole, as personality, as a direct manifestation or reflection of the individual life force, the monad.

This synthesis has been called the Triad of Personality Projection; its particular function is to project, or externalize, the personalizing forces of the self in a creative and personally significant manner.

# PLANETARY GROUPING: THE REALM OF MULTIFUNCTIONAL INTEGRATION

*The human individual operates fundamentally in two realms: the realm of dualistic soli-lunar relationship ("life"), and that of complex organic relationships established between the periodic motions of the planets within the solar system as a whole.*

DANE RUDHYAR

## TWO TYPES OF PLANETS

Humanistic astrology deals with two types or categories of planets: the "lights," the Sun and Moon, whose bipolar activity symbolizes the very source of life itself; and the solar system as a whole, with *all the planets,* including the Sun and Moon, contained within it. This second group of planets channels the bipolar life generated by the soli-lunar relationship and makes it manifest in vast and varied forms. It is these planets of "multifunctional integration" that symbolize the various organic functions operative within any whole. In the span of the next several pages, we'll explore the realm of multifunctional integration and examine the various functions as they are operative within personality. Most important, it should be remembered that the archetypal pattern of relationship described by the lunation cycle can, and should, be applied to the planetary pairs given below, with significant results.

## FOUR BASIC FUNCTIONS

The planets of multifunctional integration may be correlated to the four basic urges, drives, or functions that are a part of the psychological being of every integrated organism.

THE FOUR ESSENTIAL FUNCTIONS*

1) The urge to be a "particular" being. The formation of the ego.
2) The urge to maintain the particular form and quality of this particular being.
3) The urge to reproduce its particular quality.
4) The urge to transform in accordance with some purpose. The urge to evolve.

Any one of the above may be:

a) expressed in a positive (constructive) or negative (destructive) manner, in terms of personal integration;
b) overwhelmed by its own desire element, and in turn overwhelm the entire organism—unless checked by other functions and kept within its proper limits by the structuring or regulating power of the organism. If any one of the four essential functions takes on a condition of abnormal proportion (over- or underdevelopment), a distinct condition may develop.

## AN ASTROLOGICAL SURVEY
## OF THE FOUR ESSENTIAL FUNCTIONS

1) *The urge to be a particular being*

The formation of the individual, differentiated ego is symbolized by the Saturn function, which provides the ego structure, and by the lunar function, which provides the life contents of this structure. These two planets compose (in this context) a bipolar relationship and function together as the Dyad of Identification and Adaption.

2) *The urge to maintain the particular form and quality of this particular being*

The Jupiter function preserves what has been defined by Saturn

* Adapted from *An Astrological Study of Psychological Complexes,* by Dane Rudhyar.

and established by the Moon. This process is carried out in close co-operation with the Mercury function, the principle of relatedness and association. The bipolar activity of Jupiter and Mercury compose the Dyad of Preservation and Association.

3) *The urge to reproduce the particular quality of being*

The particular quality of the organism is reproduced biologically through sex and creatively through the creation and projection of internal forms, ideals, and values. Venus, in this context, symbolizes the seed, while Mars represents the process of germination. Together, Venus and Mars operate as the Dyad of Sex.

4) *The urge to transform the individual being in accordance with some purpose; the urge to become greater*

The urge to go beyond the area defined and limited by Saturn is symbolized by the three trans-Saturnian planets, Uranus, Neptune, and Pluto, which together function as the Triad of Transformation and Self-Transcendence.

## PSYCHOLOGICAL COMPLEXES AND HUMANISTIC ASTROLOGY

An imbalance in the functional operation of any organism is bound to result in some sort of difficulty, especially if the imbalance is prolonged or isolated in one part of the organism. "Abnormal" development of any function is likely to produce or indicate what has been called a "complex" in modern psychology.

C. G. Jung explains that the contents of a complex are experiences that have been cut off from the whole of personality, repressed by the conscious mind, but continuously making their presence known by hindering the harmonious operation of the conscious mind and the individual's daily life. The origin of a complex is generally believed to be some kind of severe emotional shock. In simpler terms, one may describe a complex as a weak spot in the personality or an inability to accept the whole of one's own nature.

As we'll see in the following pages, certain types of psychological complexes may be related to particular astrological factors. Nothing in a birth-chart will, however, cause a complex. What these factors do is point to the source of a particular condition *if* the condition is present and indicate how the condition may be adjusted. The interpretation of these factors requires great skill, objectivity, and wisdom on the part of the astrologer, for he or she must understand the nature of personality as well as be free from prejudice toward any individual person or astrological factor, at least at the moment of interpretation.

## DYAD OF IDENTIFICATION AND ADAPTION

The Dyad of Identification and Adaption is the symbolic molding force behind the establishment (Moon) of the ego (Saturn) and its gradual development (Moon) into a distinct individual (Saturn).

In this process of becoming, Saturn and the Moon represent the archetypal father and mother images. The result of this process determines to a great extent the personal identity and how one will react to one's self and one's individual life experiences.

### MOON AS MOTHER IMAGE

As the mother image, the Moon symbolizes what the traditional mother is to her child: the provider of nourishment, the protector against any harm that may befall the tiny ego, the adjuster of day-to-day necessities, and perhaps most of all, the essence of inner security and comfort.

If the mother function, and the experiences given the ego by the mother, have been "normal" (neither excessive nor inadequate), the individual should be capable, upon reaching maturity, of his own adjustments to life, of providing his own nourishment and making his own way through life as a self-sustaining individual. In other words, if the mother function has been well balanced, the person should be prepared to cope with and adjust to life experiences and circumstances without difficulty.

### SATURN AS FATHER IMAGE

Just as the Moon represents all the traditional mother is to her child, Saturn symbolizes the traditional father image. Saturn becomes the mediator between the outer world and the individual, the provider of material substance, and the ideal manifestation of outer strength and security.

If the father function and the experiences given the ego by it have been well balanced, the individual should be able to meet life experiences (Moon) with enough outer strength to prevent being overwhelmed by them and should have a stable enough sense of identity to remain essentially what he *is* through any experience, no matter how difficult it may be.

## PARENTAL COMPLEXES

An imbalanced or inharmonious relationship between Saturn and the Moon indicates the possible presence of what has been called a "parental complex." The actual presence of such a condition affects the personality and the manner and attitude in which the individual reacts to himself and to his life experiences. If a full-scale complex is not present, the examination of the relationship between Saturn and the Moon may reveal certain distinctions.

### A Positive Saturn-Negative Moon Situation

When Saturn is emphasized in a birth-chart (by house, sign, aspects, etc.), while the Moon is relatively unemphasized, a positive Saturn-negative Moon condition may be present.

This condition denotes a person who seeks order, form, pattern, and structure in everything. Such a person attempts to analyze and systematize life, often at the expense of the immediate situation. There may be a search for the universal father in the form of wisdom and understanding, or in later life, a search for a transcendental mother image to provide and protect the person on a psycho-spiritual level. Such a desire may be fulfilled by emotional involvement with such things as religion, philosophy, love of country, etc.

If Saturn overwhelms (is much more emphasized than) the Moon, the individual may assume a very structured, overconfident, and cold attitude toward life and relationship. He may have a positive force-against-force attitude, going about thinking he can get anything he wants if he meets force with a greater force.

### A Positive Moon-Negative Saturn Situation

This situation is indicated by a well-placed or emphasized Moon and a relatively unemphasized Saturn. It represents a personality with a weak or undefined sense of individuality, lacking self-confidence and fearing authority, yet seeking identity through acceptance of dogma, rules, and laws or by becoming attached to some organization, movement, or church. Such a person is constantly searching for a "mother" who will provide for and protect him, make decisions and adjustments concerning his everyday affairs.

If the Moon overshadows (is much more emphasized than) Saturn, the individual may have a negative attitude toward life, constantly feeling at the mercy of overwhelming forces beyond his personal control. Such an individual may display pessimism and a defeatist attitude, possibly turning toward religion or political movements for meaning.

## THE CYCLES OF SATURN AND THE MOON

One may reach a deeper understanding of the Dyad of Identification and Adaption by noting the *phase of relationship* existing between Saturn and Moon, interpreting it in the manner of the lunation cycle.

The cycle of Saturn and the Moon, and the process symbolized by them are particularly significant. They represent the forces that enable the person to function as an individual. They bring into usable focus the energies of self and personality. Without a Moon, there would be nothing to protect and provide for the defenseless and still self-unconscious ego. Without Saturn, there would be nothing to give definition, no focus, nothing to contain one's still developing potential; nothing would have form or definition, and there would be no individual existence.

The Moon may be seen, in a way, as a microcosm of Saturn. Saturn defines the realm of particulars—while the Moon defines the earth's realm of organic life and the individual's realm of personal existence. It is significant that the term of the lunation cycle is 29-½ days, while the cycle of Saturn is 29-½ years.

## DYAD OF PARTICIPATION AND ASSOCIATION

Jupiter and Mercury compose a polarity representing the interplay between preservation and participation of the individual with a social whole and the interchange and association of the contents of that social whole. In these terms, Jupiter represents the basic social function, the preservation of any established form, and the general increase and expansion of the organic unit. Mercury is the "servant" of Jupiter: the symbol of the technique of gathering and associating knowledge and its efficient application. In an ideal condition of equilibrium, these functions may be described by the following formula:

Jupiter (assimilation of the social/individual content and social participation within the realm of personal integration) and Mercury (knowledge, technique, and efficiency) means preservation and prosperity for all.

## COMPLEXES DEALING WITH JUPITER AND MERCURY

An imbalanced condition within the Dyad of Participation and Association may act as a significator of two types of complexes:

a involving selfhood and assimilation,

b involving participation and sharing.

Such conditions may be present if the Dyad of Identification and Adaption is weak or unemphasized, giving Jupiter and Mercury very little to sustain, preserve, and participate in and associate with. This means that Jupiter and Mercury will probably attempt to compensate by channeling excess energies elsewhere, probably to:

a *The field of personality*

Here the individual may try to hide his own sense of weakness and insecurity through the development of mental acuteness (Mercury), which will enable him to take control of situations. The personality may also become aggressive (if Mars is emphasized) and manifest a cover-up superiority complex. On the other hand, the individual may cultivate a charming, pleasant personality if Venus is emphasized in the birth-chart.

b *The social-religious field*

The individual may also attempt to compensate for a weak sense of self by committing himself to some kind of social (Jupiter) or political movement (revolutionary, if Uranus is emphasized), or religious involvement (Neptune).

If the Dyad of Participation and Association acts in the above manner (by the development of a sharp mind, an aggressive ego or a charming personality, or by compensative involvement in a social-political-religious movement) to compensate for a weak sense of identity provided by the Dyad of the Moon and Saturn, it may overstrain and overdevelop its own function, creating a rigid condition and the development of more serious "complexes," including the so-called father complex (heavy Jupiter), guilt complexes (Jupiter-Mercury), messiah complexes (Jupiter and

Mars), fanatical conditions (Neptune), and other social-religious complexes.

If, however, Jupiter and Mercury do not compensate in such a manner, attention should be focused upon the transcendental realm: on the "soul" or the higher self, a condition of Jovian aspirations over ego emphasis.

## Conditions Symbolized
## by an Unemphasized Mercury
## and an Emphasized Jupiter

When Mercury fails to operate or is overwhelmed by a heavily emphasized Jupiter, a condition of imbalance results. This situation may be described as a "fattening process," in which hunger for more wealth and more power and more self-aggrandizement and more and more of everything becomes almost uncontrollable. In this situation, Mercury becomes nothing more than a slave to Jupiter, providing more and more useless information. If Saturn and/or Mars is also emphasized, the personality may be extremely egocentric (Saturn) or aggressive and violent (Mars).

## Conditions Symbolized
## by an Emphasized Mercury
## and an Unemphasized Jupiter

This situation indicates an addiction to knowledge, facts, information, any kind of data; yet the individual may be unable to put all this knowledge and information to a creative or spiritual use to assist well-balanced growth, harmony, and participation. If Saturn is strong, the mind may be extremely rigid, narrow, and cold.

The basic structure of the lunation cycle, the archetypal cycle of relationship, should, of course, also be applied to the Dyad of Participation and Association, as well as all dyadic relationships.

## THE DYAD OF SEX

Mars and Venus represent the most primary and personally intimate polarization of the basic solar potential acting upon the emotional nature of human beings. These two planets, which are found immediately within and immediately outside of the orbit of the earth, symbolize the individual's most personal realization of the basic duality of manifested life. Mars stands for all activities, desires, and urges that compel or urge one to change or disrupt any condition of equilibrium. It is the desire in man to emerge as an individual being capable of making an impression on the world. Normally, people act because there is a reason (Mercury) for action, which implies a value. In other words, desire for experience, sensation, and action (Mars) is the result of a value (Venus) being placed on the desired thing and associated with the memory of the thing or the experience associated with it.

The pairing of planets symbolizes the polarity that is responsible for all forms of creative expression. Everything externalized by the person, everything through which he expresses himself, is symbolized by the Dyad of Sex. Mars and Venus should not, however, be mistaken for the primal source, which is responsible for the generation of duality and is symbolized by the soli-lunar relationship; rather, this polarity serves as the most direct and personal channel through which these energies flow. It may be said that the Sun and Moon symbolize cosmic duality, while Mars and Venus represent personal duality, which is a reflection of cosmic duality. One's personality is polarized by the Sun and Moon, but his or her emotional life is polarized and directed by the Martial desire for emergence and the Venusian urge toward inner communion. Mars should be the "servant" of Venus and Mercury, representing the "machine of action" that expresses and externalizes the emotional and mental directives of these two principles.

## IMBALANCES IN THE DYAD OF SEX

### Mars Dominating Venus

This situation is symbolic of what might be called "animal sex," in which Venus is subservient to Mars, and sex (in the most inclusive meaning of the word) is an unconscious, compulsive act; while, in a Venus-determined situation, sex is conscious and personalized, acting as a creative release. However, Venus and Mars represent much more than this merely physical aspect of sex.

An individual with Mars dominating Venus in his or her birthchart may be exploitive and involved in getting whatever he or she desires, often without consideration of others. Values and ideals are worthless if they do not assist one in the immediate satisfaction of the more mundane desires of life. If the person is an "artist" he will be of the "commercial" type; more concerned with the worth of his art in terms of dollars, cents, and fame than the ideal behind it or its aesthetics.

### Venus More Emphasized Than Mars

In this configuration we find Venus positive and determining. Sex and all forms of creative expression become a very personal and conscious field of activity and participation for the release of the powers of personality. In this situation the urge toward expression is a directive factor, rather than the desire for immediate fulfillment. Mars, however, plays an important role in all forms of life, and a serious condition may arise if Venus overwhelms Mars.

### Other Imbalances Involving Mars and Venus

a   A compulsion to act without:

1   purpose (strong Mars—weak Sun)
2   reason (strong Mars—weak Mercury)
3   value or consideration (strong Mars—weak Venus);

b   An inability to act when need is present, because of:

1   physical weakness (weak Mars, Jupiter, or Sun-Moon)
2   lack of insight or mental confusion (weak Mercury)
3   inability to see the value of acting upon a situation (weak Venus).

## THE TRIAD OF TRANSFORMATION AND
## SELF-TRANSCENDENCE

The three trans-Saturnian planets are symbolic of the sacred process of transformation and self-transcendence, a process that makes the person more than just human, more than just a man or woman, but a whole and integrated individual. Such a person is conscious of his or her place and function within the universal scheme and at harmony with the lesser universes that compose his or her own body. This process involves sequence and order, each planet of the triad performing a specific function in order to bring about a particular change in the consciousness of the individual, and all (ideally) in harmony with the whole.

Until quite recently, the nature, and even the existence, of this process had been kept secret, especially in the West. In the past, Saturn was thought to be the planet defining the outermost realm of the solar system, only because human consciousness, as a whole, had not yet developed the ability to see the three bodies whose orbits extend beyond the orbit of Saturn. Because of this, humanity as a whole was not able to respond to the urge of self-transcendence, and those few who did respond to the call were forced to seek a teacher and usually sworn to the strictest secrecy. To become involved with such activities may have been dangerous. The mystery schools and the alchemists, for example, had to invent fronts and symbolic languages to cover up their operations and to disguise their traditions in order to prevent persecution. A person who desired to partake in the teachings had to prove himself worthy by undergoing many dangerous "tests."

The situation is much different today. Humanity has begun to respond to the higher frequencies of the solar system and the universe; witness the discovery of the three trans-Saturnian planets. Certain types of knowledge that had been kept secret for centuries are now being given out rather freely and, despite what many may claim, a teacher is no longer needed (at least on the physical plane) if one wishes to "tread the spiritual path." It may be true, as many astrologers claim, that most people today have not yet developed the capacity for responding to the trans-Saturnian planets in a positive manner. However, the fact remains that a growing number of persons have.

## URANUS AS THE "MASTER OF TRANSFORMATIONS"

The ancient Chaldean astrologers were probably unaware of the three planets with orbits beyond Saturn. Modern science didn't discover Uranus, the first planet beyond Saturn, until 1781, when it was sighted by the great astronomer Herschel.

Both Saturn and Uranus have astronomical peculiarities that make them unique in our solar system. Saturn, which for thousands of years defined the boundaries of our solar system, is surrounded by flat, disklike rings, which bring to mind the "ring-pass-not" of occult philosophy. Uranus, which defies the traditional authority of Saturn and is the symbol of change (it was discovered during a period of worldwide revolt), rotates in a direction radically different from any other planet in our solar system. That is, its polar axes are east-west rather than north-south; it rolls on its belly.

It is the Uranian urge that initially takes the individual outside the safe, secure, and familiar realm of conventional living defined by Saturn. It may take place within or beyond the control of the person. It is often a disruptive and bewildering experience, which may leave the person temporarily disoriented; his world has been scattered by the shock of the realization that there is something beyond the traditional way of life and a power greater than one's own ego. This first phase, the first step of the process that will transform the individual into something greater, may come in many ways. It may be the result of gradual discontentment with convention, or the result of certain drug experiences, or one may even be born with the urge for transformation.

However, it is only one step, one of many steps; one may even say that it is *the step,* and it must be repeated endlessly, or until one reaches the shrine of the eternal life of self. Saturn and Uranus are constantly interacting. The new experiences provided by Uranus quickly become absorbed by Saturn and Moon and eventually conventionalized and assimilated by Jupiter into the fabric of the culture. This process can be seen today with the establishment of the "counter-culture" and its superficial assimilation by the conventional culture. The truly integrated individual, transformed by Uranus, Neptune, and Pluto, lives outside of all culture, yet realizes culture has a place in the evolution of his own personality and the evolution of humanity in general. The transforming person never stops placing one foot in front of the other. Every time he or she breaks through a barrier, another barrier is discovered, more inclusive but still a barrier. Such a person is constantly expanding his realm of integration, but the "I" principle isn't there in the normal sense. True, there is individual consciousness, but not the normal type of ego-centered consciousness. The person transformed by Uranus, Neptune, and Pluto will appear to be an extremist to others, because those still set in conventional ways of life are not used to witnessing a whole person living as an integrated individual. When an entire culture is misguided by distorted values, anyone living a more harmonious life, outside of that culture, will appear to be "misguided." There is no one way, and the only way is found within one's self.

Saturn is a remarkable rebounder; as soon as Uranus tears down a Saturnian barrier, it builds a newer, more expansive one. It is in this manner that Saturn and Uranus are in eternal competition with one another in an endless though not meaningless race. Each time Saturn and Uranus act upon one another, a new form of experience is realized. The race may never end, but the participants become greater in the process.

### URANUS AND MARS AS THE DYAD OF TRANSFORMATION

The process of expanding the consciousness of a human being beyond the boundary set by Saturn requires more than simply Uranian forces. Uranus must be assisted by Mars, which provides the needed power and externally directed force. Without Mars, the Uranian function wouldn't be strong enough to keep up with Saturn. In this way, Mars may be seen as the "right-hand man" of Uranus. It should be revealing to note that Mars is the first planet of a translunar nature, while Uranus is the first trans-Saturnian planet. Together, these two bodies work as a team that drives the individual toward transformation (if Uranus is directive) or meaningless acts of disruption (if Mars is directive). As is the case with all dyadic relationships, these two planets should be related to the framework of the archetypal cycle of relationship.

## NEPTUNE AS THE "UNIVERSAL SOLVENT"

Once the Saturnian walls have been penetrated and broken up by the Uranian urge, Neptune comes in and dissolves the disintegrating remains with a strong acid, the "universal solvent" of the alchemists, which will eat through anything. In this phase of the process of self-transcendence the person is taken into a fluid state of unfocalization and disorientation. As may be expected, the individual usually reacts with fear and confusion when he finds himself in such a limbo-like state, in which everything seems so meaningless. At this point he may come to one of two conclusions: 1) that everything is meaningless and the only way to preserve sanity is by escaping into a nullistic state, perhaps with the help of opiates and alcohol, or 2) that, despite appearances, there is some higher principle and meaning in existence.

Reorientation is most important for the person at the Neptune phase. He must reorganize and re-evaluate all that he has known and taken for granted in the past, examining it in the light of a new, transformed world. Once one has passed through the portal of Uranus, new meanings and values must be given to everything, everything must be reassociated. One must reorient one's energies toward the realization of a new purpose, a purpose that transcends both the personal and social realms of existence, of planetary and universal significance. In this way, Neptune is symbolic of compassion and selflessness.

Religious or social fanaticism and self-abnegation form the dark side of Neptune, quite an easy thing to slip into when one's entire conventional or personal world has been destroyed before one's eyes. Established unconventional religious or social movements may be the first place one prematurely reaching the Neptunian phase may turn. Here he will find others, who have also experienced the effect of the "universal solvent" upon their personal and social lives. Here the individual may find something that sheds light upon the confused and meaningless world, something to relax his troubled mind. But one should not stop here, simply to erect another barrier and adopt another authoritarian, dogmatic philosophy.

### NEPTUNE AND JUPITER AS THE DYAD OF REORIENTATION

Neptune and Jupiter are operationally connected in much the same way as Uranus and Mars. Neptune is symbolic of the reorientation of the individual's consciousness from personal-social values to universal significance, while Jupiter stands for the assimilation of the collective realm of experience by the individual and the preservation of the personality within the social sphere. On one hand, Jupiter helps Neptune in the process of universalization, and on the other it works against Neptune through the preservation of the established norm defined by Saturn. Together, Neptune and Jupiter work for the reorientation of the individual's consciousness directed toward the goal of self-transcendence (if directed by Neptune) or self-aggrandizement (if directed by Jupiter). The quality of relationship active within the Dyad of Reorientation may be revealed by referring the phase of relationship to the archetypal cycle of relationship.

## PLUTO AS "COSMIC INTEGRATOR"

The third trans-Saturnian planet, Pluto, was, strangely enough, discovered eighty-four years (one cycle of Uranus) after the discovery of Neptune. This planet, which has an extremely eccentric orbit, can reach a latitude of as much as 18° and, for a short period during each orbit, is found within the orbit of Neptune. When Pluto was first discovered, in 1930, many astronomers thought it might be a wandering satellite of Neptune because of its eccentric orbit and its relatively small size (at that time Pluto was believed to be about the size of Mercury).

Pluto is symbolic of the process of refocalization of consciousness once it has been reoriented toward the realization of a higher or universal ideal, which enables the person to clearly see his relation to and place within the universal scheme. In this way, Pluto acts as integrator and represents the final stages of individuation, or in occult terms, initiation.

The so-called "New Age" and all other forms of renewed consciousness are symbolized by Pluto. It should be understood, however, that new forms are not actually new but simply old forms that have been transformed, reoriented, and refocused by the triad of trans-Saturnian planets. These planets transform "old" and forgotten forms into something *more,* giving to them a new quality of consciousness. The seed pattern remains the same, though the individual organism becomes more capable of fulfilling the potential latent within its archetypal pattern.

When one completes the Pluto phase and forms a positive relationship with the whole of life, he has symbolically completed the process of self-transcendence and emerges as a transfigured individuated being, more than human. This is an extremely difficult process, a process through which most human beings are not yet able to pass successfully. This is not to say, however, that the urge for self-transcendence is not operative within all beings, at least on an unconscious level. The triad of Uranus, Neptune, and Pluto are operative everywhere, within all things, not within just those few who are able to achieve total self-transcendence right now. It seems, however, as if the results of these planets make themselves more apparent and obvious on the social-cultural-collective level than within the individual; indeed, it may be easier to revolutionize a culture than to transform an individual.

### PLUTO AND SATURN AS THE DYAD OF REFOCALIZATION

What Saturn is to the personal-social identity of a person, Pluto is to his or her spiritual-universal identity. On one hand, Pluto may be seen as the higher octave of Saturn, and on the other, Saturn's archrival. Saturn acts as the structuring agent within the realm of particulars, while Pluto restructures and redefines what has been broken down and dissolved by Uranus and Neptune, refocalizing the consciousness that animated the old Saturnian forms within a more transcendental and universal frame of reference. In a way, Pluto does the same thing as Saturn, only in a more universal and less ego-centered way. Pluto, the symbol of new forms, is, however, a threat to the old, established forms of Saturn, which are constantly being transformed, reoriented, and refocused by Uranus, Neptune, and Pluto. It is a threat and a fearful symbol only when consciousness hangs onto antiquated forms; otherwise it is a natural organic function, beneficial to the entire organism.

The Sun gives its light to the Moon, which transforms solar light into organic life, which is passed on to Saturn, which gives individual consciousness and identity to lunar organisms and is in turn passed on to Pluto, which calls forth the eternal light dwelling within the individual, giving consciousness of its divine source.

# 7

# DIRECTIVE FACULTIES:
# GUIDES TO LIVING

*To be responsibly self-directing means that one chooses—and learns from the consequences.*

CARL ROGERS

In addition to the four essential functions and their symbolic planetary groupings, which drive or urge individuals toward active participation within the realm of personal experience and growth, every person possesses certain directive faculties, which guide him toward the fulfillment of the particular way of life most meaningful and purposeful to him as an individual. In the next several pages we'll be discussing how these directive faculties may be recognized as guides to creative and individual living through the process of astrological interpretation.

## A BRIEF SURVEY OF THE FIVE DIRECTIVE FACULTIES

### 1. DIRECTIVE MOTIVATION

The relationship between Jupiter and Saturn acts as a significator of the directive motivation of the individual. Together, Jupiter and Saturn function as the Dyad of Internal/External Relatedness.

## 2. DIRECTIVE INTELLECT

The cycle of Mercury and its relationship with the Sun represents the mental temperament of the individual. This particular area of astrological study has been termed *mental chemistry* by Marc Edmund Jones.

## 3. EMOTIONALLY DIRECTED RESPONSIVENESS

The cycle of Venus and its relationship with the Sun reveals the emotional temperament of the individual and the manner in which he or she uses emotions as a guide to living.

## 4. DIRECTIVE UTILIZATION

The manner in which one goes about getting what he wants and the way in which he uses his natural abilities to assist him in his affairs are determined by various factors, discussed below.

## 5. DIRECTIVE COMPATIBILITY

The Sun, Moon, and ascendant, and the Dyad of Sex are the primary significators of the faculty that directs the individual to seek relationships with certain types of people.

## DIRECTIVE INTELLECT: THE CYCLE OF MERCURY

Traditional astrology has ignored the geocentric phenomenon created by the orbit of Mercury. This planet, which is never more than 28° from the Sun, has an extremely eccentric orbit (the only planet with a more eccentric orbit is Pluto) and forms two distinct types of solar conjunctions. At its most accelerated speed of daily motion it is the quickest-moving of all planets. While at its point of maximum brightness (within 14° of the Sun), Mercury is the third-brightest body in the sky, second only to the Sun and Moon.

## TWO TYPES OF MERCURIAL-SOLAR CONJUNCTIONS

Because Mercury occupies a position in the solar system heliocentrically within the orbit of the earth, it becomes involved in two types of geocentric solar conjunctions, an inferior conjunction and a superior conjunction.*

**The Inferior Conjunction:** Mercury is heliocentrically conjunct and closest to the earth, mediating between the Sun and earth, having the quality of a New Moon (new Mercury). It takes place when Mercury is retrograde, and begins the *promethean* cycle.

**The Superior Conjunction:** Mercury is heliocentrically opposed to the earth. It takes place when Mercury is direct (and has the quality of a Full Moon). The *epimethean* cycle begins.

### THE PROMETHEAN CYCLE

The promethean cycle (promethean means progressive) of Mercury corresponds to the waxing hemisphere of the solar-Mercurian relationship. This cycle is characterized by a Mercury function that "runs ahead of the Sun"; that is, Mercury rises, or crosses the ascendant (in a clockwise direction), before the Sun. There are two phases of the promethean cycle; one with Mercury retrograde, the other with Mercury direct.

**Promethean Retrograde.** Begins at the inferior conjunction, when Mercury is accelerating in speed of motion, thus transmitting energy to earth in its most focalized condition. The mind of a person born during this period should be highly focused and in direct rebellion against the instinctive nature, the mind seeking independence.

**Promethean Direct.** Begins when Mercury is at its greatest distance from the Sun. The mind becomes established in its own nature. When Mercury's speed becomes greater than the Sun's, the Mercury function becomes very intense and projective. Mercury's speed is almost at its greatest when the superior conjunction takes place.

* See Appendix VI for a more detailed astronomical explanation of this phenomenon.

The epimethean cycle (epimethean means conservative) of Mercury corresponds to the waning hemisphere of the solar-Mercurian relationship. This cycle is characterized by a Mercury that rises after the Sun. As was the case with the promethean cycle, there are two phases: one with Mercury direct, the other with Mercury retrograde.

**Epimethean Direct.** Begins when Mercury's speed of daily motion begins to decelerate, at the superior conjunction. The mental functions are reflective and objective, and reasoning out precedents, becoming the master of the present. The mind doesn't run ahead of itself, as is the case with the promethean cycle, but runs people and things.

**Epimethean Retrograde.** The mind is philosophical, yet still somewhat bound to tradition. Mental introspection directed toward inner realization.

## MERCURY AS SIGNIFICATOR OF DIRECTIVE INTELLECT

The cycle of Mercury provides the basic structure for a system of examination that should reveal, or at least indicate, the individual's ability and manner of using his mind as a directive faculty. This system calls for the consideration of:

**a**  Mercury's configuration with the Sun,
**b**  the daily motion (speed) of the Moon,
**c**  aspects formed between Mercury, Venus, and Mars.

### Mercury's Configuration with the Sun

The configuration of Mercury with the Sun characterizes the individual's particular type of human mentality.

*Mercury 14° to 28° ahead of Sun.* The mind is eager and untrammeled, free from interference by inner reactions or feelings. It is functioning in its own realm and leading the individual in and out of life experiences.

*Mercury 0° to 14° ahead of Sun.* The mind is eager, though censored by the will; more self-conscious and restrained than the above.

*Mercury 14° to 28° behind the Sun.* The mind is deliberate, using experience and judgment as guides, though often lacking confidence and operating in a detached manner.

*Mercury 0° to 14° behind the Sun.*  The mind is deliberate, though self-conscious and within the realm and control of personality.

## Consideration of the Moon's Daily Motion

The average daily motion of the Moon is 13°10'. Anything less than the average is considered "slow," while anything more than this average is considered "fast." In the birth-chart, the Moon's speed of daily motion indicates the person's way of responding to life experiences.

**Fast Moon.**  The person is quick to respond to life experiences and the needs they pose. Perceptive and active.

**Slow Moon.**  The person's acts are deliberate and cautious. He may be slow and lax in responding to the needs and challenges posed by life, but he is less inclined toward rash acts and poor judgment than most.

## Consideration of the Cycle of Mercury
## in Relation to the Moon's Speed

The cycle of Mercury considered in relation to the speed of the Moon characterizes the individual's way of handling life experiences and his over-all mental temperament.

**a**  Promethean Mercury and slow Moon; or epimethean Mercury and fast Moon: indicates a well-balanced sense of directive intellect.

**b**  Epimethean Mercury and slow Moon: characterizes a person who may be mentally withdrawn and unsocial. Rationalizations and conclusions are often based largely upon one's personal views and understanding of the subject. The person is liable to experience difficulty when attempting to effect change within his own field of experience.

**c**  Promethean Mercury and fast Moon: such a person may have unusual mental comprehension, though is liable to be impatient and wasteful of energy.

## Consideration of Aspects to Mercury from Venus and Mars

Aspects to Mercury from Venus and Mars indicate the person's mental disposition and attitude.

*Mercury Not in Aspect to Either Venus or Mars.*  Denotes a person with an abstract nature and little or no inclination toward practical affairs.

*Mercury conjunct Mars.* Symbolizes an aggressive and uncompromising mind.

*Mercury conjunct Venus.* Denotes mental appreciation.

*Mercury sextile Mars.* Refers to an ease of mental functioning.

*Mercury sextile Venus.* Denotes the type of mind that works well in close association with others but is easily impressed.

*Mercury square Mars.* Indicates an argumentative, intellectually ambitious, and confident nature.

*Mercury trine Mars.* Refers to an open-minded and confident personality.

*Mercury opposed Mars.* Denotes the type of person who may be critical and condescending toward the mental dullness of others. Creative insight.

## EMOTIONALLY DIRECTED RESPONSIVENESS:
### THE CYCLE OF VENUS

The cycle of Venus, like that of Mercury, has two types of solar conjunctions: inferior and superior. Venus is at superior conjunction when its motion is rapid (about 1°15′ is its maximum daily motion, reached just after superior conjunction) and direct and it is farthest from the earth. It is one of the two points (the other being when it reaches maximum latitude) at which Venus is most intense and operative within its own sphere. Venus reaches inferior conjunction with the Sun when it is closest to the earth, slow, and in retrograde motion.

## VENUS AS SIGNIFICATOR
## OF EMOTIONALLY DIRECTIVE RESPONSIVENESS

The relationship between Venus and the Sun serves as an indicator of the individual's emotional temperament and the manner in which the individual approaches and relates to situations and people.

### VENUS AS LUCIFER (BEARER OF LIGHT)

When Venus rises ahead† (being of a lesser degree of zodiacal longitude) of the Sun, it may be seen in the morning sky, whence the name "the morning star." Venus as Lucifer refers to a basic type of

---

† Venus is never more than 47° from the Sun; when it reaches this maximum distance, a crisis of emotional reorientation may take place.

human emotional responsiveness, which may be described as impulsive and spontaneous. The person who has this configuration in his or her birth-chart should be responsive and eager in relationships. The tendency of rushing into situations and relationships may result in disappointments and emotional rejection by others, the emotional stress of which may "force" the person into adopting a cold or indifferent attitude as a compensation or mask.

The person with Venus as Lucifer should have a high sense of ideals (generally speaking) and will probably try to project them upon himself and others, unmercifully if Venus is retrograde, being critical when they are not realized to his satisfaction.

Finally, it could be said that persons with Venus rising ahead of the Sun should rely upon their emotions and intuitions as directives and guides to living. The further ahead of the Sun Venus happens to be, the more pronounced and obvious this type of temperament will be, especially if Venus is also ahead of Mercury.

### VENUS HESPERUS

Venus rising after the Sun is symbolic of the type of personality that feels after the act, judging the performance of an act (by himself or others) after it has been transacted, on the basis of aesthetics, procedure, or its reception.

Emotions may be just as intense as the Lucifer type, though not as likely to be as unrestrained or spontaneous, and possibly they may be directed toward destructive or negative channels of release. Generally, the Venus Hesperus personality does not allow his emotions to directly guide him through his daily life, employing his emotional nature instead in an evaluative or judicial manner.

If the Sun rises before both Mercury and Venus, the personality may be guided and directed by the self, by pure inner directives, rather than by the intellect or emotions. In cases in which both Venus and Mercury rise before the Sun, the personality will be directed by both the intellect and the emotions, but primarily by that signified by the body rising first.

### The Significance of Venus Retrograde

Venus is one of the planets most seldom found in retrograde (the other is Mars)—about six weeks every 584 days.

Venus retrograde in a birth-chart symbolizes an ascetic type of personality, whose values, incentives, and modes of expression seem to be in contradiction with natural life instincts. This may be due to a desire to attain some high and sublime state of transcendence; or, on the other hand, it may be symbolic of disintegrative forces within the emotional or psychological make-up of the personality. A person with a retrograde Venus may be in tune with a more personal type of aesthetics.

## DIRECTIVE MOTIVATION: BEING AND DOING

The relationship between Saturn (individual identity) and Jupiter (the social sense) reveals the basic condition of balance and interchange existing between the person's consciousness as an independent entity and his experiences as a social entity.

Each person is an individual, a complete whole, as well as a part of a greater (social-racial-planetary) whole. The condition of psychological equilibrium between these two principles varies from person to person. One may emphasize and attempt to develop his uniqueness as an individual, while another may focus his attention and energies upon a movement or cause, regarding himself as first an agent of that cause and secondly as an individual. In both cases there is relatedness, though the direction may differ. The pairing of Saturn and Jupiter produces the Dyad of Internal/External Relatedness.

## DYAD OF INTERNAL/EXTERNAL RELATEDNESS AS SIGNIFICATOR OF DIRECTIVE MOTIVATION

A significator of directive motivation may be determined by the examination of the condition of balance between Saturn and Jupiter.

(a)   If Saturn is more emphasized than Jupiter, the person should be able to function in a creative and meaningful manner within the realm of personal interest.

(b)   If Saturn overshadows Jupiter, the person should be motivated by individual experiences, values, ideals, and interest. Social activity may be subservient to the individual's personal goals, purposes, and desires.

(c)   If Jupiter is more emphasized than Saturn, the person should be concerned with social-collective-religious affairs and activities, receiving personal inspiration from his or her involvement with them.

(d)   If Jupiter overshadows Saturn, the person may be subservient to the group or society, having a weak sense of identity and being motivated by external (social-collective-religious) experiences, ideals, values, and goals.

## SIGNIFICANCE OF ASPECTS BETWEEN SATURN AND JUPITER

Any major aspect found between Saturn and Jupiter (aspects, particularly between planetary pairs, should be considered as phases of a cycle) may serve as a significator of directive motivation in terms of the individual's ability to integrate the two poles of relatedness.

*Saturn-Jupiter Conjunct.* A new form of internal/external relationship is represented here. There is great freedom of direction, but perhaps a lack of discrimination.

*Saturn-Jupiter Sextile.* One's internal/external relationships assist and co-operate with one another in a positive, productive manner. The individual should be able to maintain himself well in both the internal and external scheme of things.

*Saturn-Jupiter Square.* Basic conflict between one's internal and external affairs, between one's responsibility to himself as a person or to his own self-actualization, and his relationship to the outer world or the establishment.

*Saturn-Jupiter Trine.* The individual should be able to function and express himself (if he is able to differentiate) equally well within both the internal and the external realms of experience.

*Saturn-Jupiter Opposed.* Awareness of the contrast existing between the individual and collective values and the attempt to maintain a functional balance between the two. The person may, however, find himself torn between two worlds, and if the balance breaks, the two poles may become severely divorced within the individual's personality.

## DIRECTIVE UTILIZATION:
## PROFICIENCY AND APTNESS

The study of directive utilization reveals the manner in which the person should be best equipped to utilize the immediate opportunities of a situation and his or her special or unique skills and abilities.

To gain insight into this, we'll be examining:

(a)   the planet of oriental appearance,

(b)   the medium coeli and the tenth house,

(c)   the significator of dynamic aptness.

## PLANET OF ORIENTAL APPEARANCE AS PRACTICAL DIRECTOR

Each person has been given special skills and abilities to help him fulfill himself as an individual and as a purposeful member of society. Through the technique of directive utilization, we are able to recognize these personal gifts and understand how they may be utilized and developed.

The term "planet of oriental appearance" was coined to designate the planet crossing the eastern horizon immediately before the Sun on any given day. The planet of oriental appearance at the time of our birth serves as the significator of practical direction. This planet will act as the agent of the personality within the field of practical, everyday affairs and life experiences. It provides the individual with a method and a direction of action to assist him in the handling of the immediate demands of life.

The planet of oriental appearance also reveals the particular things one should be good at: the areas of activity and experience that should provide the person with the richest harvest for his efforts. It represents how one's unique skills and faculties can be put to their best possible use and how one may fulfill his potentiality for practical and productive activity.

The significator of practical direction at the time of birth is the planet in the birth-chart immediately preceding the Sun in a clockwise direction—the planet immediately preceding the Sun in the zodiac. For instance, if the Sun occupied the thirteenth degree of Scorpio on the day of my birth while Neptune occupied the twelfth degree of Libra, Neptune would be my oriental-appearing planet if no other planet is found between the twelfth degree of Libra and the thirteenth degree of Scorpio.

### Mercury as Practical Director

The person with Mercury rising directly before the Sun is a thinking type. He is able to think and reason his way through problems and difficulties confronting him, arriving at the best way to deal with a situation. The mind is sharp and alert. It should be allowed to guide the person through his or her everyday experiences.

One born with Mercury in oriental appearance should be able to deal directly with a job, function, or technique without conflict or external interference. Efficiency, practicality, and reliability may be this type of person's forte, though he should try to cultivate creativity.

## Venus as Practical Director

This type of person should be concerned with the value and ideals behind his work, insisting upon making a personal impression on everything he touches. Aesthetics, beauty, value, and meaning are very important if Venus is in oriental appearance, and one should use them as guides to practical living. This type of person is sensitive and appreciative of people, things, and situations, and this should assist him in realizing their value (and disadvantage) as they relate to his life and work.

The Venusian sensitivity represented here is constantly seeking creative expression and fulfillment in all that one does, and for this reason the person with Venus in this position should seek out employment, or earn his living, in a field that leaves room for creative expression and artistic judgments. Such persons should find work as artist, designer, decorator, or buyer to be rewarding and fulfilling.

## Moon as Practical Director

Refers to a person who has a special ability for keeping the practical, functional affairs of his life running smoothly. He or she is equally at ease running a household or managing a business, and both may be essential for this individual's happiness. However, if one's Moon is in oriental appearance, one should be careful not to become obsessively concerned with the maintenance and upkeep of his home or office.

The lunar response represented here may be well utilized by involving oneself in assisting and guiding others in their everyday lives. For this reason, it is an excellent significator for the manager, counselor, or teacher.

## Mars as Practical Director

Characterizes the type of person who becomes totally involved in whatever he or she is doing, often to the point of self-abnegation. The Martian temperament found in persons having Mars rising directly before the Sun enables them to, sooner or later, accomplish almost everything they set out to do, and they are usually not satisfied until their ambitions are finally realized.

The person with Mars in oriental appearance has a great asset in his ability to stick with things, and for this reason he should be highly productive. However, an awareness and sensitivity of others should be developed, as he may be inclined toward exploitiveness as a means of actualizing success. This configuration is symbolic of the businessman, the promoter, and the athlete.

### Jupiter as Practical Director

Such a person usually has a great number of personal resources and a vast array of skills, enabling him to get things done easily; he should experience little difficulty in the handling of practical affairs. There is a good deal of social sense here; often, fulfillment can be found through social activity and involvement.

If Jupiter is in oriental appearance, the person should have ability for organizational work and dealing and relating with others, though he should also try to develop a deeper understanding of those who occupy a lower social station than himself.

Symbolic of the social worker and organizer.

### Saturn as Practical Director

Characterizes the type of person who should be able to exercise great self-discipline and endurance in achieving his or her objective. Such an individual has a deep understanding of things on the structural level, having a special ability for knowing how things run and what makes things happen.

The Saturnian temperament represented here gives one a position and air of authority, though one should be careful not to abuse this power, as persons born with Saturn in oriental appearance often find their way to influential positions in the fields of politics, science, and academics.

### Uranus as Practical Director

The type of person with Uranus in oriental appearance is out to change everything he comes in contact with. The individual represented here is particularly suited to promoting and developing the type of changes in the meaning, value, and understanding of existence (both individual and collective) necessary for the realization of the new age. One with Uranus in this position should understand, however, that the premature destruction of conventional institutions and forms can pose as great a danger to social harmony as the antiquated forms one hopes to transform.

The Uranian temperament represented here may find fulfillment in the development and innovation of concepts and principles of personal and social significance in the field of the material and natural sciences, as well as in the realm of philosophy and the arts.

### Neptune as Practical Director

Characterizes the type of person who has a special ability for directing his or her energies toward psychological, mystical, or transcendental experiences. Such persons often have definite intuitive feelings, which may provide them with a valuable guide in practical matters. However, there may be some difficulty experienced in the process of bringing these special Neptunian perceptions into a clear and reliable focus, and one with Neptune in this position may profit by attempting to develop his sense of form and definition.

Persons with this arrangement may find conventional employment difficult and frustrating. They may find the role of poet, occultist, or astrologer more fulfilling.

### Pluto as Practical Director

The person with Pluto rising immediately before the Sun is particularly apt at the development and perfection of new forms and systems. This process is, however, more closely associated with the process of giving new meaning and new significance to old and forgotten forms. In reality, "there is nothing new under the sun," only new ways of looking and relating.

Pluto in oriental appearance is symbolic of the men and women who are ahead of their time, often painfully ahead of the established mentality and morality of the time. Persons with this arrangement in their birth-charts should find fulfillment by involving themselves in the reorganization and re-examination of social, intellectual, religious, and political concepts.

### IMPORTANCE OF THE HOUSE

The house occupied by the planet of oriental appearance reveals the quality and type of individual experience that provides the most fertile ground for the expression and fulfillment of the practical skills, abilities, and ways of handling everyday affairs and opportunities symbolized by the significator itself. In other words, the planet of oriental appearance represents the special skills of the person, things he is naturally good at, while the house occupied by this planet reveals the type of experience through which these skills can be actualized. For instance, if Neptune (my significator of directive utilization) is found in the eleventh house of my birth-chart, I should channel my special psychological, mystical, transcendental skills toward eleventh-house experiences, such as the experience of working with others on a social-professional level of co-operation. Perhaps I would find work as an astrologer, meditation instructor, or therapist fulfilling and personally rewarding.

### Significator in the First House

The person's skills and abilities can be best fulfilled when integrated into the field of personality and the basic experiences of being. One should be able to consciously control and use his special gifts at will.

### Significator in the Second House

One's special skills can find fulfillment through handling immediate situations. This asset may be particularly valuable when dealing with matters that require an active relationship with substance or matter.

### Significator in the Third House

The skills and abilities symbolized by the significator may be actualized and most useful in situations requiring the application of practical knowledge and the use of the concrete mind.

### Significator in the Fourth House

The person's special skills and abilities may be best used when applied to matters of personal integration, of bringing the various facets of his personality together as an operative whole.

### Significator in the Fifth House

The person can best use his unique skills and abilities in experiences of self-expression and creativity, of personalizing his day-to-day duties, and discovering his own unique and individual way of doing things.

### Significator in the Sixth House

The skills and abilities symbolized by this type of person's significator of directive utilization are best used when applied to the process of growth through introspection and self-knowledge.

### Significator in the Seventh House

The skills symbolized by the significator are best used when applied to matters of personal relationships, in experiences that require deep understanding of and co-operation with others.

### Significator in the Eighth House

The skills and abilities symbolized by the planet of oriental appearance may be best utilized when applied to active participation within a social whole, such as in the field of group activity and co-operation.

### Significator in the Ninth House

One's special skills may be best utilized in assisting him in understanding the nature of existence and the underlying relationship existing between all things. The individual should use these abilities in the formulation of concepts and systems.

### Significator in the Tenth House

The person's special skills find fertile ground by seeking expression in the outer world of professional activity. They can be valuable personal assets in the field of social, political, or spiritual activity.

### Significator in the Eleventh House

The skills and faculties symbolized by the oriental-appearing planet should be utilized in the field of experience associated with working and co-operating with others on a social or professional level.

### Significator in the Twelfth House

The person may best utilize his or her special abilities by channeling them toward experiences that involve reorientation of personal and social values and the questioning of conventionally accepted concepts and beliefs. Such a person may find working in isolation or work dealing with little-known or abstract matters rewarding.

## MEDIUM COELI AS PRACTICAL SIGNIFICATOR

In addition to the routine examination of the planets placed around the medium coeli and the planetary aspects formed to it, one should also consider the balance of weight carried by the area around the M.C. in relation to the area around the twelfth house and ascendant.

(a)   If the houses surrounding both the ascendant and the M.C. are occupied, the individual should have little or no difficulty coordinating his personal, private interests with his business, professional, or practical affairs.

(b)   If the houses surrounding both the M.C. and the ascendant are unoccupied, the individual is unlikely to be so absorbed by either his personal interests or his practical or business affairs that a conflict between the two would result.

(c)   If the ninth and tenth houses are full and the twelfth and first houses empty, the individual's attention should be focalized upon his practical responsibilities and affairs. This type of person is inclined to be active in social-political movements.

(d)   If the twelfth and first houses are full and the ninth and tenth houses empty, there is a general disinterest in the practical affairs of life, and a lack of "social responsibility." This type of person may be concerned with personal matters, having a sound sense of self and identity.

## DYNAMIC APTNESS AS SIGNIFICATOR OF PRACTICAL ATTAINMENT

Dynamic aptness serves as an indicator of the individual's way of getting what he wants and of his characteristic way of approaching the area within which he desires to express himself.

In a birth-chart, the square, opposition, semisquare, or sesquiquadrate of the most exact orb acts as the indicator of dynamic aptness. Here one must consider:

1   the nature of the aspect,
2   the nature of the planets involved,
3   the applying and separating planets.

### THE NATURE OF THE ASPECT

*Square.*   Achievement and success depend upon the individual's assumption of direct concern and responsibility for his own actions.

*Opposition.*   The individual must employ subtle or indirect methods if he wishes to achieve his goals.

*Semisquare or Sesquiquadrate.*   The individual may achieve his goals through dynamic and intense activity.

### THE NATURE OF THE PLANETS INVOLVED

The nature of the planets involved symbolizes the organic functions that will be utilized by the individual for the purpose of practical attainment. If the two planets are complements, such as Mars-Venus, the particular dyadic relationship will be a great personal and practical asset.

### THE APPLYING AND SEPARATING PLANETS

The *applying planet* is the quicker-moving planet if the aspect has not yet reached exact orb, or the slower-moving planet if the aspect has already reached exact orb. The *separating planet* is the quicker-moving planet if the aspect has already reached exact orb, or the slower-moving planet if the aspect has not yet reached exact orb.

The *applying planet* is the focal planet of dynamic aptness. It indicates the functional operation that will bring about practical success and fulfillment.

The *separating planet* indicates the area of experience to be acted upon by the applying planet in order to bring about practical attainment.

## DIRECTIVE COMPATIBILITY:
## THE TECHNIQUE OF SYNASTRY

The Triad of Personality Projection is the primary significator of interpersonal compatibility. There are several techniques for determination of compatibility based on the comparative examination of this triad as it relates to the Sun, Moon, and ascendant of another person's chart.

## COMPATIBILITY DETERMINATION THROUGH ELEMENTAL COMPARISON

This technique is based upon the consideration of the status of elemental compatibility existing between the Triad of Personality Projection of one individual and that of another. For instance, the Suns of two persons' charts are said to be compatible if they are found in the same or a compatible element (fire-air or earth-water). On the other hand, if they are not found in compatible elements (fire-water or air-earth), a *cross stimulus* is said to be active within the field of relationship.

### Two Compatible, One Cross Stimulus

This arrangement is indicative of a comfortable and fundamentally compatible relationship; the contrasting factor will act as a release for the power of the relationship and provide it with new experiences.

*Cross Stimulus Between Suns* is symbolic of a mutual respect of the other's individuality and differences, though they may frequently clash.

*Cross Stimulus Between Moons* denotes a mutual respect and sensitivity toward the other's feelings and manner of adjusting to life experiences, even though there may be great contrast in this area of the relationship.

*Cross Stimulus Between Ascendants* refers to a mutual appreciation of the other's uniqueness and special characteristics.

### Two Cross Stimuli and One Rapport

Such a relationship will be more difficult to maintain, requiring greater attention and more-frequent adjustments, than the "ordinary" relationship. There is, however, a greater chance for individual freedom of expression and development within such a relationship.

### Three Cross Stimuli and No Rapport

This situation is symbolic of a relationship that is unique (if a positive relationship is able to evolve at all) and based on an experience not found in the ordinary type of relationship; there is some unique and extraordinary factor involved here (karma?).

### Three Rapports and No Cross Stimulus

Denotes a static state of affairs with little or no excitement, because of the lack of new or different energies entering the relationship.

## COMPATIBILITY DETERMINATION THROUGH MODAL COMPARISON

This technique is based upon the status of the relationship existing between the modes of the Triad of Personality Projection of a person's chart to that of another.

### Two of the Same Mode, One Different

Denotes a basically functional relationship.

### One of the Same Mode, Two Different

Indicative of a relationship in which there may be conflict rising from the individual's particular manner of functioning. There is also the possibility of combining the contrasting factors into a very deep relationship.

### Three of the Same Mode, None Different

Symbolic of a relationship in which both individuals tend to do the same things in the same ways, with little improvisation.

### Three Different, None in the Same Mode

Denotes a relationship in which the two individuals are unable to get their energies together at all; or are able to work together, each in his own individual way, in an outstanding manner.

## DETERMINATION OF COMPATIBILITY THROUGH THE CONSIDERATION OF ASPECTS FORMED WITHIN THE TRIAD OF PERSONALITY PROJECTION

This is perhaps the one area of astrological application where there has been a good deal of "scientific" investigation,‡ and the actual proof of the validity of this technique may be easily obtained. It is based on aspects that are formed between the Sun, Moon, and ascendant of one person's chart and the positions of the Sun, Moon, and ascendant in another person's birth-chart.

Trine or sextile aspects formed between one of these three factors and any of the three as they are positioned in another's chart are said to be indicative of a lasting and satisfying relationship, while squares or oppositions may be symbolic of a relationship of a more conflicting or difficult nature. In any case, the orbs for such aspects mean a great deal and should be kept small and considered carefully, along with the nature of the factors, signs, houses, and so on.

A quincunx aspect formed between any of these three factors is most interesting and difficult to describe. The two individuals will be drawn to one another by some mysterious force, and their relationship may be highly productive and mutually satisfying in some areas, though very weak or disappointing in others.

## DETERMINATION OF COMPATIBILITY BY THE CONSIDERATION OF PLANETARY ASPECTS TO THE SUN, MOON, AND ASCENDANT

The moon and Venus are the traditional significators of the type of woman a man is said to be most receptive to and compatible with. By the same tradition (which may be seen as somewhat rigid), the Sun and Mars serve as significators for the type of man a woman is said to be most compatible with. These significators are most potent when aspecting one another or the Sun, Moon, or ascendant of another's chart.

When the position of Uranus in one person's chart is aspecting the Sun, Moon, ascendant, Venus, or Mars of another person's chart, a compulsive relationship may be indicated.

‡ See Jung's *Interpretation of Nature and Psyche.*

Actually, any aspect formed between any planet in one chart and any in another is significant and should be approached with an open mind, without overstressing biological sex.

## IMPORTANCE OF THE HOUSES

The houses are of considerable importance in synastry, particularly in terms of individuality and experience. Much may be revealed by comparing how the planets of one person's chart fall into the house structure of another person's chart and vice versa.

## A TRADITIONAL SYNASTRIC TECHNIQUE

A technique that has been used since the time of Ptolemy is the determination of "marriage significators" by the application of a man's natal Moon and the examination of aspects to a woman's natal Sun. Here we should use the loosest possible definition of the terms *marriage, wife,* and *husband.*

### PTOLEMY'S "MARRIAGE SIGNIFICATORS"

In a man's chart, his "wife" is indicated by the planet with which the Moon is in APPLYING aspect. If more than one planet is in such an aspect, several relationships are indicated, partners being described by the respective planets and the qualities of the relationships described by the respective aspects. If no applying aspects are present at birth, the Moon should be "applied" until an aspect is formed.

In a woman's chart the "husband" is indicated by the planet forming an aspect with the natal Sun, providing the planet is from 0° to 180° behind the Sun in the zodiac. If more than one planet is in such an aspect, each partner is described by the respective planets and the qualities of relationship by the respective aspects.

The more closely aspected planets generally indicate earlier relationships. In other words, if a man's Moon has two applying aspects, one with a 2° orb and the other with a 4° orb, the planetary aspect with the 2° orb is indicative of an early relationship, while the planet with the 4°-orb aspect is symbolic of a later relationship.

8

# SYNTHETIC POINTS:
# INDICATORS OF STRENGTH
# AND SENSITIVITY

*[Synthetic points] refer to the operation of personality as a unified whole and as a unit in the infinitely complex interweavings of social relationship.*

DANE RUDHYAR

The numerous mid-points and parts formed by planetary groupings and the nodal axes of the Moon and planets serve as important indicators of personal strength and sensitivity. These abstract factors point to the more complex and diversified reaches of personal experience and relationship.

There are literally hundreds of synthetic points in every astrological chart; for this reason, we'll confine our presentation here of this valuable and almost boundless realm of astrological symbolism to a selection of the most readily understood and applied points.

## PLANETARY MID-POINTS

As stated in Part Two, planetary mid-points represent the points through which the dynamic forces generated by a relationship existing between any two bodies (or, for that matter, any two astrological factors) are released in their most operative, concrete, and externalized form. Because there are hundreds of such points, it is best to select only those mid-points formed between two planets forming particularly important aspects, those that have a third planet activating them, and those composing planetary dyads (in addition, of course, to quadrant mid-points), for general use.

## MID-POINTS FORMED
## BETWEEN TWO ASPECTING PLANETS

This type of mid-point represents the point in the birth-chart where the meaning, quality, and purpose of the particular aspect (determined by the nature of the aspect, its orb, and the planets, houses, and signs involved) are released in the most operative and apparent manner.

## MID-POINTS ACTIVATED
## BY A THIRD PLANET

If a third planet is within a degree or two of the mid-point of two other planets, the third planet's function should be intimately involved in the process symbolized by the particular mid-point.

## DYADIC MID-POINTS

The mid-point of a dyad, or planetary pair, is particularly significant because it represents the point of release for an important facet of multifunctional integration. When interpreting this type of mid-point, it is important to consider not only the particular function of the dyad but also the phase of relationship and the houses and signs involved.

The following statements concerning dyadic mid-points are necessarily brief and general because of the abstract nature of these factors and are meant to serve as basic guidelines rather than as rigid definitions.

SOLI-LUNAR MID-POINT

### The Point of Meaning

The mid-point of the Sun and Moon represents the externalization, or practical realization, of one's purpose and the meaning of personal existence.

The inverse point represents one's inner awareness, or intuition, of one's purpose and the meaning of life.

### The Point of Identification and Adaptation

The Moon-Saturn mid-point represents the point in space (in terms of the circle of houses and the zodiac) where the interfunctional relationship of identification and adaptation is released in its most operative and concrete manner.

Its inverse point symbolizes the process of internalization and the spiritual release of the forces of identification and adaptation.

MERCURY-JUPITER MID-POINT

### The Point of Associative Participation

The mid-point of Mercury-Jupiter represents the externalization of the individual's powers of creative and associative participation within the social sphere.

The inverse point symbolizes the individual's manner of giving personal meaning to his or her social participation and associations.

VENUS-MARS MID-POINT

### The Point of Sex

The mid-point of Venus-Mars symbolizes how duality is externalized and operative within the field of the individual's personality. The person's sensitivity to people and situations and his or her characteristic manner of approaching a situation is also represented here.

The inverse point is symbolic of the process of internalization of duality and the manner in which the individual handles interpersonal relationships and his or her own sexuality.

JUPITER-SATURN MID-POINT

### The Point of Creativity

Creativity is the result, or the synthetic factor, of the individual's relationship to the internal and external realms of relatedness. A fine line divides the two worlds: the world within and the world without. The internal realm provides one with a unique and individual existence and a specific point of view, while the external realm provides the vast and varied forms of the universe to captivate the imagination.

The mid-point of Jupiter-Saturn is symbolic of the creative process that gives meaning and individual expression to interplay between the microcosm and the macrocosm, which is responsible for individual consciousness. The house and sign of this point serve as indicators of the type of experience and activity through which the individual is most able to relate, in a creative manner, to the realm of internal-external activity.

The inverse point may be considered an indicator of the source of inspiration, which gives personal and spiritual meaning to the creative process.

## MARS-URANUS MID-POINT

### The Point of Transformation

The functional operation of the process of transformation is symbolized by the Mars-Uranus mid-point. This is the point in the birth-chart where the forces of transformation are most intense, and focused and directed toward an external change.

The inverse point is representative of the process of the internal or spiritual transformation, or transformation directed toward an internal change.

## JUPITER-NEPTUNE MID-POINT

### The Point of Reorientation

The mid-point of Jupiter-Neptune refers to the manner in which the process of reorientation is operative within the individual's personality and the point in the birth-chart where the meaning of this process is released in an external manner.

The inverse point is representative of the release of the internal or spiritual meaning of the process of reorientation.

## SATURN-PLUTO MID-POINT

### The Point of Self-Refocalization

The mid-point of Saturn-Pluto represents the process of refocalization and the manner in which it is operative within the individual's personality and life. The point in the birth-chart where this factor is found refers to the release of the interfunctional relationship existing between Saturn and Pluto (the Dyad of Refocalization) and the point where this relationship will be most operative in terms of concrete or apparent refocalization of one's energies and consciousness.

The inverse point refers to the type of experience that brings about an awareness of this process itself, as well as the release of the spiritual or internal significance of the act of refocusing one's consciousness.

## PLANETARY PARTS

Planetary parts serve as indicators of the points of greatest inter-functional ease and sensitivity and are composed of any two planets and the ascendant (or any other angle). Any triad is also a septenary (organic whole made up of seven principles); the relationship between the Three and the Seven is one of the most primary and essential of all occult teachings. When the principles of a triad are brought together as an operative whole, something takes place that makes the triad more than just an assemblage of parts and more than a triad in two-dimensional space. This synthesis of the Three gives birth to an additional factor, a factor born out of the wholeness of the triadic relationship. The fourth, or synthetic, principle transforms the triad into a tetrad, a transformation that takes the relationship from a two-dimensional plane to a three-dimensional, "solid" space form. In addition, the synthetic principle combines the Three in such a way that it is able to manifest itself in the form of four individual aspects.

The synthetic principle of the tetrad is symbolically composed of four *indices* or *parts* of personality projection, which are actually the four facets of the unified nature of the original triad. The part of fortune is the primary part evolving from the Triad of Personality Projection and serves as an archetype for all other planetary parts.

## THE PART OF FORTUNE AS AN INDEX FOR PERSONALITY PROJECTION

The part of fortune is today the most widely (and usually only) used of the dozens of planetary parts developed centuries ago by the mathematically inclined Arabian astrologers. The part of fortune is the lunation cycle focused through the ascendant and is symbolic of the point of expression for the power generated by the soli-lunar relationship. It is a highly personal and intimate symbol (as is any part involving the ascendant), because it is the synthesis of the Triad of Personality Projection.

This part is not exclusively, or even primarily, a significator of material wealth and fortune. Rather, it characterizes the quality and type of personality that the individual will most likely develop and project. It is the point of greatest interfunctional ease and is symbolic of the individual's line of least personal resistance. The part of fortune is a point of personal strength and happiness and operates through the same process as that represented by the waxing hemisphere of the lunation cycle; that is, the part of fortune is connected with the development of organic structures.

One may say simply that the part of fortune is the point of most natural externalization of personality. The placement of this part in relation to the entire birth-chart is significant. The house (the most important factor to consider when interpreting parts) in which the part of fortune is found symbolizes the circumstances and type of experiences in which the individual will find the greatest ease of function. The sign in which the part of fortune is found represents the type of activity the individual will find most rewarding and will respond to with the greatest ease.

When a planet is contacting (conjunctions and oppositions are the only aspects to be used with planetary parts) the part of fortune, the planetary function will be involved with the individual's search for happiness within the personal realm of experience. The planet's characteristics will also be externalized and made evident (if not dominant) within the personality.

### CONTACTS BETWEEN THE PART OF FORTUNE AND THE PLANETS

*Sun and Part of Fortune:* Characterizes an individual seeking a personal and self-directed life-style.

*Moon and Part of Fortune:* Is symbolic of a person who should be involved and at ease with personal and mundane affairs. May also represent an extremely sensitive individual.

*Mercury and Part of Fortune:* Refers to a personality with an "intellectual" temperament.

*Venus and Part of Fortune:* Characterizes an introverted person, who should be concerned with internal and personal matters. Personal charm.

*Mars and Part of Fortune:* Refers to a person with great personal strength or aggressiveness.

*Jupiter and Part of Fortune:* Characterizes an optimistic personality that functions well within the social sphere.

*Saturn and Part of Fortune:* Denotes a serious and profound attitude, with the possibility of pessimism and a sense of destiny. Such a person's approach to things may be highly structured.

*Uranus and Part of Fortune:* Is representative of the type of person who must constantly break down walls and overcome limitations in order to feel at ease with life. Such an individual's life should always be changing and expanding its field of relationships.

*Neptune and Part of Fortune:* Is indicative of a person who wishes to participate in some kind of vast social or spiritual movement. Such a person may be concerned with so-called "mystical" things, often on a very subjective level.

*Pluto and Part of Fortune:* Characterizes the type of person who should feel inclined to pursue and be at ease within political activities and when participating in various forms of social agitation. On the other hand, such a person may be concerned with the process of refocalizing his energy to a higher level of activity.

### THE POINT OF ILLUMINATION

The point of illumination is the polar opposite of the part of fortune and carries the significance of the waning hemicycle of the lunation cycle. This part is an expression of the release of the creative meaning of the inner, or spiritual, self. It deals with the internalization of the lunation cycle; the part of fortune deals with its externalization.

When the point of illumination is contacting a planet, the particular function symbolized by the planet will be involved in the individual's search for happiness within the spiritual realm of creative meaning.

### THE PART OF SPIRIT

This part may be considered a "retrograde" index to the lunation cycle. The formula for this part is ASC + Sun − Moon, meaning it is a solar-dominant index. Actually, the part of spirit has very little to do with spirit. Tradition and social-cultural conditioning are symbolized by this part. It also refers to the hold the past and traditional values have on the individual.

At the first and third quarters of the lunation cycle, the part of fortune and the part of spirit are in opposition, referring to the conflict between the past and the future, or between memory and expectation.

### THE PART OF INSPIRATION

This is the polar opposite of the part of spirit and is symbolic of the individual's inspiration and the type and quality of experience he is moving toward or motivated by.

## PARTS OF THE DYAD
## OF IDENTIFICATION AND ADAPTATION

The synthesis of the Dyad of Identification and Adaptation with the ascendant produces two parts: one with the Moon dominant, the other in which Saturn is dominant.

### TETRAD OF ADAPTIVE POINTING

*Formula:*   Moon + ASC − Saturn

*Meaning:*   The point in the birth-chart where the individual should experience the greatest ease in adapting and adjusting to external circumstances.

*Inverse:*   The point where the individual is most able to adapt and adjust to internal and creative needs.

### TETRAD OF IDENTITY POINTING

*Formula:*   Saturn + ASC − Moon

*Meaning:*   The type of experience through which the person is most likely to realize his or her personal identity.

*Inverse:*   The point in the birth-chart where the person is most likely to realize his or her spiritual or creative identity.

The synthesis of the Moon with the I.C. and Saturn with the M.C. produces two more significant parts:

### TETRAD OF GROWTH

*Formula:*   Moon + I.C. − Saturn

*Meaning:*   The type of experience through which the individual is most likely to achieve outward growth and fulfillment.

*Inverse:*    The point in the birth-chart where the person is most able to make progress in terms of inward growth and fulfillment.

### TETRAD OF ATTAINMENT

*Formula:*    Saturn + M.C. − Moon

*Meaning:*    The type of experience through which the individual is most able to realize and fulfill his place in the collective-planetary-universal scheme of things.

*Inverse:*    The point in the birth-chart where the individual is most able to realize growth in terms of personal identity.

## PARTS OF THE DYAD OF PARTICIPATION AND ASSOCIATION

### TETRAD OF SOCIAL POINTING

*Formula:*    Jupiter + ASC − Mercury

*Meaning:*    The individual's point of greatest ease in terms of social participation and contribution.

*Inverse:*    The type of social experience and activity the individual should find spiritually valuable and beneficial.

### TETRAD OF ASSOCIATION

*Formula:*    Mercury + ASC − Jupiter

*Meaning:*    The point in the birth-chart where the mind should experience the greatest ease of operation in terms of social contribution and education.

*Inverse:*    The point where the mind is most functional in the realm of spiritual and creative association and education.

## PARTS OF THE DYAD OF SEX

### TETRAD OF EXPRESSIVE POINTING

*Formula:*    Venus + ASC − Mars

*Meaning:*    The point in the birth-chart where the individual should experience the greatest ease of emotional expression.

*Inverse:*    The type of experiences through which the individual should be most able to express himself in a creative or spiritual manner.

### TETRAD OF FULFILLMENT POINTING

*Formula:*  Mars + ASC − Venus

*Meaning:*  The type of experience the individual should find most fulfilling and through which he or she is most likely to seek self-fulfillment.

*Inverse:*  The type of experience through which the person should find creative and inner fulfillment and satisfaction.


## PARTS OF THE DYAD OF INTERNAL/EXTERNAL RELATEDNESS

### TETRAD OF PERSPECTIVE POINTING

*Formula:*  Saturn + ASC − Jupiter

*Meaning:*  The point in symbolical space from which the individual views the world (both internal and external) and the perspective from which he is most capable of defining existence.

*Inverse:*  The point from which the individual is most capable of defining his own place, as an individual, within the world.


### TETRAD OF SUBJECT-MATTER POINTING

*Formula:*  Jupiter + ASC − Saturn

*Meaning:*  The area in the birth-chart from which the individual (the artist) chooses his subject matter and draws his materials.

*Inverse:*  The spiritual value or principle that stands behind the subject matter and the tradition chosen by the individual.


## PARTS OF THE DYAD OF TRANSFORMATION

### TETRAD OF TRANSFORMATION

*Formula:*  Uranus + ASC − Mars

*Meaning:*  The type of experience through which the individual is most capable of effecting change and transformation and the area in which one is most likely to succeed in penetrating barriers.

*Inverse:*  The spiritual or creative purpose that directs the process of transformation.

## PARTS OF THE DYAD OF REORIENTATION

### TETRAD OF REORIENTATION

*Formula:*   Neptune + ASC − Jupiter

*Meaning:*   The type of experiences through which the individual is most able to respond to the need of reorientation.

*Inverse:*   The spiritual or creative ideal that motivates the individual to reorient his consciousness.

## PARTS OF THE DYAD OF REFOCALIZATION

### TETRAD OF SELF-REFOCALIZATION

*Formula:*   Pluto + ASC − Saturn

*Meaning:*   The area in which the individual should place particular attention upon the process of self-refocalization and the type of experiences that will serve the individual as vehicles for the expression of new forms of consciousness.

*Inverse:*   The spiritual, transcendental, or creative value of experience that motivates the individual toward self-refocalization.

## PLANETARY NODES

We have seen how planetary mid-points act as symbolic portals through which combined planetary functions are released in a dynamic and externalized manner, and how planetary parts serve as indicators of areas where the relationship existing between a pair of planets functions with the greatest ease in terms of one's individual life experiences. In closing this chapter we'll explore how a planetary orbit, when referred to the ecliptic, represents the entire cycle of a planet as a dynamic element of the solar system, not as just a point in space.

### THE LUNAR NODAL AXIS

Planetary orbits are never perfect circles and are never entirely perpendicular to the plane of the ecliptic. As discussed elsewhere in Part Three, this situation gives rise to the planetary cycle of latitude and its nodal axis. During half of its orbit, a planet is north of the ecliptic, and it is south of the ecliptic for the remaining half. When the plane of a planet's orbit meets, or intersects, the plane of the ecliptic, the planet is at its north node (completing the southern-latitude cycle and beginning its travel through the northern hemisphere of its cycle of latitude) or at its south node (completing the northern-latitude cycle and commencing its route below the ecliptic).

Because the Moon is a satellite of the earth, it completes its cycle much more rapidly than any satellite of the Sun, and for this reason, in addition to reasons discussed in "The Lunation Cycle: the Archetypal Cycle of Relationship," the lunar nodal axis is considered as an archetype in this brief presentation of the meaning of planetary nodes.

### THE MOON'S LATITUDE CYCLE

The maximum lunar latitude is 5°17' north or south of the ecliptic. At these points it is squaring its nodes and is most distant, in both space and function, from the earth, therefore most active and independent in its own sphere. At maximum latitude the lunar function, or one's manner of adjusting to the needs of life, operates in a spontaneous and detached manner.

When in the northern hemisphere of its latitude cycle, the lunar function is of a very personal nature, dealing with the survival and adjustment of the person in the outer world, often with very ambitious designs. In the southern latitude of its cycle, the lunar function is focused upon the discovery of the meaning of life through social, political, or spiritual participation. Persons born with the Moon in this hemisphere may seek to attain self-fulfillment through the release of self by engaging the self with a social or spiritual movement. One should, however, not place too much emphasis upon the Moon's latitude (and likewise upon the latitudes of the planets) unless other factors are involved, such as emphasis on the nodes.

### THE MEANING OF THE NORTH LUNAR NODE

The position of the north lunar node symbolizes the area in the birth-chart where the person should be able to act most freely and should receive the greatest return (in terms of personal integration) for his or her efforts. It is the symbolic point of intake and integration of lunar materials (experiences, adjustments, etc.) that build the personality and the organic structures of self. The north lunar node is the symbolic mouth of self—through which new experiences are taken in, used, and assimilated by the entire organism.

The house (the most important factor to consider when studying nodes) represents the type of experiences that, involving the greatest amount of exertion on the part of the person, should also produce the most beneficial and needed results.

The sign of the north node symbolizes the type of "food" or "fuel" that is most readily assimilated by the organism for propelling the lunar (or planetary) function through experience.

## THE MEANING OF THE SOUTH LUNAR NODE

This node may be related to the spontaneous creative act or the release of the seed, as well as to anything no longer needed by the organism. It symbolizes the area of the birth-chart where the individual may expand his personality, while the north node represents the area where the individual may build his personality. The south lunar node is also the point of release for the contents of personality directed toward the service of a greater whole. In addition, it represents the establishment of habit through the repetition of an act, while the north node represents gradual progress made through personal effort. One may consider the south node a symbol of the unconscious, of spontaneous or habitual activity.

The house of the south lunar node represents the type of experience in which the person is most likely to become entangled, repeating the same experiences, or the same mistakes, time after time. These experiences may be seen, from the person's point of view, as the line of least resistance.

The sign of the south lunar node refers to the type of activities about which the individual is most likely to be passive, or approach in a negative or unconscious manner.

### The Moon Contacting Its Nodal Axis

Persons born with the Moon near its north node may be strongly influenced by the mother principle. Such a highly focused lunar nature may enable the person to "feel" his or her way through life by developing a tactful and diplomatic manner, which may be channeled toward the guidance of others.

Persons born with the Moon near its south node may repudiate the mother principle and its influence. This may also refer to a desire for some kind of transcendental mother image (such as a church or organization) or even to the desire to exercise maternal authority over others.

### Lunar Nodal Axis Contacting the Horizon-Meridian

This situation represents the lunar function acting upon the basic structure of individual selfhood in the most focused manner possible. The personality should, in this case, display a lunar nature and act as an agency for the release of the lunar function in all fields of experience.

## THE MEANING OF PLANETARY NODES

The framework described above may be applied to other planets (excluding the Sun, of course, which has no latitude cycle and therefore no nodal axis). The north node of a planet represents the body's point of integration and assimilation, while the south node represents the release of the contents of the planet's function and the accumulated past (habit) of the planetary function.

If one planet is on another's node, the node will "overtone" the operation of the planet, adding contrast and color to its expression.

The one major difference between lunar and planetary nodes is that planetary nodes are almost stationary in terms of zodiacal reference; they all move less than one minute of arc annually. This means that the positions of a planet's nodes in the zodiac refer to how the meaning of that planet should be (or is becoming) manifest within the whole of humanity, in order to meet the call of a collective or planetary need. The house positions of a planetary node, however, refer to how the principle of the particular node relates to the person as an individual and to his or her individual life experiences.

# 9

# THE BIRTH-CHART AS A WHOLE

*Your birth-chart is a message—a set of instructions outlining in broad terms the best way for you to become what you are only potentially at birth—that is, what place and function you were meant to fulfill by being born at a precise place and moment.*

DANE RUDHYAR

On the preceding pages I have attempted to give an approach and a procedure for the interpretation of the birth-chart more thorough than any presentation previously given on the subject in one volume. One who wishes to facilitate the various techniques given here is advised to relate all his or her findings to a cohesive, comprehensive, and relevant framework; the use of techniques alone, without an organic structure of significance, will provide nothing but confusion and a mass of unrelatable and meaningless information.

The birth-chart is, firstly, a symbolic statement, and secondly, a unit containing limitless symbolic factors, which reveal their significance (their symbolic syllable) only when considered in active relationship to all other symbolic factors within the birth-chart as a whole, and to the whole person the chart represents. After one has studied the symbolic factors with the chart one desires to make use of (there are limitless symbolic factors within every astrological chart, so one must select the most pertinent to the purpose of one's interpretation), one should meditate upon the birth-chart so that the symbolic statement contained by the chart may be revealed as an expression of *being*, as a statement of the person's *dharma* as an individual.

Of course, such an experience of at-one-ment is not easily reached, and one who is seriously interested in this approach to astrology should not be considered a "failure" simply because this particular faculty of perception has not yet actualized its potential.

It might be convenient at this point to mention, for the reader who has not already assumed it, that the astrological technique can and should be practiced upon the astrologer himself. The field of astrological "self-practice" or "self-therapy" has been virtually untouched by traditional astrologers, though one can expect to see it given more attention and consideration in the future by those involved with the symbolic life.

# PART THREE

## *Notes*

Introductory quotes are from the following sources: Chapter 1: *The Practice of Astrology*, by Dane Rudhyar (Penguin Books, 1970); Chapter 2: *Guide to Horoscope Interpretation*, by Marc Edmund Jones (Sabian Publishing Society, 1969); Chapter 3: *Essentials of Horoscope Analysis*, by Marc Edmund Jones (Sabian Publishing Society, 1960); Chapter 4: *Holism and Evolution*, by Jan C. Smuts (The Viking Press, 1961); Chapter 5: *The Lunation Cycle*, by Dane Rudhyar (Shambala Publications, 1971); Chapter 6: *An Astrological Study of Psychological Complexes*, by Dane Rudhyar (Servire N.V., 1969); Chapter 7: *On Becoming a Person*, by Carl R. Rogers (Houghton Mifflin, 1961); Chapter 8: *The Astrology of Personality*, by Dane Rudhyar (Doubleday, 1970); Chapter 9: an extract from a paper delivered by Dane Rudhyar to the 1972 convention of the American Federation of Astrologers.

The essay "First Steps in the Study of Birth-Charts," now included in *Person-Centered Astrology*, by Dane Rudhyar, was very useful in reference to Chapter 2. The scheme of focal points (Chapter 3) is based on the concept of *determinators of focal emphasis*, originated by Marc Edmund Jones and presented in *Essentials of Horoscope Analysis*.

The concept of the soli-lunar relationship and its eight soli-lunar types was originated by Rudhyar and thoroughly discussed in *The Lunation Cycle*.

Chapter 6, "Planetary Grouping," was inspired by *An Astrological Study of Psychological Complexes*, as were parts of Chapter 7.

"Pythagorean Astrology," a study course by Marc Edmund Jones, was a particularly useful reference for Chapters 7 and 8.

# 4

---

# the birth-chart and time:

TECHNIQUES
OF ASTROLOGICAL TIME ANALYSIS

# 1

# THE CONCEPT
# OF ASTROLOGICAL TIME ANALYSIS

*What constitutes a dynamic horoscopy fundamentally is the projection of the planets, either by purely symbolic motion or by employment of the actual movements, to establish their significant relations with the various positions of themselves and others.*

MARC EDMUND JONES

A true understanding of an individual person as an evolving entity constantly involved in the process of personal unfoldment requires, from the astrological approach, a *time analysis* of the birth-chart. Here the birth-chart represents the archetypal pattern of individual *being,* remaining as an unchanging factor throughout the life of each person. One's personality is, however, in a constant state of unfoldment, from birth to death. Obviously, a newborn infant does not, at the moment of birth, have a fully integrated personality, though the singular event of birth provides the potential of *developing* a fully integrated personality if proper conditions are present. In the course of one's growth and development, certain potentials symbolized within the birth-chart may be realized, in one manner or another; the person experiences certain turning points and crucial periods that if properly met can quicken his personal unfoldment. The time analysis of the birth-chart, through the use of *progressions* and *transits,* may reveal the nature and meaning of these turning points (past, present, and future), providing one with a more complete understanding of the individual he wishes to aid by means of astrology in the process of self-actualization and personal unfoldment.

## THE USE OF ASTROLOGICAL TIME ANALYSIS

This form of astrological analysis has been greatly abused by both astrologers and the public. The media, too, have projected a distorted image of astrology in which astrology, if it is given any validity at all, is primarily seen as a type of fortunetelling. According to this popular image, with the advice of an astrologer one can "make it big," an astrologer being able to, supposedly, foretell specific events. In turn, many astrologers specialize in the abuse of progressions and transits, or overemphasize their importance in order to capitalize on the neurotic curiosities, pet phobias, or financial preoccupations of those who actually believe astrology is a means of fortunetelling. True astrology, and most certainly the humanistic approach to astrology, is not fortunetelling.

The time analysis of the birth-chart is used by the humanistic astrologer to discover the crucial period of the individual's life in order to assist him in his own personal unfoldment; the prediction of events, whether fulfilled or not, is potentially destructive to the psychological being of the person, and is at best a superficial distraction. Although it is beyond the scope of this present work to give a complete presentation of the philosophy, symbolism, and practice of astrological time analysis (indeed, it would require at least an entire volume), a practical guide to this area of astrological study will be presented in the following pages.

## THE BIRTH-CHART AND SYMBOLIC TIME

Astrological progressions and symbolic directions are not based upon objective duration; rather, they deal with symbolic or subjective time, which has significance only when related to an individual factor (the birth-chart). Some symbolic directions are founded upon the idea that one year of objective time is equal to one day or one degree in terms of subjective duration. Other systems are of a more numerological origin. Generally, all systems of symbolic direction (of which there are many) are valid in terms of their frame of reference and deal primarily with the gradual unfoldment of personality and potentiality.

## THE BIRTH-CHART AND MANIFESTED TIME

Planetary transits refer to the actual and objective day-to-day positions of planetary bodies in the sky. Considered in relation to the birth-chart, they may reveal information regarding the collective and external forces that act upon the individual's personal existence.

### VARIETIES OF PROGRESSIONS AND SYMBOLIC DIRECTIONS

Below, we will outline the several different methods of symbolic direction and progression. Although the information derived from each system is different, it is generally applied to the birth-chart in the same manner. The various techniques for the application of these progressions and symbolic directions will be discussed immediately following the outline below.

### Secondary Progressions

*Formula:*   One year of life equals one day in the ephemeris.*

*Philosophy:*   Birth is a continuing process. The day is the reflection of the solar year. This system relates the collective factor (orbital revolution of the earth) to the individual life process (axial rotation of the earth).

*Considerations:*   The solar factor (day-year) is dominant, conditioning all information derived by this system.

*Consensus:*   Probably the most widely favored by present-day astrologers.

### Primary Directions

*Formula:*   One year of life is equal to about one degree on the M.C.

*Philosophy:*   Relates the life process to the structure of individual selfhood (horizon-meridian).

*Considerations:*   Special tables and complex calculations are required. Exact time of birth must be known (an error of four minutes equals one year). Planetary progression (movement) is almost nonexistent.

*Consensus:*   Widely used in the past, though not very popular today.

* Mathematical calculations for the various systems of symbolic direction are outlined in Appendix IV.

### Radix, or Solar Arc, Directions

*Origin:* Developed by Valentine Naibod during the sixteenth century and popularized by the Victorian astrologer Sepharial.

*Formula:* One year of life is equated to the daily motion of the Sun. Increment may be added to all natal positions.

*Philosophy:* The solar factor is dominant in individual existence. Solar motion is related to the individual life process.

*Considerations:* Daily lunar motion may also be used as annual increment, giving a lunar nature to all directions.

*Consensus:* Popular in England and Europe.


### One-Degree Measure

*Formula:* One year of life is equal to one degree. Increment may be added to all natal factors.

*Philosophy:* Relates the archetypal solar symbol (the degree) to one year of the life process.

*Considerations:* Archetypal and solar in origin and significance. Combines the best of the primary and radix systems. Easy to use, very significant and useful.

*Consensus:* Widely used and favored.


### Duodenary Measure

*Origin:* Introduced by Charles Carter about fifty years ago, though he does not claim to have invented it.

*Formula:* One year of life is equal to $2\text{-}1/2°$. Increment may be added to all natal factors.

*Philosophy:* Employs pure astrological numerology by dividing $30°$ by 12, resulting in the increment of $2\text{-}1/2°$.

*Considerations:* The natal positions progress or move through the signs, houses, etc., more quickly by this system than most others, because of its larger increment, thus providing more frequent significators. Purely numerological. May provide significant information that may not be obtained by another system.

*Consensus:* Seldom used, though often recognized as significant.

### Septenary (Point of Life) Measure

*Formula:* One year is equal to 4-2/7°. Increment may be added to all natal positions.

*Philosophy:* One year of the life process is correlated to one seventh of 30°.

*Considerations:* Carries the symbolic meaning of 7. Related to the destiny and structure of individuality. Correlated to the 84-year cycle of Uranus. Particularly useful when related to the horizon-meridian.

*Consensus:* Seldom used.

### Point of Self Measure

*Formula:* One year of life is equated to 12-6/7°. Increment may be added to all natal factors.

*Philosophy:* Annual increment is found by the division of the quadrant (90°) by 7, or by the division of 360° by 28.

*Considerations:* Annual increment is point of life measure times 3. Divides the Uranian cycle of 84 years into three smaller cycles, of 28 years each. The 28-year cycles may be correlated to the progressed lunation cycle of 28-1/2 years and the transiting Saturnian cycle of 29 years. Can give significant information concerning the unfoldment of individuality, particularly when applied to the horizon-meridian.

*Consensus:* Seldom used.

## CHOICE OF SYSTEMS

Each system of symbolic direction and progression is valid and significant within its own sphere: each is theoretically best suited for a particular type of time analysis, and each potentially reveals a particular type of life experience more reliably than the other systems. However, the practical variations among systems and their relative validity have not been clearly accounted for by significant in-depth research; therefore, any statement concerning the validity or suitability of one system over another must be very limited.

Unless one is very experienced with the use of these techniques, or unless a particular type of information is desired for which one specific technique is obviously best suited, one should concentrate on the use of the one-degree measure or secondary progressions.

## SIGNIFICANCE OF PROGRESSED POSITIONS

The increment given by a system of symbolic progression is added to the natal positions, resulting in the progressed natal positions. Progressed positions have very little significance in themselves; they reveal their meaning in terms of the personal existence of the individual when they are applied or related to the birth-chart.

## PROGRESSED ASPECTS

When a progressed position forms an aspect to a natal position (extremely narrow orbs should be used, since in some cases one degree may equal several years of living), the function symbolized by the natal factor will be modified by, channeled through, or actualized with the assistance of the progressed factor. The progressed positions act as conditions through which the archetypal and unchanging natal forces become manifest. The "meaning" of a progressed aspect is generally the same as that of a natal aspect (a square is always a square); progressed aspects, however, reveal their significance in terms of becoming, while natal aspects are related to the structure of being (the birth-chart).

In addition to aspects formed between a progressed position and a natal position, aspects formed between two progressed planets are also significant, though more abstract. Of particular importance are progressed aspects formed between dyadic complements (such as Mars and Venus).

## ACTUALIZATION OF NATAL ASPECTS

A natal aspect may become actualized, releasing its great potential of creative energy, during the time of life when the progressed-to-natal or the progressed-to-progressed relationship reaches an angular value of 0° to 180°. A natal aspect progressed to conjunction may become actualized in terms of *activity,* while a relationship progressed to opposition may become actualized in terms of *awareness.* A natal aspect progressed to a square may become actualized through constructive crises.

## PROGRESSED HOUSE AND SIGN PLACEMENT

The progressive changes of position, in terms of house and sign, can reveal the basic direction and orientation of any natal factor for the date of progression. For instance, if a person's natal Mars is in his natal twelfth house, as Mars progresses into the first house, the Martial function should become more apparent within the personality (particularly as Mars contacts the ascendant), and he will probably become more conscious of the planet's symbolic function as an active force in his personal existence. The same holds true for the signs, the progressed positions acting only as conditions through which natal potentials become manifest.

# 2

# TECHNIQUES
# OF SYMBOLIC TIME ANALYSIS

*Progressions, as applied to the unfoldment of the human person, year after year, refer to the gradual demonstration and actualization of [the] powers of understanding and intelligent adjustment of life. . . .*

DANE RUDHYAR

## SOLI-LUNAR TECHNIQUES

The progressed lunation cycle is the most primary and personal index for the basic crises and turning points experienced by the individual person in the process of becoming. It is best here to employ the secondary system of progression, because it deals with the natural rhythm of the lunation cycle—New Moon to New Moon—which it translates into a 29½-year cycle. Generally, the progressed lunation cycle is based upon the same structure as the archetypal lunation cycle described earlier in the text, except that the progressed cycle refers to the dynamic process of *unfoldment* and *becoming,* while the natal lunation cycle is symbolic of *being.*

## PROGRESSED NEW MOON

The progressed New Moon occurs when the progressed Sun and progressed Moon occupy the same degree of the zodiac. It represents a period when old and familiar patterns adopted in the past are potentially revealed as antiquated and useless vehicles that may have been of value in the past but are now dead weight. Here the person may experience temporal disorientation, and his life may change dramatically as he adopts an entirely new frame of reference.

Obviously, such a turning point may leave the individual in an uncomfortable situation, and he may experience feelings of isolation and disorganization. For this reason, the period immediately preceding the New Moon should be a time for the reorientation and redirection of one's life. The progressed New Moon is indeed a symbolic rebirth, and within the moment of the New Moon is contained the seed for the next 29½ years of unfoldment and realization.

## PROGRESSED FIRST QUARTER

The progressed First Quarter occurs when the progressed Moon is 90° ahead of the progressed Sun in terms of the zodiac. During this period of life, the individual should experience external confrontations that may generally affect his basic instinctual and emotional natures. This is a time when the instinctual and emotional natures are at their apex in terms of the consciousness of the individual, as well as a period of great emotional crisis. In addition, if these emotional crises are not recognized and dealt with in a positive manner, the personality may suffer deep frustrations, which could repress one's emotional nature throughout the cycle.

## PROGRESSED FULL MOON

The progressed Full Moon takes place when the progressed Moon is 180 degrees ahead of the progressed Sun. This is a time of fulfillment and decision. The individual must recognize the direction of his life at this time and attempt to clarify his life purpose, personal desires, and aims. During this period, one must face the basic issues of life, order them according to his own nature, and give them creative meaning in terms of his own existence.

Of course, the age of the person experiencing the progressed Full Moon (as well as any other progressed significator) must be considered. For instance, if the person is very young we cannot speak of an actual individual fulfillment, for what is being fulfilled is the child's social-cultural background. One born during the waxing phase begins to build his individuality within the structure and in terms of his racial-social-cultural background. On the other hand, if he was born during the waning Moon he would experience his first New Moon before his first Full Moon; meaning, he is more likely to clarify his life purpose creatively and experience some kind of individual fulfillment when his first Full Moon does occur. That is, if he was able to free himself from cultural conditioning at the time of his first progressed New Moon.

## PROGRESSED THIRD QUARTER

The progressed Third Quarter takes place when the progressed Moon is 90° behind the progressed Sun. This may be a time of crisis in terms of thinking or consciousness. The experiences encountered by the person during this period may drastically repolarize his beliefs, thinking, and consciousness.

### PROGRESSED LUNATION CHARTS

Because these turning points (progressed lunar phases) are so important, it is a good practice to calculate the secondary progressed planetary positions for the moment of the progressed lunation and locate them within the basic structure (horizon-meridian) of the birth-chart. This progressed New Moon chart symbolizes the seed or pattern of unfoldment for the entire 29½-year cycle—and it is a good idea to use it as a starting point when considering any type of progressed information.

There are five factors to consider when examining a progressed soli-lunar chart:

**1.** *Progressed soli-lunar aspects to other progressed bodies.* The aspected planet will be involved, as well as the nature of the aspect, in the process symbolized by the particular phase of the soli-lunar relationship.

**2.** *Progressed soli-lunar aspects to natal positions* act as channels through which the process symbolized by the phase of the soli-lunar relationship may manifest itself objectively.

**3.** *The natal house occupied by the progressed Sun and Moon* refers to the circumstances involved in the manifestation of the process symbolized by the particular soli-lunar phase.

**4.** *The signs of the progressed Sun and Moon* indicate the type of experience involved in the process.

**5.** *Aspects between progressed planets and natal planets* represent forces operative during the same time period as the progressed lunation.

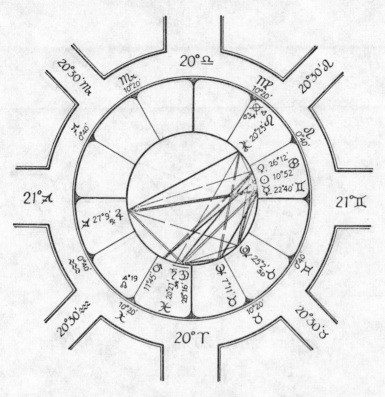

Hermann Hesse

We may now turn our attention to the birth-chart and progressed
(second) New Moon chart of Hermann Hesse. Hesse was one of
the most popular and widely read German novelists before the out-
break of the First World War. During the war, his entire past life
fell apart, losing for him all of its value. There were several experiences during this period (1914–17) that Hesse has stated "totally
transformed [his] concept of life." He writes that 1914 brought the
second major turning point in his life (the first being his decision
to be a writer, at age thirteen, close to the progressed First Quarter
Moon): ". . . through this experience I crossed, for the first time,
over the threshold of life." During 1916, his father died, his son became very ill, and his wife "lost her sanity"; also during this year,
Hesse himself entered a private mental hospital, where he experienced
seventy-two sessions with a Jungian psychiatrist.

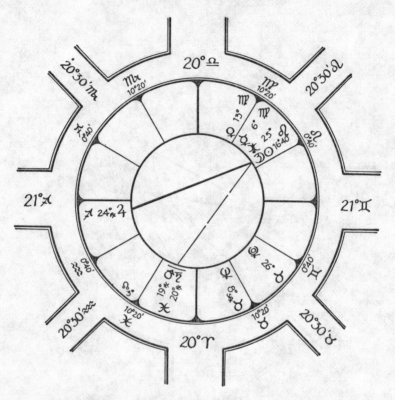

Hermann Hesse (2nd New Moon Chart)

*Demian,* his first post-1914 novel, was published in 1919 under a pseudonym, because Hesse felt that he was no longer the person the public had identified with the name Hermann Hesse. This was Hesse's first symbolic novel and is said to be the story of his rebirth and experiences with Jungian psychology. During the following years he wrote the outstanding works *Siddhartha, Journey to the East, Steppenwolf, Narcissus and Goldmund,* and *The Glass-Bead Game,* the book that won the Nobel Prize for Literature in 1946.

Hesse's birth-chart reveals a complex nature and a disseminating Moon (he experienced his first New Moon while still quite young). His second progressed New Moon occurred in mid-1914. The chart for this occasion reveals that it took place in the seventeenth degree of Leo, which is trine to his natal ascendant and very close to the mid-point of the upper-western quadrant. In addition, the New Moon forms a loose septile to Mercury (natal), which occupies the seventh house, and the twenty-third degree of Gemini, as well as being the planet of oriental appearance, obviously a significator of Hesse's writing talent.

The only progressed planetary bodies aspecting this progressed New Moon are the very tight conjunction of Mars, stationary retrograde, and Saturn retrograde in the third natal house occupying the sign of Pisces. These two planets form a quincunx to the progressed New Moon, and this conjunction may be regarded as representing the force that transformed (through its "destructive" as well as "constructive" powers) the course of Hesse's life. This conjunction was at closest orb (0°20′) during Hesse's lifetime during 1916 (both bodies at that time retrograding), the most difficult period of his life as well as the year he began his relationship with Jungian psychology.

### NEW-MOON-BEFORE-BIRTH CHARTS

The New Moon before birth is representative of the seed moment of the cycle upon which the individual was born—thus is a basic significator of the past. A chart may be drawn for the moment of the last New Moon before birth, placing the planetary positions within the framework of the natal chart.

In the examination of the New Moon chart, one should consider:

**1.** Whether the New Moon before birth took place in the same sign as the natal Sun. If so, the quality of the natal Sun's sign will pervade the personality and nature of the individual; if not, the personality will manifest a basic dualism in terms of quality.

**2.** Whether the New Moon before birth took place in the same house as the natal Sun. If so, no conflict between fields of operation is indicated; if not, the personality will be influenced by or active within two distinct fields of operation.

**3.** Contacts between the New Moon and natal planets. The natal planet will serve as a channel for destiny fulfillment.

**4.** Aspects between the New Moon and other planets within the New Moon chart. These are symbolic of additional forces that may tend to be related to the individual's past.

When referring to a New Moon chart, one may speak of karma, inherent qualities, preconditioning, etc., as long as it is understood that the New-Moon-before-birth chart represents the essence of the cycle the individual "came in on." That is, it is basically a tool for

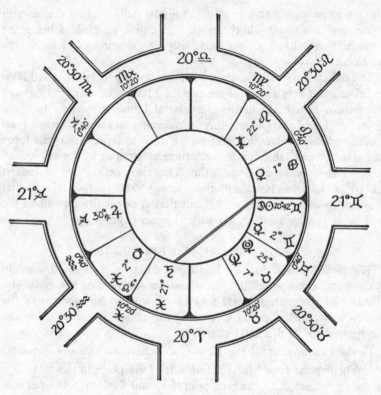

Hermann Hesse (New Moon Before Birth Chart)

determining the special and unique forces operative within the individual's "soul-field."

Now let's look at the New-Moon-before-birth chart of Hermann Hesse. The planetary positions are calculated for the moment of the New Moon (June 11, 1877, 14:32 G.M.T.) and referred to the framework of Hesse's birth-chart. The New Moon occurred at 20°42′ Gemini, within the same house as the natal Sun, though in a different sign, indicating a dualistic nature in terms of solar quality. One will also notice that the natal Mercury is 2° from the position of the New Moon, suggesting that Hesse's literary talent was an "inherent gift" or "brought over from the past"; by any means, Hesse appears to have been born to write. Further investigation will reveal a very close square between the New Moon and the natal (and New-Moon-before-birth) Saturn, representative of the close connection existing between Saturn and the emergence of Hesse's true identity. There is also a sextile between the New Moon and the New-Moon-before-birth Uranus, indicating that the natal Uranus-Saturn quincunx is a key factor behind Hesse's unusual capability of self-transformation.

## PLANETARY TECHNIQUES

After the progressed soli-lunar relationship has been considered, the next phase of symbolic time analysis is the examination of progressed planetary positions.

When examining the progressed planetary positions, one should consider:

**1.** the sign occupied by the planet and the time of life during which a planet progresses into the following sign;

**2.** the house occupied by the planet, noticing any changes in house placements in the recent past or near future;

**3.** aspects between progressed planets and natal factors;

**4.** aspects between progressed positions; and

**5.** the over-all progressed planetary pattern.

### PROGRESSED DYADIC RELATIONSHIPS

The progressed phases of dyadic relationships may be examined in the same manner as the soli-lunar relationship.

### CHARTING THE PROGRESSED PLANETS

The progressed planetary positions should be charted, using the natal-house cusps, on a form specially designed for this purpose. If more than one system of planetary progression is used, a separate form should be used for each.

## SYMBOLIC TECHNIQUES

### THE POINT OF SELF AND THE CYCLE OF UNFOLDMENT

The gradual process of unfoldment of individuality may be revealed by the use of a factor, a purely symbolic point, called the point of self. This point is found by assigning twenty-eight months of life to each of the twelve houses, beginning at birth with the ascendant. A complete cycle occupies twenty-eight years. This divides life into three 28-year cycles of unfoldment symbolizing the individual's particular relationship to the archetypal energies of his birth-chart in terms of unfoldment of individuality.

The progression of this point through the houses indicates the symbolic unfoldment of individuality in terms of experience. Perhaps the most suitable method of examining the progression of the point of self, through its 28-year cycle from ascendant to ascendant, is to relate it to the archetypal structure of the lunation cycle, by hemisphere, quadrant, and biquadrant.

The first 28-year cycle of the point of self corresponds to the process of mental development; the second cycle, from twenty-eight years of age to fifty-six, is related to the expansion and control of the personal field of experience; the third, to the realization of spiritual identity and the completion of the process of individualization at the age of eighty-four. The last few years of each cycle, the twelfth-house stage, are usually extremely critical, because they symbolize periods of reidentification and form the crucial steps to the building of the individuality. The first few years of each new cycle denotes the emergence of a new meaning of life.

3

# THE STUDY OF TRANSITS
# IN ASTROLOGICAL TIME ANALYSIS

*A transit is a focused manifestation of the unending pressure applied by Nature upon the natal, archetypal structure of our selfhood.*

DANE RUDHYAR

## TRANSITS

A planet's transit position is its position as it is found in an ephemeris for a particular day and hour; in other words, transits refer to the present positions of the planets in the sky. Thus, they deal with manifested, or objective, time. Basically, the transiting positions are representative of the external or collective pressures or forces that act upon human beings. The study of planetary and dyadic cycles can be very significant (when approached with a proper attitude) applied to the individual's life experiences.

In the examination of transiting positions one should consider:

1. the planetary position in terms of house and sign placement;
2. aspects between transiting positions and natal positions;
3. aspects between transiting positions and progressed positions;
4. transit retrograde cycles; and
5. aspects between transit positions, particularly polarities.

### Charting Transit Positions

The transit positions should be charted in a manner similar to the charting of progressed planets, preferably on a form that provides an area for transits as well as progressions.

## SOLAR AND LUNAR RETURNS

This technique is widely used by many astrologers. It involves casting a chart for the exact moment of the Sun's return to the exact position it occupies in the natal chart each year (called a solar return chart), and casting a chart for the exact moment the Moon returns to its natal position each month (lunar return chart). These charts are supposed to reveal the pattern of unfoldment for the following solar and lunar periods, when related to the birth-chart.

It may be more organic to substitute or implement solar and lunar returns within a soli-lunar return chart. Such a chart would be cast monthly, for the exact moment the transiting soli-lunar cycle returns to the natal relationship, revealing the pattern of the next month in terms of the individual's soli-lunar temperament.

## SOLI-LUNAR RETURNS AND THE FERTILITY CYCLE

Research has been done by a Czechoslovakian psychologist, Dr. Eugen Jonas, that shows, with 87 per cent accuracy, that a woman is fertile when the transiting soli-lunar cycle is at the same phase as it was at the time of her birth. In other words, a woman born under, for instance, a First-Quarter Moon, can conceive only when the soli-lunar relationship in the sky is also in its first quarter. In addition, Dr. Jonas has discovered that if conception does occur, the sex of the child may be determined by the sign the Moon occupied at the time of conception, the traditional positive signs (fire and air) signifying a male child, and the negative signs (earth and water) signifying a female child.

# PART FOUR

## *Notes*

The opening statement for Chapter 1 is from *Scope of Astrological Prediction,* by Marc Edmund Jones (Sabian Publishing Society, 1969). Those for Chapters 2 and 3 are extracted from *The Practice of Astrology,* by Dane Rudhyar (Penguin Books, 1970).

The concept of the progressed lunation cycle and progressed lunation charts was originated by Rudhyar and is more thoroughly treated in *The Lunation Cycle* (Shambala Publications, 1971). The concept of the point of self was also originated by Rudhyar and is discussed in his *The Astrology of Personality* (Doubleday, 1970) and *The Astrological Houses* (Doubleday, 1972).

# epilogue

## THE PERSONAL SIGNIFICANCE
## OF ASTROLOGICAL STUDY

# THE PERSONAL SIGNIFICANCE OF
## ASTROLOGICAL STUDY

Astrology has been with us, though certainly not always retaining its original outward form, since the dawn of mind. It is difficult to ascertain what kind of faculty led the first astrologer to the realization of the relationship existing between man and the universe. We can say, however, that any person who is an astrologer, in the true sense, perceives life as an endless and remarkably complex web of relationship. All existents—from the most minute cell in one's body to the universe—are in some way intimately related and essentially inseparable. Astrology is essentially an application of the law of correspondence, and when applied to the life experiences of individual human beings can be seen as a means of recognizing and actualizing one's potential as a whole person. When seen in this way, it becomes apparent that astrological study can and should effect a change in the consciousness and evolutionary stature of the person who studies it.

The initial process before the man or woman who wishes to approach the astrological path is one of mental discipline and the development of holistic perception. The experiences of the individual during this process encourage one to see and understand all things as wholes—as patterns composed of interrelated and interdependent factors that reveal their significance only when they are perceived in their structural totality (wholeness). The individual gradually becomes aware that the present is just one point—simply one moment—of an entire cycle of complex and intricate relationship. As the abstract mind emerges into the realm of symbolic cognition, astrology becomes a highly sophisticated system of universal symbolism, which gives the person the power to comprehend the secret of trans/interfunctional relationships existing between wholes on any level of existence. When fluent in the symbolic language of astrology, the holistic perception of archetypal and evolving forms, one has within one's reach a valuable tool for integration and perfection through active self-actualization.

Knowledge of the law of correspondence and the wise application of such knowledge toward the integration of one's self constitutes astrological "self-therapy." Astrological self-therapy, or self-practice, differs from the conventional type of astrological practice, which necessitates two parties: an "astrologer," one who knows and understands, and a "client," one who is seeking knowledge and understanding concerning his or her own personal existence. It differs because astrological self-practice reveals directly to the individual the meaning and significance of his or her personal existence. When an individual's consciousness penetrates beyond the superficial realms of experience, one may make *direct* contact with the ageless body of symbolic wisdom manifest within all things. This essence of astrological wisdom, when assimilated by the consciousness, reveals the nature of all things.

Astrology is an effective instrument of self-actualization, and in a larger sense, self-perfection, when applied directly to the individual experiences of the astrology student, and it is this concept of self-perfection that should be a motivating factor in one's study of astrology. Astrological study should be a process that commences with the development of the mental faculties, both concrete and abstract, and is completed when its primary purpose is accomplished: the transformation of the individual into something *more*. This something *more* has the characteristic of transcending duality through the reconciliation and synthesis of opposites.

When viewed from this perspective, there is no real distinction between true astrology and other "evolutionary vehicles," such as tantrism and alchemy. Indeed, the processes achieve the same thing: the transformation of the individual's consciousness through the inner communion of self.

# appenòixes

# APPENDIX I

## INSTRUCTIONS FOR CASTING THE BIRTH-CHART

# INTRODUCTION

## LEARNING TO CAST THE BIRTH-CHART

There are two basic requirements for learning to cast the birth-chart: a basic knowledge of arithmetic, and patience. There is no real reason why anyone cannot master the process. Many, of course, become frustrated or confused at certain points, but if one step is taken at a time and mastered before going on to the next, many headaches will be saved. And, of course, it always takes longer to perform a structured routine the first few times, before one has become familiar with the process and confident in his or her ability to perform well. Although the procedure may seem inordinately laborious to the beginner, an experienced astrologer can cast the basic birth-chart in fifteen or twenty minutes.

In the following pages, I've tried to present the process of casting the birth-chart in the simplest and clearest way possible. Sample exercises are included, with answers in the back, for those who wish to check their progress as they go along step by step.

I've used a *noon* ephemeris for the examples here, for the simple reason that the ephemeris most astrologers use (*Die Deutsche Ephemeride*) is calculated for *noon* for the years 1850–1930 and for *midnight* thereafter. It is easier to master the procedure for using a midnight ephemeris after one has learned to use a noon ephemeris than vice versa.

# PART ONE

EQUIPMENT NECESSARY TO CAST THE BIRTH-CHART*

Before we can begin to cast a birth-chart, we must have on hand the necessary information and equipment.

1. The first thing needed is the correct BIRTH DATA:
   a. the NAME of the person for whom we wish to cast the chart
   b. the DATE of his or her birth: the day, month, and year
   c. the PLACE of the birth: the city or town, the state or province, and the country
   d. the TIME of the birth, as accurately as possible, in hours and minutes, carefully noting whether the birth took place in the A.M. or the P.M.

Example of proper birth data:
```
      NAME:  Example
BIRTH DATE:  August 27, 1945
BIRTHPLACE:  New York, New York, U.S.A.
BIRTH TIME:  5:45 A.M.
```

2. An EPHEMERIS for the year of the birth will be needed. Ephemerides are published for each year; the ephemeris for one year is not interchangeable for the ephemeris of any other year. There are many fine ephemerides available; they are individually reviewed in Appendix II.

   The ephemeris gives the positions of the planets (the Sun and Moon are called "planets" to avoid confusion) for each day, as they relate to the ecliptic of the zodiac. The ephemeris also gives Sidereal Time, which is used to determine the ascendant and house cusps.

3. A TABLE OF HOUSES will also be needed as a reference in finding the ascendant and house cusps.

4. TIME-CHANGE REFERENCES are needed to determine whether or not Daylight-Saving Time was in use at the time and place of birth. The principal work you'll need is *Time Changes in the U.S.A.*, by Doris Doane.

5. TABLES OF LONGITUDE AND LATITUDE are used to determine the latitude and longitude of the birthplace. The latitude is used as a factor in finding the ascendant in the table of houses, while the longitude is used as a factor in finding Local Sidereal Time. A table of latitude and longitude may be found in some ephemerides and tables of houses.

* An analysis of astrological equipment is given in Appendix II.

6. TIME-ZONE REFERENCES are needed to determine the time zone in which the birth took place. Time-zone references are given in some ephemerides and atlases, as well as in *Time Changes in the U.S.A.*

7. CHART FORMS are the blank forms in which the ascendant, cusps, planets, etc. are placed to make up the birth-chart, or "horoscope."

8. A TABULATION SHEET is simply a sheet of paper on which all the vital information and factors are recorded for easy reference. Having all the important factors in one orderly place saves much confusion and frustration. A sample tabulation sheet is given below.

---

NAME_____

BIRTH DATE_____

BIRTHPLACE_____ LAT _____ LONG_____

BIRTH TIME _____ AM _____ PM_____DST or WT _____

CONVERTED TIME_____ TLT _____ LST _____

GMT_____ GREENWICH DATE_____

ASC_____          SUN _____

2nd _____          MOON _____

3rd _____          MERCURY_____

10th _____          VENUS _____

11th _____          MARS _____

12th _____          JUPITER_____

                                     SATURN _____

                                     URANUS _____

PART OF FORTUNE_____          NEPTUNE_____

LUNAR NODES _____          PLUTO_____

---

This tabulation sheet is for recording the most basic information needed to cast a birth-chart.

# OUTLINE OF THE FIRST PHASE:

## FINDING LOCAL SIDEREAL TIME

1.  Have birth data on hand.

2.  Find Converted Time.

3.  Find Greenwich Mean Time.

4.  Find True Local Time.

5.  Find Greenwich Noon Sidereal Time.

6.  Adjust Sidereal Time for time of birth.

7.  Find Local Sidereal Time.

(1)  Example:
     August 27, 1945
     New York City, 73°57′ W Long., 40°45′ N Lat.
     5:45 A.M. War Time

(2)  5:45     Given Time
     −1:00    to correct War Time
     ‾‾‾‾‾
     4:45     Converted Time

(3)  4:45     Converted Time
     +5:00    Time WEST of Greenwich
     ‾‾‾‾‾
     9:45     GMT

(4)  4:45        Converted Time
     + :04:12    1°03′ EAST of time center
     ‾‾‾‾‾‾‾‾
     4:49:12     TLT

(5)  10:21:25    Sidereal Time, Noon GMT, August 27, 1945
     −    :22    Adjustment Factor for Interval
(6)  ‾‾‾‾‾‾‾‾
     10:21:03    Adjusted Sidereal Time
     − 7:10:48   Interval between TLT and Noon
(7)  ‾‾‾‾‾‾‾‾
     3:10:15     Local Sidereal Time

# PART TWO

CALCULATIONS NECESSARY TO CAST THE BIRTH-CHART

### Phase I: Finding Local Sidereal Time (LST)

Local Sidereal Time is the key factor involved in finding the ascendant and house cusps. When we have found Local Sidereal Time we may turn to the table of houses, and using the latitude of the birthplace and Local Sidereal Time as cross references, we will then know the ascendant and cusps of the houses.

A brief outline of the procedure used in calculating LST is given above. If you examine the outline, you will notice that it involves the use of several different variations of time. An explanation of each variation is given in the tabulation below.

### The Variations of Time That Are Used in
### Casting the Birth-Chart

1. GIVEN TIME is the time of birth according to the clock.
2. CONVERTED TIME is Given Time with any of the necessary corrections made for time changes, such as Daylight-Saving Time or War Time.
3. TRUE LOCAL TIME (TLT) is the *actual* or *solar* time at the time and place of birth.
4. GREENWICH MEAN TIME (GMT) is the time it is at Greenwich, England, or 0° longitude, at the time of birth.
5. SIDEREAL TIME (ST) is the key to the ascendant. Sidereal Time is given daily in the ephemeris, calculated for either noon or midnight GMT, depending on the ephemeris. Sidereal Time measures the year in terms of 24 "hours," beginning with the vernal equinox and progressing at a rate of about four minutes a day.
6. ADJUSTED SIDEREAL TIME (ADJUSTED ST) is the Sidereal Time, as given in the ephemeris, adjusted to the time of birth by GMT.
7. LOCAL SIDEREAL TIME (LST) is the Adjusted ST, calculated for the place of birth.

We will also be dealing with:

TIME CHANGES, such as Daylight-Saving Time and War Time;

TIME ZONES, which are certain predetermined areas where all clocks are set to a standard time;

TIME CENTERS, which are the longitudes within the time zone where Converted Time is also True Local Time.

## Time Zones

The surface of the globe is divided into sections formed by imaginary lines extending from north to south. These lines are called meridians of longitude, and their positions are indicated in degrees. The earth being a sphere, there are, of course, a total of 360 degrees of longitude. Greenwich, England, has been designated as 0° Longitude; all locations *west* of Greenwich for a distance of 180° are considered West Longitude. Conversely, all locations *east* of Greenwich for 180° are considered East Longitude. The International Date Line is roughly on the 180th meridian.

The Sun appears to progress along the horizon at the speed of 15° of longitude per hour, or one degree every four minutes. Because of the fact that 15° is equal to one hour, most standard time zones are positioned at intervals of 15° longitude. There are four time zones in the continental United States:

1.  the Eastern Time Zone, 5 hours west of Greenwich;

2.  the Central Time Zone, 6 hours west of Greenwich;

3.  the Mountain Time Zone, 7 hours west of Greenwich; and

4.  the Pacific Time Zone, 8 hours west of Greenwich.

Within a time zone all clocks are synchronized to a standard time; that is, all clocks read the same time within a time zone, with the possibility of inconsistencies in regard to Daylight-Saving Time. While this system of standard times tends to eliminate much confusion with regard to commerce, it does not assure true, or actual, time.

To cite an example: New York City and Pittsburgh are both within the Eastern Time Zone and both use the same standard time, even though New York, being approximately at 74° West Longitude, is several hundred miles east of Pittsburgh, which is at approximately 80° West Longitude. Now, when the sun is "on the meridian," it is noon by true time. However, when the sun is directly overhead at New York, the clocks read 11:56 A.M., and, on the other hand, when the sun is at the noon position in Pittsburgh, the clocks read 12:20 P.M. Because of this discrepancy, we must make the proper adjustments to Converted Time to find True Local Time.

## PHASE I: STEP 1
## PREPARATION OF THE BIRTH DATA

Before we can cast the birth-chart, the time, place, and date of birth must be known. To cast an *absolutely* accurate chart, the exact time of birth must be known, right down to the second. However, very few people know their birth times within such a fine margin of exactitude. Although it is preferable to know the time of birth within the minute, this also is not always known; a margin of ten or fifteen minutes will assure a reasonably accurate chart with a three to five degree margin of error on the angles.

Once we have the proper birth data on hand, we should transcribe it onto the tabulation sheet, along with the longitude and latitude of the birthplace, as well as the time zone.

### How to Find Latitude and Longitude

To find the latitude and longitude of the birthplace, refer to the references given in Part One of this appendix. You will also find a sample table of latitudes and longitudes in Appendix III. The sample gives the latitude and longitude for most cities in the U.S.A., along with their time zones and the hours west of Greenwich. You will notice that at the head of the two left columns is printed "Lat. N" and "Long. W," meaning Latitude North and Longitude West. The numbers in these columns correspond to the cities given in the extreme left. In the case of locations in the Eastern Hemisphere, the longitude would be east; for the Southern Hemisphere, the latitude would be south.

> Example:  The latitude of New York City is 40°45′ North;
> the longitude of New York City is 73°57′ West.

The interval between the birthplace and Greenwich may be found in the section headed "Hours WEST of Greenwich" in the sample.

> Example:  The time zone for New York City is the Eastern
> Time Zone, six hours West of Greenwich.

EXERCISES:

1. Find the latitude and longitude for San Francisco, California.

2. Find the latitude and longitude for Chicago, Illinois.

3. Find the latitude and longitude for New Haven, Connecticut.

4. Find the latitude and longitude for Denver, Colorado.

5. Find the time zone for Madison, Wisconsin.

6. Find the time zone for Boise, Idaho.

7. Find the time zone for Ann Arbor, Michigan.

8. Find the time zone for Las Vegas, Nevada.

# PHASE I: STEP 2
# FINDING CONVERTED TIME

## Time Changes

If the birth took place during a time change, one hour must be *deducted* from the Given Time; the result is called Converted Time. The two types of time changes practiced in the U.S.A. are War Time (WT) and Daylight-Saving Time (DST).

## War Time

War Time was practiced in this country in the entire years of 1918 and 1919 and from February 9, 1942, 2:00 A.M. to September 30, 1945, 2:00 A.M. If the birth took place during War Time, one hour must be deducted from the Given Time.

## Daylight-Saving Time

Daylight-Saving Time is a source of much confusion for the astrologer. Daylight-Saving Time is practiced, in some areas, from April to October. *Time Changes in the U.S.A.*, by Doris Doane, gives a complete listing of time changes in the United States and is an essential reference for every astrologer. If the birthplace was on Daylight-Saving Time at the time of birth, one hour must be deducted from the Given Time.

Example:    August 27, 1945
            New York City
            5:45 A.M. Daylight-Saving Time

            5:45   Given Time
           −1:00   To correct DST
            4:45   Converted Time.

## If Birth Was Not During a Time Change

If the birth did not take place during a time change, Converted Time will be the same as Given Time.

## Adjusting for the 24-Hour Clock System

The Converted Time should now be adjusted for the 24-hour clock system and entered on the tabulation sheet. The purpose of the 24-hour clock system is to eliminate the possibility of confusing an A.M. birth with a P.M. birth.

> EXAMPLES of the 24-hour clock system:
>
> 12:00 midnight = 00:00; 3:00 A.M. = 3:00;
>
> 6:00 A.M. = 6:00; 9:00 A.M. = 9:00;
>
> 12:00 noon = 12:00; 3:00 P.M. = 15:00;
>
> 6:00 P.M. = 18:00; 9:00 P.M. = 21:00.

EXERCISES:

9. Find Converted Time for 2:30 A.M., January 2, 1944, Iowa City, Iowa.

10. Find Converted Time for 6:11 P.M., December 10, 1933, Seattle, Washington.

11. Find Converted Time for 5:02 P.M., September 30, 1945, Los Angeles, California.

12. Find Converted Time for 8:54 A.M., DST.

13. Adjust 11:33 P.M. to the 24-hour clock system.

14. Adjust 7:34 A.M. to the 24-hour clock system.

15. Adjust 3:12 P.M. to the 24-hour clock system.

16. Adjust 10:47 A.M. to the 24-hour clock system.

## PHASE I: STEP 3
## FINDING GREENWICH MEAN TIME (GMT)

Ephemerides record the Sidereal Time and the positions of the planets but once a day, for either noon or midnight Greenwich Mean Time, depending on the ephemeris. We must know the GMT of the birth if we wish to make the necessary adjustments to the figures given in the ephemeris. The process of adjusting the planetary positions and the Sidereal Time assures a greater degree of accuracy with regard to the positions of the ascendant and the planets.

## Calculating Greenwich Mean Time

To find GMT we must first know the time difference between the birthplace and Greenwich. To find this time difference, we may refer to the
sample Table of Latitudes and Longitudes given in Appendix III. The
second column from the right gives the hours from Greenwich for the
corresponding city.

Once we know the time difference between the birthplace and Greenwich, GMT may be found by the following rule:

If the longitude of the birthplace is WEST of Greenwich, ADD the
time difference to Converted Time. The result will be the GMT.

If the longitude of the birthplace is EAST of Greenwich, SUBTRACT
the time difference from the Converted Time.

EXAMPLE 1:     4:45    Converted Time, New York City.
                        New York is 5 hours, or 5 time zones,
                        WEST of Greenwich.

                        4:45    Converted Time
                     +5:00    WEST of Greenwich
                        9:45†   GMT.

EXAMPLE 2:    15:43    Converted Time, Berlin, Germany,
                        one hour EAST of Greenwich.

                       15:43    Converted Time
                      − 1:00    EAST of Greenwich
                       14:43    GMT.

## How to Know if Longitude Is East or West

When referring to the Table of Longitudes and Latitudes: if the degrees
of longitude are followed by the letter "E," the longitude is EAST; if the
longitude is followed by "W," the longitude is WEST.

## When Greenwich Mean Time Exceeds Twenty-Four Hours

Often, when working with GMT, the calculated GMT exceeds twenty-
four hours. In such cases, twenty-four hours should be subtracted from the
figure and the Greenwich Date will be a day later than the local date.

† GMT should always be adjusted to the 24-hour clock system.

EXAMPLE:   22:43   Converted Time, July 4, 1934
         + 8:00   WEST of Greenwich
         ─────────
           30:43
         −24:00
         ─────────
            6:43   GMT, July 5, 1934.


## When Time Difference Is Greater Than Converted Time

There are also cases in which the time difference between Greenwich and the place of birth is greater than the Converted Time. In these cases, twenty-four hours should be added to the Converted Time. The Greenwich date will then be a day earlier than the local date.

EXAMPLE:   1:13   Converted Time, March 27, 1958
         − 3:00   EAST of Greenwich

           1:13   Converted Time, March 27, 1958
         +24:00
         ─────────
           25:13
         − 3:00   EAST of Greenwich
         ─────────
           22:13   GMT, March 26, 1958.


## When GMT Changes Date

When the Greenwich date is different from the local date, we must keep in mind that it will be necessary to use the Greenwich date when referring to the ephemeris. The GMT and the Greenwich date should now be entered on the tabulation sheet.

EXERCISES:

**17.**  Find the Greenwich Mean Times for the following Converted Times:

a.  3:10, Boston, Massachusetts

b.  13:57, Boulder, Colorado

c.  5:34, Cleveland, Ohio

d.  21:53, Portland, Maine, August 6, 1945

e.  9:10, Berlin, Germany (one hour east of Greenwich)

f.  14:22, Sydney, Australia (ten hours east of Greenwich)

g.  8:11, Athens, Greece (two hours east of Greenwich)

h.  16:53, Madrid, Spain (0 hours east of Greenwich)

## PHASE I: STEP 4
## FINDING TRUE LOCAL TIME (TLT)

True Local Time is the actual time of birth and is used in the calculation of Local Sidereal Time. To find the True Local Time, we must know the longitude of the birthplace, the time zone, and the zone's time center.

### What Is a Time Center?

The standard time for each time zone is based on the actual, or local, time at the time center, or meridian. Thus, the only longitude within the time zone where the Standard Time is also the True Local Time is the longitude occupied by the time center. The time centers are positioned at regular intervals of 15° of longitude (with a few exceptions), beginning with 0° Longitude (Greenwich).

The time-zone centers for the continental United States are: Eastern Time Zone, 75° West Longitude; Central Time Zone, 90° West Longitude; Mountain Time Zone, 105° West Longitude, Pacific Time Zone, 120° West Longitude.

### How to Find True Local Time

To find True Local Time, the difference between the birthplace and the time center must be determined. This interval may be found in the Table of Longitudes and Latitudes under the column headed VARIATION BETWEEN STANDARD TIME AND TLT. If the place of birth is not listed, or if you are using a table that does not give this information, follow this rule:

If the birthplace is EAST of the time center (a place east of the time center will be of a lesser degree of longitude in the Western Hemisphere and larger in the Eastern), ADD 4 minutes to the Converted Time for each degree the birthplace is EAST of the time center.

If the birthplace is WEST of the time center (a place west of the time center is of a larger degree of longitude in the Western Hemisphere and is lesser in the Eastern), SUBTRACT 4 minutes from the Converted Time for each degree the birthplace is west of the time center.

EXAMPLE 1:    4:45   Converted Time, New York City,
                        73°57′   West Longitude

            4:45:00   Converted Time
          + ___4:12   one degree EAST of time center
            4:49:12   TLT.

EXAMPLE 2:   9:43   Converted Time, Des Moines, Iowa,
             93°38′   West Longitude

             9:43:00   Converted Time
          —    14:32   four degrees WEST of time center
             9:29:32   TLT.

After True Local Time has been calculated, it should be entered in its proper place on the tabulation sheet.

EXERCISES:

**18.**   Find the True Local Time for the following Converted Times:

  a.   12:24, Chicago, Illinois

  b.   4:56, Baltimore, Maryland

  c.   21:15, Eureka, California

  d.   15:45, Poughkeepsie, New York

  e.   3:46, Las Vegas, Nevada

  f.   18:50, Omaha, Nebraska

  g.   7:10, Easton, Pennsylvania

  h.   22:32, Gary, Indiana

## PHASE I: STEP 5
## FINDING SIDEREAL TIME (ST)

Sidereal Time is given in the ephemeris once for each 24-hour period, calculated for noon GMT (or midnight GMT if you are using a midnight ephemeris). By referring to the ephemeris for the proper year and month, you may easily find the Sidereal Time.

In the sample ephemeris found in Appendix III you will notice that the day of the month is given in the extreme left column. Next to the day column you will find the column where the Sidereal Times for each day are given, in hours, minutes, and seconds; this column is headed s.t. To find the proper Sidereal Time, first locate the Greenwich date of birth in the day column; the figure directly to the right of the day, in the st column, is the Sidereal Time for the date of birth and should be transcribed.

EXAMPLE:   The Greenwich Noon Sidereal Time for
           August 27, 1945, is 10:21:25.

EXERCISES:

**19.** Find the Greenwich Noon Sidereal Time for the following days:

    a.  August 3, 1945

    b.  August 23, 1945

    c.  August 11, 1945

    d.  August 29, 1945

    e.  August 17, 1945

    f.  August 8, 1945

# PHASE I: STEP 6
## ADJUSTING SIDEREAL TIME

Because the ephemeris gives Sidereal Time but once daily, for noon (or midnight) ‡ GMT, and because Sidereal Time is in a state of constant progression, an adjustment must be made to it if the GMT of birth is not noon. In other words, the ephemeris gives us Sidereal Time for the day, and we must then adjust it for the time of birth.

Adjusting Sidereal Time involves three steps: (1) finding the interval between GMT and noon; (2) finding the adjustment factor, which is based on the interval between GMT and noon and the daily progression of Sidereal Time; (3) adjusting the Sidereal Time, which is done by either adding or subtracting the adjustment factor from the noon Sidereal Time.

### 1. Finding the Interval Between GMT and Noon

If GMT is before noon (less than 12:00), SUBTRACT GMT from 12 hours. The result will be the interval.

If GMT is after noon (more than 12:00), SUBTRACT 12 HOURS from GMT. The result will be the interval.

      EXAMPLE 1:   12:00

               −  9:45   GMT (before noon)

                 2:15   Interval between GMT and noon.

      EXAMPLE 2:  16:15  GMT (after noon)

              −12:00

                4:15   Interval between GMT and noon.

‡ From this point on, our examples are based on the use of a *noon* ephemeris. The procedure for using a midnight ephemeris is found on page 315.

## 2. Finding the Adjustment Factor

Sidereal Time progresses at a steady rate of about 3 minutes 56 seconds per day. The tables below give the correct proportion of this movement to use when adjusting Sidereal Time.

To find the adjustment factor, ADD the factor for the hours of interval to the factor for the minutes of interval. The result will be the adjustment factor.

EXAMPLE:   For an interval of 2:15

2 hours ----------- 20 sec.   factor
15 minutes ---------- 2 sec.   factor
2:15 -------------- 22 sec.   Adjustment Factor.

### TABLE A

| Hours of Interval | Factor |
|---|---|
| 1 | 10 sec. |
| 2 | 20 sec. |
| 3 | 29 sec. |
| 4 | 39 sec. |
| 5 | 49 sec. |
| 6 | 59 sec. |
| 7 | 1 min. 9 sec. |
| 8 | 1 min. 18 sec. |
| 9 | 1 min. 28 sec. |
| 10 | 1 min. 38 sec. |
| 11 | 1 min. 48 sec. |
| 12 | 1 min. 58 sec. |

### TABLE B

| Minutes of Interval | Factor |
|---|---|
| 0–3 | 0 sec. |
| 4–9 | 1 sec. |
| 10–15 | 2 sec. |
| 16–21 | 3 sec. |
| 22–27 | 4 sec. |
| 28–33 | 5 sec. |
| 34–39 | 6 sec. |
| 40–45 | 7 sec. |
| 46–51 | 8 sec. |
| 52–57 | 9 sec. |
| 58–60 | 10 sec. |

## 3. Adjusting the Sidereal Time

If GMT is BEFORE noon, SUBTRACT the adjustment factor for the interval from the Sidereal Time. The result will be the Adjusted Sidereal Time.

If GMT is AFTER noon, ADD the adjustment factor for the interval to the Sidereal Time. The result will be the Adjusted Sidereal Time.

EXAMPLE 1:  10:21:25  ST, 9:45 GMT, August 27, 1945
            10:21:25  ST, noon GMT, August 27, 1945
        −      :22  Adjustment Factor for 2:15
            10:21:03  Adjusted Sidereal Time.

EXAMPLE 2:   8:54:41  ST, 16:15 GMT, August 5, 1945
             8:54:41  ST, noon GMT, August 5, 1945
        +      :41  Adjustment Factor for 4:15
             8:55:22  Adjusted Sidereal Time.

EXERCISES:

**20.** Find the interval between GMT and noon for the following times:
a. 15:43 GMT
b. 9:21 GMT
c. 23:10 GMT
d. 5:22 GMT

**21.** Find the adjustment factors for the following intervals:
a. 9:55
b. 0:33
c. 5:10
d. 3:53

**22.** Find the Adjusted Sidereal Times for the following times:
a. 3:53:33 ST, 18:10 GMT
b. 9:22:47 ST, 4:32 GMT
c. 5:36:11 ST, 14:45 GMT
d. 1:49:18 ST, 7:24 GMT

# PHASE I: STEP 7
## FINDING LOCAL SIDEREAL TIME (LST)

We have now come to the seventh, and final, step in calculating Local Sidereal Time, which will enable us to find the ascendant and the house cusps. In this step we will adjust the Adjusted Sidereal Time for the place of birth.

Finding Local Sidereal Time involves the following procedure: (1) finding the interval between TLT and noon, and (2) adding or subtracting the interval to or from the Adjusted Sidereal Time.

## 1. Finding the Interval Between TLT and Noon

If the birth is BEFORE noon TLT, SUBTRACT TLT from 12 hours. The result will be the interval.

If the birth is AFTER noon TLT, SUBTRACT 12 hours from TLT. The result will be the interval.

EXAMPLE 1:  12:00:00
− 4:49:12  TLT (BEFORE noon)
7:10:48  Interval between TLT and noon.

EXAMPLE 2:  18:25  TLT (AFTER noon)
−12:00
6:25  Interval between TLT and noon.

## 2. Finding Local Sidereal Time

If the birth is BEFORE noon TLT, SUBTRACT the interval between TLT and noon from the Adjusted Sidereal Time. The result will be the Local Sidereal Time.

If the birth is AFTER noon TLT, ADD the interval between TLT and noon to the Adjusted Sidereal Time. The result will be the Local Sidereal Time.

Once the Local Sidereal Time has been calculated, it should be entered onto the tabulation sheet.

EXAMPLE 1:  10:21:03  Adjusted ST
− 7:10:48  Interval, 4:49:12 TLT
3:10:15  Local Sidereal Time.

EXAMPLE 2:  8:42:21  Adjusted ST
+ 2:10:11  Interval, 14:10 TLT
10:52:21  Local Sidereal Time.

## When Local Sidereal Time Exceeds Twenty-Four Hours

In some instances, the addition of the interval to the Adjusted ST results in a figure greater than 24 hours. In such a case, 24 hours should be subtracted from the figure. The result will then be a usable Local Sidereal Time.

EXAMPLE:   18:05:39   Adjusted ST
            +10:00:00   Interval
             28:05:39
            −24:00:00
              4:05:39   Local Sidereal Time.

## When Interval Is Greater Than Adjusted Sidereal Time

Often when dealing with births before noon TLT, the interval is found to be greater than the Adjusted Sidereal Time, from which it must be deducted. In such a case, 24 hours should be added to the Adjusted Sidereal Time.

EXAMPLE:   2:11:53   Adjusted ST
              5:03:00   Interval

              2:11:53
            +24:00:00
             26:11:53
           −  5:03:00   Interval
            21:08:53   Local Sidereal Time.

## Should the Seconds in Local Sidereal Time Be Dropped?

If the exact time of birth is not known, LST should be rounded off to the nearest minute. If the exact time of birth is known, little accuracy will be lost by rounding off LST to the nearest minute; the matter is left to the astrologer's personal preference.

EXERCISES:

23. Find the interval between TLT and noon for the following times:
    a. 10:50 TLT
    b. 3:23 TLT
    c. 23:45 TLT
    d. 15:13 TLT

24. Find Local Sidereal Time for the following times:
    a. 6:55 Adjusted ST, 3:15 TLT
    b. 11:23:29 Adjusted ST, 14:47 TLT
    c. 3:27:21 Adjusted ST, 22:38 TLT
    d. 20:58:14 Adjusted ST, 7:20 TLT

**25.** Find Local Sidereal Time from the following birth data:
   a.  August 2, 1945, Kansas City, Missouri, 1:15 P.M. War Time
   b.  August 30, 1945, Albany, New York, 3:23 A.M. War Time
   c.  August 12, 1945, Toledo, Ohio, 10:25 P.M. War Time
   d.  August 22, 1945, Erie, Pennsylvania, 7:49 A.M. War Time

# PHASE II: ASCENDANT AND HOUSE CUSPS

## PHASE II: STEP 1
## FINDING THE ASCENDANT AND HOUSE CUSPS

Now that we have calculated the Local Sidereal Time, our next task is to find the ascendant and the house cusps, adjust the ascendant, and place the ascendant and the cusps on the chart form.

To find the ascendant and houses, we must know the latitude of the birthplace and the Local Sidereal Time. We must also have on hand a table of houses, a sample of which is given in Appendix III.

### Finding the Ascendant

Most tables of houses include tables for 0° to 60° latitude. The first thing to do is find the section of the tables for the latitude nearest the birthplace. We then locate the figure in the column headed ST, which is the nearest to the Local Sidereal Time (the figures in the ST column are given at intervals of about four minutes). When we have found the figure, which we shall call the "Nearest Sidereal Time," the ascendant may be found directly to the right in the column headed *ASC*. The ascendant is given in degrees and minutes; the sign of the ascendant is the first sign inserted directly above the figure for the ascendant.

The ascendant may be rounded off to the nearest degree, adjusted to assure the utmost possible accuracy, or entered into the tabulation sheet directly from the table.

### Finding the House Cusps*

### Equal House System

If you wish to use the Equal House System, the degree of each cusp will be the same as the degree of the ascendant. The signs for the cusps will progress in their natural order from the ascendant to the twelfth house.

* A discussion of the various systems of house division can be found in Part Two of the text.

EXAMPLE:    Ascendant for 40°45′ North Latitude,
3:10:15 LST, is 27°23′ Leo.

ASC    27°23′ Leo
2nd    27°23′ Virgo
3rd    27°23′ Libra
and so on to
12th    27°23′ Cancer.

*Finding the Medium Coeli for the Equal House Chart.*

The tenth-house cusp by the Equal House System is not always of the same degree as the medium coeli (the tenth-house cusp by the Quadrant House System, given in the Table of Houses). The degree and sign found in the tenth-house column that corresponds to the Nearest ST in the Table of Houses should be used as the M.C. in the Equal House chart.

## Quadrant House System

If you prefer to use a Quadrant House System, the house cusps may be found in the Table of Houses, on the same horizontal line as the ascendant. The column headed *12* is the 12th-house cusp, *11* gives the 11th-house cusp, *10* gives the 10th-house cusp (which is always the same as the medium coeli by Quadrant House Systems), *2* gives the cusp for the second house, and the column headed *3* gives the third-house cusp. The remaining six houses may be found through oppositions.

EXAMPLE:    40°45′ North Latitude, 3:10:15 LST

| ASC | 27°23′ Leo | DEC | 27°23′ Aquarius |
|---|---|---|---|
| 2nd | 20° Virgo | 8th | 20° Pisces |
| 3rd | 19° Libra | 9th | 19° Aries |
| 10th | 20° Taurus | 4th | 20° Scorpio |
| 11th | 25° Gemini | 5th | 25° Sagittarius |
| 12th | 28° Cancer | 6th | 28° Capricorn. |

There are several quadrant house-division systems, each giving slightly different house cusps for the same LST. The most widely used is the Placidus System (the system used in the sample Table of Houses in Appendix III); it was, until recently, difficult to obtain tables for any other systems.

### Porphyry System of Quadrant Division

If you prefer to use the Porphyry System (a quadrant system), the house cusps may be calculated by the division of the number of degrees within each house of that (and the opposing) quadrant. The ascendant and medium coeli are, of course, the same as by the Placidus System.

EXERCISES:

26.  Find the ascendants for the following LST's:
     a.  2:34:48 LST, 41° North Latitude
     b.  0:59:00 LST, 41° North Latitude
     c.  4:22:37 LST, 41° North Latitude
     d.  1:33:00 LST, 41° North Latitude


# PHASE II: STEP 2

## ADJUSTING THE ASCENDANT (optional)

This step should be taken if the exact time of birth is known; it is optional for the beginning student. It involves adjusting the ascendant from the Nearest ST to the LST.

Because Sidereal Time is listed in the Table of Houses at intervals of about four minutes, we must make an adjustment to the ascendant that corresponds to the Nearest ST if we wish to assure the utmost possible accuracy. Of course, if the Nearest ST is the same as, or very close to, the LST, this step is not necessary.


### How to Adjust the Ascendant

To adjust the ascendant, follow this procedure of interpolation:

1.  Find the interval between Nearest ST and LST.

    EXAMPLE:     2:16:09   LST
              −2:14:42   Nearest ST
              _____
                 1:27   Interval
                  :87   Converted to seconds.

2.  Find the interval between Nearest ST and Next Nearest ST in seconds of value.

    EXAMPLE:     2:18:35   Next Nearest ST
              −2:14:42   Nearest ST
              _____
                 3:53
                  :233   Interval in seconds.

3. Find the interval between Nearest ASC and Next Nearest ASC in minutes of value.

> EXAMPLE:    16°31′  Leo, Next Nearest ASC
>             −15°45′  Leo, Nearest ASC
>                46′  Interval in minutes.

4. Divide (2) by (1).

> EXAMPLE:   $233 \div 87 = 2.6$.

5. Divide (3) by the quotient of (4); the result is the Adjustment Factor.

> EXAMPLE:   $46′ \div 2.6 = 18′$ Adjustment Factor.

6. If LST is GREATER than Nearest ST, ADD Adjustment Factor to Nearest ASC. The result will be the adjusted, or exact, ascendant.

   If LST is LESS than Nearest ST, SUBTRACT Adjustment Factor from Nearest ASC. The result will be the adjusted ascendant.

> EXAMPLE:    15°45′  Leo, Nearest ASC.
>           +    18′  Adjustment Factor
>           16°03′  Leo, Adjusted Ascendant.

# PHASE III: PLANETARY POSITIONS

## PHASE III: STEP 1
## FINDING THE POSITIONS OF THE PLANETS

After we have calculated the ascendant and the house cusps and placed them on the chart form, our next phase is finding the planets' positions. The Greenwich noon position of the planets may be found in an ephemeris (midnight positions are given in the case of a midnight ephemeris). Naturally, because the positions are given for a predetermined time, some adjustment is likely to be necessary if accuracy is desired.

### Finding the Positions of the Planets in the Ephemeris

If you turn to the sample ephemeris in Appendix III, you will notice that the month and year of the particular table, and the time for which the positions are calculated, are given in the heading. Also at the head, you will notice that the table is for the longitudes of the planets. Some ephemerides also include tables for the latitudes and declinations of the planets whose symbols are given at the head of the column.† Once we have found the Greenwich date in the day column, the calculated longitudes of the planets may be found in their respective columns directly to the right, on the same horizontal line as the day.

The sign in which a planet is located at the first of the month is given at the head of each column, just below the planet's symbol. However, some planets change signs during the month, and in such cases the newly entered sign's symbol is inserted into the column at the day of the sign change. One must be careful to remember that the sign given at the head of the column is not necessarily the sign a planet is in on any day but the first of the month. Failure to consider this is an error frequently made by the beginner.

> EXAMPLE:    Venus was in 26°42′ Gemini on August 1.
> On August 27, Venus was in 26°25′
> Cancer.

† The location of Pluto in the ephemeris varies, depending on the year and the publisher. In the sample ephemeris, Pluto appears at the foot of the table, given once monthly.

EXERCISES:

**27.** Find the noon GMT positions of the following planets:
   a.  August 10, 1945; Mercury, Venus, and Moon
   b.  August 21, 1945; Sun, Jupiter, and Neptune
   c.  August 4, 1945; Mars, Saturn, and Uranus
   d.  August 16, 1945; Sun, Mercury, Venus, and Moon

# PHASE III: STEP 2
## ADJUSTING THE POSITIONS OF THE PLANETS
## WITH PLANETARY-MOTION TABLES

A simple method of accurately adjusting the position of the planets is given below, using tables of planetary motion. You will find a complete set of these tables in Appendix III; a small section of a table appears below as an example.

### How to Use Tables of Planetary Motion

Planetary-motion tables provide an easy and accurate method of planetary adjustment. If you look in Appendix III, you will notice that there are three sets of tables, one for the Sun, another set for the Moon, and another for the remaining planets. To adjust the planets' positions, follow this procedure:

1.  Have the interval between GMT and noon on hand.
2.  Find the *daily motion* of the planet, which is the degrees and/or minutes that the planet progressed in longitude, or regressed in the case of retrogradation, during the twenty-four hours before or after the noon Greenwich date.‡ To find the planet's daily motion, follow this procedure:

    If the birth is BEFORE noon GMT, SUBTRACT the planet's noon position for the day BEFORE birth from the planet's position on the day of birth. The result will be the daily motion of the planet. However, if the planet is in retrograde, the process should be reversed.

    If the birth is AFTER noon GMT, SUBTRACT the noon position of the planet for the day of birth from the planet's position for the day AFTER. The result will be the daily motion. If the planet is in retrograde, reverse the process.

3.  Go to the proper table and find the vertical column headed by the degree and/or minutes nearest to the daily motion of the planet.

‡ When a planet appears to be moving backward, it is called retrogradation. A letter "R" is inserted into the planet's column on the day it begins to retrograde. A "D" is inserted when the planet is no longer in retrograde.

4. Then go down the column until you come to the line that is on the same horizontal as the Hours of Interval. The figure given on that line is the Adjustment Factor for the Hours of Interval.

5. At the bottom of the table is a section used for finding the Adjustment Factor for the Minutes of Interval.

6. When you have found the Adjustment Factor for the Minutes of Interval, ADD it to the Adjustment Factor for the Hours of Interval; the sum will be the Adjustment Factor for the planet.

### How to Adjust the Planet's Position

If GMT is AFTER noon, ADD the Adjustment Factor to the noon position of the planet.

IF GMT is BEFORE noon, SUBTRACT the Adjustment Factor from the noon position of the planet.

## DAILY MOTION OF THE PLANETS

| INTERVAL IN HOURS | 0°30′ | 0°35′ | 0°40′ | 0°45′ | 0°50′ |
|---|---|---|---|---|---|
| 1 | 1′15″ | 1′27″ | 1′40″ | 1′52″ | 2′05″ |
| 2 | 2′30″ | 2′55″ | 3′20″ | 3′45″ | 4′10″ |
| 3 | 3′45″ | 4′22″ | 5′00″ | 5′37″ | 6′15″ |
| 4 | 5′00″ | 5′50″ | 6′40″ | 7′30″ | 8′20″ |
| 5 | 6′15″ | 7′17″ | 8′20″ | 9′22″ | 10′25″ |
| 6 | 7′30″ | 8′45″ | 10′00″ | 11′15″ | 12′30″ |

| INTERVAL IN MINUTES | | | | | |
|---|---|---|---|---|---|
| 10 | 12″ | 14″ | 16″ | 19″ | 21″ |
| 20 | 25″ | 29″ | 33″ | 37″ | 42″ |
| 30 | 37″ | 44″ | 50″ | 56″ | 1′02″ |

Sample Table of Planetary Motion

### When Exact Position of Planet Exceeds 30°

It can happen that when the Adjustment Factor is added to the noon position, the result is greater than 30°. In such cases, 30° should be subtracted and the next sign given to the planet.

EXAMPLE:   29°54'   Libra, noon position
           +  0°23'   Adjustment Factor
               30°17'
           −30°00'
                0°17'   Scorpio, adjusted position.

## When Adjustment Factor Is Greater Than Noon Position

It can also happen that when the Adjustment Factor is to be subtracted from the noon position, the Factor is greater than the noon position. In such cases, 30° should be added to the noon position and one sign taken from the planet.

EXAMPLE:   0°13'   Cancer, noon position
           −  1°06'   Adjustment Factor

              0°13'   Cancer
          +30°00'
             30°13'   Gemini
          −  1°06'   Adjustment Factor
             29°07'   Gemini, adjusted position.

## Examples for Phase III: Step 2:

1. Mars's noon position is 18° Cancer; daily motion is 35'; GMT is 16:15.

   Adjustment Factor for Hours of Interval is 6'.
   Adjustment Factor for Minutes of Interval is 21".
   Adjustment Factor is 6'21"; round off to 6'.

     18°00'   Cancer, noon position
   +    06'   Adjustment Factor
     18°06'   Cancer, adjusted position of Mars.

2. Noon position is 5°13' Virgo; daily motion is 40°; GMT is 8:45.

   Adjustment Factor for Hours of Interval is 5'15".
   Adjustment Factor for Minutes of Interval is 26".
   Adjustment Factor is 5'41"; round off to 6'.

     5°13'   Virgo, noon position
   −    06'   Adjustment Factor
     5°07'   Virgo, adjusted position.

# PHASE III: STEP 3
## PLACING THE PLANETS IN THE HOUSES

Our final task in this phase will be the placement of the planets in the houses. This step simply involves placing the planets between the houses' cusps in which the degrees and signs of the planets fall.

EXAMPLE:     Jupiter 0°26′ Scorpio falls in the third
             house, between 23°08′ Libra and 21°
             Scorpio.

# PHASE IV: FINDING THE PLANETARY ASPECTS

We are now ready to find the planetary aspects, which are the angular relationships between two or more planets, or between two or more planets and one of the angles.

## WHEN ARE ASPECTS FORMED?

An aspect is formed when two or more planets, or two or more planets and one of the angles, are within a certain number of degrees of each other. There are many aspectual angles used in astrology; the major ones are listed below.

### Orbs

Each aspect is given an orb, which is a certain number of degrees more or less than the exact degree of the aspect allowable for the planets still to be considered in aspect. Thus, if two planets are 87° apart, they are still considered to be in square aspect to each other, even though the exact aspect is 90°. However, the size of the orbs allowed does differ a good deal, depending upon the particular planets and the astrologer, though the general tendency seems to be moving in the direction of smaller orbs at this time. The orbs given with the aspects below are the orbs recommended for initial use.

| ASPECT | SYMBOL | DISTANCE BETWEEN | ORB | KEY WORD |
|--------|--------|--------|--------|--------|
| Conjunction | ☌ | 0° | 7°-10° | Unifying |
| Semisquare | ∟ | 45° | 2°- 3° | Intense |
| Sextile | ⚹ | 60° | 2°- 3° | Productive |
| Square | □ | 90° | 5°- 6° | Constructive |
| Trine | △ | 120° | 6°- 7° | Co-operating |
| Opposition | ☍ | 180° | 8°-10° | Opposing or Complementary |

EXAMPLE 1:   Jupiter   22°35′   Leo

Saturn    20°41′   Leo

           1°54′   distance between.

Jupiter and Saturn are in conjunction, with a 1°54′ orb.

EXAMPLE 2:   Moon   29°01′   Taurus

ASC      27°23′   Leo

           1°38′   and 3 signs or 90°.

Moon is square ASC, with a 1°38′ orb.

EXAMPLE 3:   Venus   26°19′   Virgo

Mars     22°59′   Gemini

           3°20′   and 3 signs or 90°.

Venus and Mars are square, with a 3°20′ orb.

## Some Easy Rules for Finding Aspects

1.  Check the modes. Signs of the same mode are spaced at intervals of 90°. Thus, two planets in the same mode but not the same sign are most likely to form no other aspect except squares or oppositions.

    EXAMPLE:   Sun 10° Scorpio is square to Mars 12° Leo, both being in fixed signs.

2.  The same is true for the elements, only at 120° intervals, thus forming trines.

    EXAMPLE:   Moon 19° Pisces is trine with Venus 22° Cancer, both being water signs.

3.  Conjunctions are obvious, due to their closeness.

4.  Semisquares are always 1½ signs away from the position of the planet.

## Drawing in Aspect Patterns

Aspected planets may be connected by colored lines on the birth-chart as an aid to visual interpretations. The sextiles and trines may be done in blue ink; the semisquares, squares, and oppositions in red; and the conjunctions in green ink.

# ADDITIONAL STUDIES

## HOW TO USE THE MIDNIGHT EPHEMERIS

If you are using a midnight ephemeris, you will need to follow a slightly different procedure from the one given above.

1. The GMT is always used as the interval between GMT and midnight. In all cases in which the interval between GMT and noon is called for, simply use the GMT as the interval.

2. When adjusting the ST (PHASE I: STEP 6), find the Adjustment Factor for the GMT. The Adjustment Factor is then ALWAYS ADDED to the midnight ST, which is found in the ephemeris.

3. When finding the LST (PHASE I: STEP 7), ALWAYS ADD the TLT to the Adjusted ST.

4. When adjusting the planets' positions, ALWAYS ADD the Adjustment Factor to the midnight positions of the planets.

EXAMPLE: August 27, 1945, 9:45 GMT, 4:49:12 TLT.

```
  22:19:26   Sidereal Time, midnight GMT 8/27/45
+     1:35   Adjustment Factor for 9:45
  22:21:01   Adjusted Sidereal Time
+  4:49:12   TLT
  27:10:13
 -24:00:00
   3:10:13   Local Sidereal Time.
```

## SOUTHERN-HEMISPHERE BIRTHS

If the birth has taken place in the Southern Hemisphere (south latitude), some additional adjustments must be made:

1. ADD 12 hours to the LST.

2. The ASC and the house cusps are found by using the north latitude in the table of houses, which is of the same degree as the latitude for the birthplace. The signs for the ASC and the cusps should then be reversed.

EXAMPLE:    13:53:17   LST
          +12:00:00   for south latitude
           25:53:17
          −24:00:00   for LST over twenty-four hours
            1:53:17   LST for south latitude.

ASC for 1:53:17 for 41° north latitude is 12°
Leo; by reversing the sign, we have an ASC
of 12° Aquarius for the southern latitude
birth.

## NODES OF THE MOON

Most ephemerides include the position of the Moon's nodes, which are
not used by all astrologers though they are important as indicators of
personal strength and sensitivity. Usually the north node is given in the
ephemeris; the south node is always its polar opposite.

☊ north node,        ☋ south node.

## PART OF FORTUNE   ⊕

Some astrologers (including the writer) use one of the Arabic parts,
the *part of fortune,* which may be found by this formula: Ascendant +
Moon − Sun.

EXAMPLE:    27°   Taurus ASC   (2nd sign)
          +29°   Leo Moon    +(5th sign)
           56°   Libra        (7th sign)
          −30°
           26°   Scorpio      (8th sign)
          − 3°   Leo Sun     −(5th sign)
           23°   Gemini       (3rd sign)

The part of fortune is 23° Gemini.

## PLANETARY LATITUDE

Most ephemerides include tables for the latitudes of the planets, which
measure the distance a planet is north or south of the terrestrial equator.
The meaning of a planet's latitude is given in the text.

# DECLINATIONS

Most ephemerides also include tables for the declinations of the planets. The declination of a planet is the distance, measured in degrees, a planet lies north or south of the *Celestial Equator*.

## Parallels of Declination

When two or more planets are of the same degree of declination, they are said to be *parallel*. An orb of 1½° is usually allowed.

# ANSWERS TO EXERCISES

1. 37°47′N, 122°26′W
2. 41°52′N, 87°39′W
3. 41°18′N, 72°55′W
4. 39°45′N, 104°59′W
5. Central Time Zone
6. Mountain Time Zone
7. Eastern Time Zone
8. Pacific Time Zone
9. 1:30
10. 18:11
11. 17:02
12. 7:54
13. 23:33
14. 7:34
15. 15:12
16. 10:47
17. a. 8:10
    b. 20:57
    c. 10:34
    d. 2:53, August 7, 1945
    e. 8:10
    f. 4:22
    g. 6:11
    h. 16:53
18. a. 12:33:24
    b. 4:49:32
    c. 20:58:20
    d. 15:49:20
    e. 4:05:28
    f. 18:16:12
    g. 7:09:08
    h. 22:42:40
19. a. 8:46:48
    b. 10:05:39
    c. 9:18:20
    d. 10:27:18
    e. 9:41:59
    f. 9:06:31
20. a. 3:43
    b. 2:39

    c. 11:10
    d. 6:38
21. a. 1 minute, 37 seconds
    b. 5 seconds
    c. 51 seconds
    d. 38 seconds
22. a. 3:54:34
    b. 9:21:33
    c. 5:36:38
    d. 1:48:33
23. a. 1:10
    b. 8:37
    c. 11:45
    d. 3:13
24. a. 22:10
    b. 14:10:29
    c. 14:05:21
    d. 16:18:14
25. a. 8:40:29
    b. 00:58:22
    c. 18:15:27
    d. 4:30:20
26. a. 19°30′ Leo
    b. 0°56′ Leo
    c. 10°22′ Virgo
    d. 7°31′ Leo
27. a. Mercury 4°10′ retrograde Virgo; Venus 6°50′ Cancer; Moon 16°31′ Virgo
    b. Sun 28°00′26″ Leo; Jupiter 29°15′ Virgo; Neptune 4°50′ Libra
    c. Mars 8°13′ Gemini; Saturn 18°2′ Cancer; Uranus 16°26′ Gemini
    d. Sun 23°13′46″ Leo; Mercury 0°42′ retrograde Leo; Venus 13°31′ Virgo; Moon 28°32′ Scorpio

# APPENDIX II

## ANALYSIS OF ASTROLOGICAL EQUIPMENT

1. Ephemerides
2. Tables of Houses
3. Tables of Longitudes
   and Latitudes
4. Time-Change References
5. Miscellaneous

# ANALYSIS OF ASTROLOGICAL EQUIPMENT

It is not unusual for the active astrologer to invest a large amount of money in various tables, references, forms, etc. Often the beginner may be somewhat confused by the vast array of astrological paraphernalia, and it may be difficult for him to judge what is actually necessary and what is simply a convenience. This situation is often further complicated by a limited budget. For this reason, I have included a short analysis of the tools of the astrological trade, which I hope will be helpful.

Generally, all the many fine ephemerides available are accurate. However, some ephemerides, such as the *200 Year Ephemeris,* provide data on a monthly rather than daily basis. Such tables are not practical for regular and precise work. Other than this, the major considerations to base one's choice on are economy, ease of use, and aesthetics.

In the choice of a table of houses, the situation is basically the same. The case is different, however, when one is considering a table of longitudes and latitudes: an astrologer can get along without a table of longitudes and latitudes if he does not mind searching for the needed data in other, less convenient sources; also, these tables are available through only one publisher.

One must also consider the purchase of time-change references, which an astrologer can hardly do without. Only one publisher offers complete and reliable time-change information.

Because publication of astrological equipment and literature is a specialty field, prices may vary considerably from dealer to dealer and area to area, and, of course, in this day of economic uncertainty, prices are always subject to change.

## EPHEMERIDES

DIE DEUTSCHE EPHEMERIDE

Distributed by New York Astrology Center, 127 Madison Ave., New York, New York 10016.

| | | |
|---|---|---|
| Band I | 1850–1889; | about $14. |
| Band II | 1890–1930; | about $14. |
| Band III | 1931–1950; | about $14. |
| Band IV | 1951–1960; | about $10. |
| Band V | 1961–1970; | about $10. |
| Band VI | 1971–1980; | about $10. |

I use these ephemerides in my own work. Knowledge of the German language is not required. These ephemerides are hardbound, small, and aesthetic in appearance. They include ST, and planetary longitudes, latitudes, and declinations. Pluto is included after 1960. Bände I and II are calculated for *noon* GMT, while the remaining Bände are calculated for *midnight* GMT.

## PLUTO EPHEMERIS

Omega Associates, Chicago, Illinois.

1773–2000; about $4.

Gives the longitude and latitude of Pluto for every ten days. Interpolation tables are included to adjust position for any day. Paperback.

## RAPHAEL'S EPHEMERIS

London, England.

1860 to date, single years only; about $2 per year.

Very fine and useful. Includes, in addition to the planetary longitudes, latitudes, and declinations, a daily aspectarian listing the time of major aspects, and daily motions. Calculated for *noon* GMT. Paperback. The great disadvantage of this table is its cost, but it is one of the finest.

## ROSICRUCIAN EPHEMERIS

The Rosicrucian Fellowship, Oceanside, California.

20-year clothbound, 1860–1879; about $10.
10-year paperbound, 1880–1889 to 1960–1969; $5 each.
1-year paperbound, 1857 to date; $1 each.

This ephemeris is one of the most economical, though rumored to be not entirely reliable. It has lots of information: times for New and Full Moons are included from 1923; from 1936 it includes a daily aspectarian, the times the Sun and the Moon enter each sign, and the monthly positions of Pluto. Large print. Calculated for *noon* GMT.

## GOLGGE EPHEMERIS

Distributed by New York Astrology Center, 127 Madison Ave., New York, New York 10016.

1961–1965; about $4.
1966–1970; about $4.
1971–1975; about $4.50.

This handsome vinyl-covered, paperbound table gives the positions of
the Sun and the Moon twice daily, for *noon* and *midnight;* all other positions are calculated for *midnight* GMT. Includes daily aspects and the
date and hour of lunar phases.

## 200 YEAR EPHEMERIS

Macoy Publishing Company, Richmond, Virginia.

### 1800–2000; $15.

Gives both geocentric and heliocentric longitudes once every month,
as well as latitudes and declinations. Does not include positions for the
Moon. Calculated for *noon* GMT.

## EPHEMERIS OF THE MOON

Macoy Publishing Company, Richmond, Virginia.

### 1800–2000; $5.

A supplement to the *200 Year Ephemeris.* Gives daily positions of the
Moon in addition to the hour and minute the Moon enters each sign and
the date and time of each New and Full Moon. Hardbound. Calculated
for *noon* GMT. Very useful when calculating progressed lunations.

# TABLES OF HOUSES

## DALTON'S TABLE OF HOUSES

Macoy Publishing Company, Richmond, Virginia.

### Hardbound; about $4.

This is an excellent table. Sidereal Time is given for each whole degree
in terms of the M.C. The ascendant is given in both degrees and minutes
of arc, calculated for each whole degree of geographic latitude. Adjustments for an intermediate latitude and LST may be easily calculated.
Large, clear format.

## RICE TABLE OF HOUSES

American Federation of Astrologers, 6 Library Court S.E., Washington,
D.C. 20003.

### Hardbound; about $20.

This is the most impressive and complete table of houses I've seen.
If you can afford it, it's a good investment.

OCCIDENTAL TABLE OF HOUSES

Occidental Publishing Company, P.O. Box 38, Occidental, California 95465.

Paperback; about $8.

This newly published table of houses contains information for the Campanus, Regiomontanus, and Placidus systems of house division.

ROSICRUCIAN TABLE OF HOUSES

The Rosicrucian Fellowship, Oceanside, California.

Paperback; about $3.50.

Data are calculated for each whole degree of geographic latitude, making it easy to adjust for an intermediate latitude. Large, clear print.


# TABLES OF LONGITUDES AND LATITUDES

LONGITUDES AND LATITUDES IN THE U.S.

American Federation of Astrologers, 6 Library Court S.E., Washington, D.C. 20003.

Hardbound; about $5.

This reference is extremely useful and labor-saving. Every community in the country with a population of 2,500 or more (by the 1940 census) is included. Longitudes and latitudes are given in degrees and minutes. The inclusion of TLT (called "L.M.T." in table) variations from the standard time for each community is particularly useful.


LONGITUDES AND LATITUDES
THROUGHOUT THE WORLD [except the U.S.]

American Federation of Astrologers, 6 Library Court S.E., Washington, D.C. 20003.

Hardbound; about $5.

Basically the same format as *Longitudes and Latitudes in the U.S.* Includes over 5,000 cities and 185 countries.

# TIME-CHANGE REFERENCES

TIME CHANGES IN THE U.S.A.,

by Doris Chase Doane
Professional Astrologers Incorporated, P.O. Box 2616, Hollywood, California 90028.

Paperback—spiral bound; about $5.

Time changes have always been a major barrier to accurate astrological work, and until recently there was little reliable and easily accessible information regarding them.

*Time Changes in the U.S.A.* is essential for anyone who plans to cast charts. The time-change situation in this country has been remarkably confusing; for instance, until very recently there was no nationwide regulation of time changes. It was not uncommon for one community within a state to practice Daylight-Saving Time while others in the same state did not. *Time Changes in the U.S.A.* relieves the astrologer of the weight of this confusion. It is well laid out and easy to use. We are all indebted to Doris Chase Doane for her great contribution to astrology.

TIME CHANGES IN CANADA AND MEXICO,

by Doris Chase Doane
Professional Astrologers Incorporated, P.O. Box 2616, Hollywood, California 90028.

Paperback—spiral bound; about $4.

Similar to *Time Changes in the U.S.A.*

TIME CHANGES IN THE WORLD [except U.S.A., Canada, and Mexico],

by Doris Chase Doane
Professional Astrologers Incorporated, P.O. Box 2616, Hollywood, California 90028.

Paperback—spiral bound; about $4.

It would be impossible to record every time change throughout the world, largely because in many instances records were not kept or they were destroyed or lost. However, this reference is about as complete as possible. It includes, in addition to tables for Daylight-Saving Time and War Time, valuable information concerning the adoption of calendar revisions, time-zone and meridian adoptions, etc.

# MISCELLANEOUS

TABLES OF DIURNAL PLANETARY MOTION

American Federation of Astrologers, 6 Library Court S.E., Washington, D.C. 20003.

Spiral-bound paperback; about $5.

This table of planetary motion enables one to find the exact Adjustment Factor for planetary adjustment for every hour and every minute of the day for every minute of planetary motion.

ORMECO PLANETARY SLIDE RULE

Orbimetrix Co., P.O. Box 2252, Canoga Park, California 91306

Six-inch diameter, plastic; about $4.

Replaces tables of planetary motion and logarithms, a real time and labor saving device.

ASPECT FINDERS

There are several aspect finders available, ranging in price from one dollar up, which may help the inexperienced or less mathematically inclined astrologer in discovering aspecting planets.

CHART FORMS

There are several types of commercially available chart forms. Only forms that represent the horizon-meridian as perpendicular axes, however, are suitable for a person-centered approach. Those which emphasize the zodiac (by having the 360 degrees inscribed along the periphery) and upon which the horizon-meridian are to be drawn in by the astrologer as non-perpendicular lines, stress the factor of collective, human nature rather than the personal and individual factors of existence.

# APPENDIX III

## TABLES

# 1. EPHEMERIS

## AUGUST 1945

### Calculated for Noon G.M.T.

Longitudes of the Planets

| Day | S.T. h. | m. | s. | ⊙ ° ' | ″ | ☿ | ♀ | ☽ | ♂ | ♃ | ♄ | ♅ | ♆ |
|-----|---------|----|----|-------|---|----|----|----|----|----|----|----|----|
| 1 | 8 | 38 | 55 | 8♌50 | 27 | 3♍39 | 26♊42 | 16♉17 | 6♊13 | 25♍29 | 17♋40 | 16♊19 | 4♎13 |
| 2 | 8 | 42 | 52 | 9 47 | 53 | 4 02 | 27 49 | 0♊22 | 6 53 | 25 40 | 17 47 | 16 21 | 4 15 |
| 3 | 8 | 46 | 48 | 10 45 | 20 | 4 21 | 28 56 | 14 18 | 7 33 | 25 50 | 17 55 | 16 24 | 4 17 |
| 4 | 8 | 50 | 45 | 11 42 | 47 | 4 35 | 0♋03 | 28 05 | 8 13 | 26 01 | 18 02 | 16 26 | 4 19 |
| 5 | 8 | 54 | 41 | 12 40 | 17 | 4 44 | 1 11 | 11♋41 | 8 53 | 26 12 | 18 09 | 16 29 | 4 21 |
| 6 | 8 | 58 | 38 | 13 37 | 47 | 4 47 | 2 18 | 25 06 | 9 33 | 26 23 | 18 17 | 16 31 | 4 23 |
| 7 | 9 | 02 | 34 | 14 35 | 18 | 4 R 46 | 3 26 | 8♌19 | 10 14 | 26 34 | 18 24 | 16 33 | 4 25 |
| 8 | 9 | 06 | 31 | 15 32 | 51 | 4 40 | 4 33 | 21 16 | 10 53 | 26 45 | 18 31 | 16 35 | 4 26 |
| 9 | 9 | 10 | 27 | 16 30 | 34 | 4 26 | 5 41 | 4♍01 | 11 33 | 26 56 | 18 39 | 16 37 | 4 28 |
| 10 | 9 | 14 | 24 | 17 27 | 57 | 4 10 | 6 50 | 16 31 | 12 13 | 27 06 | 18 46 | 16 39 | 4 30 |
| 11 | 9 | 18 | 20 | 18 25 | 33 | 3 48 | 7 58 | 28 48 | 12 53 | 27 18 | 18 48 | 16 41 | 4 32 |
| 12 | 9 | 22 | 17 | 19 23 | 10 | 3 20 | 9 06 | 10♎55 | 13 31 | 27 30 | 19 01 | 16 43 | 4 33 |
| 13 | 9 | 26 | 13 | 20 20 | 46 | 2 47 | 10 15 | 22 52 | 14 10 | 27 41 | 19 07 | 16 45 | 4 35 |

| | | | | | | | | | | | | | | | | | | | | | | |
|---|---|---|---|---|---|---|---|---|---|---|---|---|---|---|---|---|---|---|---|---|---|---|
| 14 | 9 | 30 | 10 | 21 | 18 | 27 | 2 | 09 | 11 | 24 | 4 ♏ | 44 | 14 | 48 | 27 | 56 | 19 | 14 | 16 | 47 | 4 | 37 |
| 15 | 9 | 34 | 06 | 22 | 16 | 05 | 1 | 27 | 12 | 32 | 16 | 36 | 15 | 28 | 28 | 04 | 19 | 21 | 16 | 49 | 4 | 39 |
| 16 | 9 | 38 | 03 | 23 | 13 | 46 | 0 | 42 | 13 | 31 | 28 | 32 | 16 | 03 | 28 | 16 | 19 | 29 | 16 | 51 | 4 | 40 |
| 17 | 9 | 41 | 59 | 24 | 11 | 27 | 29 ♌ | 54 | 14 | 50 | 10 ♐ | 35 | 16 | 46 | 28 | 27 | 19 | 35 | 16 | 53 | 4 | 42 |
| 18 | 9 | 45 | 56 | 25 | 09 | 10 | 29 | 03 | 15 | 58 | 22 | 56 | 17 | 24 | 28 | 39 | 19 | 42 | 16 | 54 | 4 | 44 |
| 19 | 9 | 49 | 53 | 26 | 06 | 54 | 28 | 11 | 17 | 08 | 5 ♑ | 34 | 18 | 02 | 28 | 51 | 19 | 49 | 16 | 56 | 4 | 46 |
| 20 | 9 | 53 | 49 | 27 | 03 | 40 | 27 | 19 | 18 | 17 | 10 | 33 | 18 | 40 | 29 | 03 | 19 | 56 | 16 | 58 | 4 | 48 |
| 21 | 9 | 57 | 46 | 28 | 00 | 26 | 26 | 28 | 19 | 27 | 1 ♒ | 55 | 19 | 18 | 29 | 15 | 20 | 02 | 17 | 00 | 4 | 50 |
| 22 | 10 | 01 | 42 | 28 | 55 | 04 | 25 | 36 | 20 | 37 | 15 | 46 | 20 | 20 | 29 | 27 | 20 | 08 | 17 | 03 | 4 | 52 |
| 23 | 10 | 05 | 39 | 29 | 59 | 13 | 24 | 53 | 21 | 46 | 29 | 57 | 20 | 36 | 29 | 39 | 20 | 15 | 17 | 05 | 4 | 52 |
| 24 | 10 | 09 | 35 | 0 ♍ | 53 | 52 | 24 | 09 | 22 | 56 | 14 ♓ | 25 | 21 | 12 | 29 | 51 | 20 | 21 | 17 | 06 | 4 | 54 |
| 25 | 10 | 13 | 32 | 1 | 51 | 42 | 23 | 30 | 24 | 05 | 29 | 07 | 21 | 50 | 0 ♎ | 03 | 20 | 28 | 17 | 07 | 4 | 56 |
| 26 | 10 | 17 | 29 | 2 | 52 | 26 | 22 | 57 | 25 | 16 | 13 ♈ | 46 | 22 | 27 | 0 | 15 | 20 | 35 | 17 | 08 | 4 | 58 |
| 27 | 10 | 21 | 25 | 3 | 49 | 32 | 22 | 32 | 26 | 25 | 29 | 27 | 23 | 05 | 0 | 27 | 20 | 42 | 17 | 10 | 4 | 59 |
| 28 | 10 | 25 | 22 | 4 | 47 | 29 | 22 | 14 | 27 | 36 | 12 ♉ | 56 | 23 | 42 | 0 | 39 | 20 | 49 | 17 | 11 | 5 | 00 |
| 29 | 10 | 27 | 18 | 5 | 45 | 27 | 22 | 03 | 28 | 47 | 28 | 12 | 24 | 19 | 0 | 51 | 20 | 57 | 17 | 12 | 5 | 02 |
| 30 | 10 | 31 | 15 | 6 | 43 | 27 | 22 D | 00 | 29 | 57 | 11 ♊ | 11 | 24 | 56 | 1 | 04 | 21 | 03 | 17 | 14 | 5 | 04 |
| 31 | 10 | 35 | 11 | 7 | 41 | 30 | 22 | 05 | 0 ♌ | 08 | 24 | 55 | 25 | 33 | 1 | 17 | 21 | 10 | 17 | 15 | 5 | 05 |

PLUTO: August 1, 9°54' Leo
September 1, 10°42' Leo

# 2. TABLE OF HOUSES

## 41° N. Latitude

| S.T. h. m. s. | 10 ♈ | 11 ♉ | 12 ♊ | ASC ♋ | 2 ♌ | 3 ♍ |
|---|---|---|---|---|---|---|
| 0 00 00 | 0 | 6 | 15 | 19 04 | 9 | 1 |
| 3 41 | 1 | 7 | 16 | 19 50 | 10 | 2 |
| 7 22 | 2 | 8 | 17 | 20 34 | 11 | 3 |
| 11 21 | 3 | 9 | 18 | 21 20 | 11 | 4 |
| 0 14 40 | 4 | 10 | 19 | 22 40 | 12 | 5 |
| 18 20 | 5 | 11 | 20 | 22 50 | 12 | 6 |
| 22 03 | 6 | 12 | 21 | 23 32 | 13 | 7 |
| 25 41 | 7 | 13 | 22 | 24 20 | 14 | 8 |
| 0 29 23 | 8 | 14 | 23 | 25 01 | 15 | 9 |
| 33 03 | 9 | 15 | 24 | 25 48 | 16 | 9 |
| 36 44 | 10 | 16 | 25 | 26 30 | 17 | 10 |
| 40 25 | 11 | 17 | 26 | 27 15 | 18 | 11 |
| 0 44 07 | 12 | 18 | 27 | 28 00 | 19 | 12 |
| 47 49 | 13 | 19 | 28 | 28 44 | 20 | 13 |
| 51 30 | 14 | 20 | 29 | 29 26 | 21 | 14 |
| 55 13 | 15 | 21 | 29 | 0 ♌ 12 | 21 | 15 |

## 41° N. Latitude

| S.T. h. m. s. | 10 ♉ | 11 ♊ | 12 ♋ | ASC ♌ | 2 ♍ | 3 ♎ |
|---|---|---|---|---|---|---|
| 2 14 42 | 6 | 2 | 17 | 15 45 | 8 | 5 |
| 18 35 | 7 | 13 | 18 | 16 31 | 9 | 6 |
| 22 32 | 8 | 14 | 19 | 17 16 | 10 | 7 |
| 26 24 | 9 | 15 | 20 | 18 02 | 11 | 8 |
| 2 30 23 | 10 | 16 | 21 | 18 50 | 11 | 9 |
| 34 15 | 11 | 17 | 21 | 19 36 | 12 | 10 |
| 38 12 | 12 | 18 | 22 | 20 22 | 13 | 12 |
| 42 10 | 13 | 19 | 23 | 21 09 | 14 | 13 |
| 2 46 06 | 14 | 20 | 24 | 22 42 | 15 | 13 |
| 50 08 | 15 | 21 | 24 | 23 39 | 16 | 14 |
| 54 08 | 16 | 21 | 25 | 24 14 | 17 | 15 |
| 58 09 | 17 | 22 | 26 | 25 01 | 18 | 16 |
| 3 2 10 | 18 | 23 | 27 | 25 50 | 18 | 17 |
| 6 10 | 19 | 24 | 28 | 26 36 | 19 | 18 |
| 10 11 | 20 | 25 | 28 | 27 23 | 20 | 19 |
| 14 14 | 21 | 26 | 29 | 28 13 | 21 | 21 |

Table of Houses (degree/minute cusp values with sidereal time)

**Upper table**

| | | | | | | | | | |
|---|---|---|---|---|---|---|---|---|---|
| 22 | 22 | 00 | 29 | ♌ | 27 | 22 | 20 | 18 | 3 |
| 23 | 23 | 49 | 29 | 0 | 28 | 23 | 21 | 22 | |
| 25 | 24 | ♍32 | 0 | 1 | 28 | 24 | 30 | 26 | |
| 25 | 25 | 21 | 1 | 2 | 29 | 25 | 34 | 30 | |
| 26 | 26 | 10 | 2 | 3 | ♋ | 26 | 40 | 34 | 3 |
| 27 | 27 | 56 | 2 | 4 | 0 | 27 | 50 | 38 | |
| 28 | 28 | 46 | 3 | 5 | 1 | 28 | 46 | 42 | |
| 29 | 29 | 33 | 4 | 6 | 2 | 29 | 06 | 47 | |
| ♏ | 29 | 23 | 5 | 8 | 3 | 30 | 14 | 51 | 3 |
| 1 | ♎ | 58 | 5 | 9 | 4 | ♊ | 25 | 55 | |
| 2 | 1 | 18 | 6 | 10 | 5 | 1 | 35 | 59 | |
| 3 | 2 | 02 | 7 | 11 | 6 | 2 | 48 | 3 | 4 |
| 4 | 3 | 52 | 7 | 12 | 8 | 3 | 01 | 8 | 4 |
| 5 | 4 | 44 | 8 | 13 | 9 | 4 | 12 | 12 | |
| 6 | 5 | 33 | 9 | 14 | 10 | 5 | 24 | 16 | |
| 7 | 6 | 22 | 10 | 15 | 11 | 6 | 42 | 20 | |
| 8 | 7 | 12 | 11 | 16 | 12 | 7 | 54 | 24 | 4 |
| 9 | 8 | 04 | 12 | 17 | 13 | 8 | 11 | 29 | |
| 10 | 9 | 53 | 12 | 18 | 14 | 9 | 26 | 33 | |
| 11 | 9 | 43 | 13 | 19 | 15 | 10 | 40 | 37 | |

**Lower table**

| | | | | | | | | | |
|---|---|---|---|---|---|---|---|---|---|
| 15 | 22 | 56 | 0 | ♋ | 22 | 16 | 56 | 58 | 0 |
| 16 | 23 | 39 | 1 | 1 | 23 | 17 | 38 | 2 | 1 |
| 17 | 24 | 29 | 2 | 2 | 24 | 18 | 23 | 6 | |
| 18 | 25 | 08 | 3 | 3 | 25 | 19 | 05 | 10 | |
| 19 | 26 | 56 | 3 | 4 | 26 | 20 | 51 | 13 | 1 |
| 20 | 26 | 35 | 4 | 5 | 27 | 21 | 49 | 17 | |
| 21 | 27 | 18 | 5 | 6 | 28 | 22 | 19 | 21 | |
| 22 | 27 | 03 | 6 | 6 | 29 | 23 | 08 | 25 | |
| 23 | 28 | 50 | 6 | 7 | ♊ | 24 | 50 | 28 | 1 |
| 24 | 29 | 31 | 7 | 8 | 1 | 25 | 37 | 32 | |
| 25 | ♍ | 19 | 8 | 9 | 2 | 26 | 25 | 36 | |
| 26 | 1 | 01 | 9 | 9 | 3 | 27 | 10 | 40 | |
| 27 | 2 | 45 | 9 | 10 | 4 | 28 | 02 | 44 | 1 |
| 28 | 2 | 30 | 10 | 11 | 5 | 29 | 50 | 47 | |
| 29 | 4 | 14 | 11 | 11 | 6 | ♉ | 39 | 51 | |
| ♎ | 4 | 02 | 12 | 12 | 7 | 1 | 28 | 55 | |
| 1 | 5 | 43 | 12 | 13 | 8 | 2 | 17 | 59 | 1 |
| 2 | 6 | 30 | 13 | 14 | 9 | 3 | 07 | 3 | 2 |
| 3 | 7 | 15 | 14 | 15 | 10 | 4 | 57 | 6 | |
| 4 | 7 | 02 | 15 | 16 | 11 | 5 | 50 | 10 | |

## 3. TABLE OF LATITUDES AND LONGITUDES
### IN THE U.S.A.

| | Lat. N | Long. W | Hours WEST of Greenwich | TLT Variation from Standard Time | |
|---|---|---|---|---|---|
| | | | | m. | s. |
| ALABAMA: | | | | | |
| Montgomery | 32°21' | 86°18' | 6 | +14 | 48 |
| ARIZONA: | | | | | |
| Phoenix | 33°27' | 112°04' | 7 | −28 | 16 |
| ARKANSAS: | | | | | |
| Little Rock | 34°45' | 92°16' | 6 | − 9 | 04 |
| CALIFORNIA: | | | | | |
| Berkeley | 37°52' | 122°16' | 8 | − 9 | 04 |
| Eureka | 40°48' | 124°10' | 8 | −16 | 40 |
| Los Angeles | 34°03' | 118°15' | 8 | + 7 | 00 |
| Oakland | 37°48' | 122°16' | 8 | − 9 | 04 |
| Sacramento | 38°35' | 121°30' | 8 | − 6 | 00 |
| San Bernardino | 34°06' | 117°18' | 8 | +10 | 48 |
| San Diego | 32°43' | 117°10' | 8 | +11 | 20 |
| San Francisco | 37°47' | 122°26' | 8 | − 9 | 44 |
| COLORADO: | | | | | |
| Colorado Springs | 38°50' | 104°49' | 7 | + 0 | 44 |
| Denver | 39°45' | 104°59' | 7 | + 0 | 04 |
| CONNECTICUT: | | | | | |
| Hartford | 41°46' | 72°41' | 5 | + 9 | 16 |
| New Haven | 41°18' | 72°55' | 5 | + 8 | 20 |
| DELAWARE: | | | | | |
| Dover | 39°09' | 75°32' | 5 | − 2 | 08 |
| DISTRICT OF COLUMBIA: | | | | | |
| Washington | 38°53' | 77°00' | 5 | − 8 | 00 |
| FLORIDA: | | | | | |
| Miami | 25°47' | 80°11' | 5 | −20 | 44 |
| Pensacola | 30°25' | 87°13' | 6 | +11 | 08 |
| Tampa | 27°57' | 82°27' | 5 | −29 | 48 |
| GEORGIA: | | | | | |
| Atlanta | 33°46' | 84°23' | 5 | −37 | 32 |
| IDAHO: | | | | | |
| Boise | 43°37' | 116°12' | 7 | −44 | 48 |

| | Lat. N | Long. W | Hours WEST of Greenwich | TLT Variation from Standard Time | |
|---|---|---|---|---|---|
| | | | | m. | s. |
| ILLINOIS: | | | | | |
| Chicago | 41°52' | 87°39' | 6 | + 9 | 24 |
| Peoria | 40°43' | 89°35' | 6 | + 1 | 40 |
| Rockford | 42°16' | 89°06' | 6 | + 3 | 36 |
| INDIANA: | | | | | |
| Fort Wayne | 41°04' | 85°09' | 6 | +19 | 24 |
| Gary | 41°36' | 87°20' | 6 | +10 | 40 |
| Indianapolis | 39°46' | 86°10' | 6 | +15 | 20 |
| IOWA: | | | | | |
| Cedar Rapids | 41°59' | 91°40' | 6 | − 6 | 40 |
| Des Moines | 41°36' | 93°38' | 6 | −14 | 32 |
| Iowa City | 41°40' | 91°32' | 6 | − 6 | 08 |
| KANSAS: | | | | | |
| Kansas City | 39°07' | 94°38' | 6 | −18 | 32 |
| Wichita | 37°42' | 97°20' | 6 | −29 | 20 |
| KENTUCKY: | | | | | |
| Louisville | 38°15' | 85°45' | 5 | −43 | 00 |
| LOUISIANA: | | | | | |
| Baton Rouge | 30°26' | 91°11' | 6 | − 4 | 44 |
| New Orleans | 29°57' | 90°04' | 6 | − 0 | 16 |
| MAINE: | | | | | |
| Augusta | 44°19' | 69°47' | 5 | +20 | 52 |
| Portland | 43°39' | 70°16' | 5 | +18 | 56 |
| MARYLAND: | | | | | |
| Annapolis | 38°59' | 76°29' | 5 | − 5 | 56 |
| Baltimore | 39°19' | 76°37' | 5 | − 6 | 28 |
| MASSACHUSETTS: | | | | | |
| Boston | 42°22' | 71°04' | 5 | +15 | 44 |
| Cambridge | 42°22' | 71°07' | 5 | +15 | 32 |
| Pittsfield | 42°27' | 73°15' | 5 | + 7 | 00 |
| Springfield | 42°06' | 72°36' | 5 | + 9 | 36 |
| MICHIGAN: | | | | | |
| Benton Harbor | 42°07' | 86°28' | 5 | −45 | 52 |
| Detroit | 42°20' | 83°03' | 5 | −32 | 12 |
| Flint | 43°01' | 83°41' | 5 | −34 | 44 |
| Grand Rapids | 42°55' | 85°40' | 5 | −42 | 40 |
| MINNESOTA: | | | | | |
| Duluth | 46°47' | 92°06' | 6 | − 8 | 24 |
| Minneapolis | 44°59' | 93°16' | 6 | −13 | 04 |

334                                                                    APPENDIXES

|                 | Lat. N   | Long. W   | Hours WEST of Greenwich | TLT Variation from Standard Time |      |
|-----------------|----------|-----------|-------------------------|------------------|------|
|                 |          |           |                         | m.               | s.   |
| MISSISSIPPI:    |          |           |                         |                  |      |
| Jackson         | 32°18′   | 90°11′    | 6                       | − 0              | 44   |
| MISSOURI:       |          |           |                         |                  |      |
| Kansas City     | 39°06′   | 94°36′    | 6                       | −18              | 24   |
| St. Louis       | 38°38′   | 90°12′    | 6                       | − 0              | 48   |
| MONTANA:        |          |           |                         |                  |      |
| Helena          | 46°35′   | 112°02′   | 7                       | −28              | 08   |
| NEBRASKA:       |          |           |                         |                  |      |
| Lincoln         | 40°49′   | 96°42′    | 6                       | −26              | 48   |
| Omaha           | 41°15′   | 95°57′    | 6                       | −23              | 48   |
| NEVADA:         |          |           |                         |                  |      |
| Las Vegas       | 36°10′   | 115°08′   | 8                       | +19              | 28   |
| NEW HAMPSHIRE:  |          |           |                         |                  |      |
| Concord         | 43°13′   | 71°32′    | 5                       | +13              | 52   |
| NEW JERSEY:     |          |           |                         |                  |      |
| Atlantic City   | 39°22′   | 74°26′    | 5                       | + 2              | 16   |
| Elizabeth       | 40°40′   | 74°13′    | 5                       | + 3              | 08   |
| Jersey City     | 40°43′   | 74°02′    | 5                       | + 3              | 52   |
| Trenton         | 40°13′   | 74°45′    | 5                       | + 1              | 00   |
| NEW MEXICO:     |          |           |                         |                  |      |
| Santa Fe        | 35°41′   | 105°57′   | 7                       | − 3              | 48   |
| NEW YORK:       |          |           |                         |                  |      |
| Albany          | 42°39′   | 73°47′    | 5                       | + 4              | 52   |
| Buffalo         | 42°53′   | 78°52′    | 5                       | −15              | 28   |
| New York        | 40°45′   | 73°57′    | 5                       | + 4              | 12   |
| Poughkeepsie    | 41°43′   | 73°55′    | 5                       | + 4              | 20   |
| Rome            | 43°13′   | 75°27′    | 5                       | − 1              | 48   |
| Troy            | 42°44′   | 73°41′    | 5                       | + 5              | 16   |
| Utica           | 43°06′   | 75°14′    | 5                       | − 0              | 56   |
| NORTH CAROLINA: |          |           |                         |                  |      |
| Charlotte       | 35°14′   | 80°51′    | 5                       | −23              | 24   |
| Raleigh         | 35°47′   | 78°38′    | 5                       | −14              | 32   |
| NORTH DAKOTA:   |          |           |                         |                  |      |
| Bismarck        | 46°49′   | 100°47′   | 6                       | −43              | 08   |
| OHIO:           |          |           |                         |                  |      |
| Akron           | 41°05′   | 81°31′    | 5                       | −26              | 04   |
| Cleveland       | 41°30′   | 81°43′    | 5                       | −26              | 52   |
| Columbus        | 39°58′   | 83°01′    | 5                       | −32              | 04   |
| Toledo          | 41°39′   | 83°33′    | 5                       | −34              | 12   |

| | Lat. N | Long. W | Hours WEST of Greenwich | TLT Variation from Standard Time | |
|---|---|---|---|---|---|
| | | | | m. | s. |
| OKLAHOMA: | | | | | |
| Tulsa | 36°09′ | 96°00′ | 6 | −24 | 00 |
| OREGON: | | | | | |
| Portland | 45°31′ | 122°41′ | 8 | −10 | 44 |
| PENNSYLVANIA: | | | | | |
| Allentown | 40°36′ | 75°28′ | 5 | − 1 | 52 |
| Easton | 40°41′ | 75°13′ | 5 | − 0 | 52 |
| Erie | 42°07′ | 80°05′ | 5 | −20 | 20 |
| Philadelphia | 39°57′ | 75°11′ | 5 | − 0 | 44 |
| Pittsburgh | 40°27′ | 80°00′ | 5 | −20 | 00 |
| RHODE ISLAND: | | | | | |
| Providence | 41°49′ | 71°25′ | 5 | +14 | 20 |
| SOUTH CAROLINA: | | | | | |
| Charleston | 32°42′ | 79°53′ | 5 | −19 | 32 |
| SOUTH DAKOTA: | | | | | |
| Sioux Falls | 43°33′ | 96°44′ | 6 | −26 | 56 |
| TENNESSEE: | | | | | |
| Memphis | 35°09′ | 90°03′ | 6 | − 0 | 12 |
| Nashville | 36°10′ | 86°47′ | 6 | +12 | 52 |
| TEXAS: | | | | | |
| Dallas | 32°47′ | 96°47′ | 6 | −27 | 08 |
| Houston | 29°45′ | 95°23′ | 6 | −21 | 32 |
| UTAH: | | | | | |
| Salt Lake City | 40°46′ | 111°54′ | 7 | −27 | 36 |
| VERMONT: | | | | | |
| Montpelier | 44°16′ | 72°35′ | 5 | + 9 | 40 |
| VIRGINIA: | | | | | |
| Arlington | 38°53′ | 77°06′ | 5 | − 8 | 24 |
| Norfolk | 36°51′ | 76°18′ | 5 | − 5 | 12 |
| WASHINGTON: | | | | | |
| Seattle | 47°37′ | 122°20′ | 8 | − 9 | 20 |
| Spokane | 47°40′ | 117°25′ | 8 | +10 | 20 |
| WEST VIRGINIA: | | | | | |
| Charleston | 38°21′ | 81°38′ | 5 | −26 | 32 |
| Wheeling | 40°04′ | 80°44′ | 5 | −22 | 56 |
| WISCONSIN: | | | | | |
| Madison | 43°05′ | 89°24′ | 6 | + 2 | 24 |
| Milwaukee | 43°02′ | 87°55′ | 6 | + 8 | 20 |

| | Lat. N | Long. W | Hours WEST of Greenwich | TLT Variation from Standard Time | |
|---|---|---|---|---|---|
| | | | | m. | s. |
| WYOMING: | | | | | |
| Casper | 42°51′ | 106°18′ | 7 | − 5 | 12 |
| Cheyenne | 41°09′ | 104°49′ | 7 | + 0 | 44 |
| ALASKA: | | | | | |
| Anchorage | 61°10′ | 149°55′ | 10 | + 0 | 20 |
| Fairbanks | 64°51′ | 147°43′ | 10 | + 9 | 08 |
| Juneau | 58°18′ | 134°25′ | 8 | −57 | 40 |
| HAWAII: | | | | | |
| Hilo | 19°44′ | 155°05′ | 10.5 | + 9 | 40 |
| Honolulu | 21°19′ | 157°52′ | 10.5 | − 1 | 28 |
| PUERTO RICO: | | | | | |
| San Juan | 18°28′ | 66°07′ | 4 | −24 | 28 |

## 4. TABLES OF PLANETARY MOTION

| INTERVAL IN HOURS | MOTION OF THE SUN | | | | | |
|---|---|---|---|---|---|---|
| | 57' | 58' | 59' | 1° | 1°01' | 1°02' |
| | m. s. | m. s. | m. s. | m. s. | m. s. | m. s. |
| 1 | 2 20 | 2 25 | 2 27 | 2 30 | 2 32 | 2 35 |
| 2 | 4 40 | 4 50 | 4 55 | 5 00 | 5 05 | 5 10 |
| 3 | 7 00 | 7 15 | 7 22 | 7 30 | 7 37 | 7 45 |
| 4 | 9 20 | 9 40 | 9 50 | 10 00 | 10 10 | 10 20 |
| 5 | 11 40 | 12 05 | 12 17 | 12 30 | 12 42 | 12 55 |
| 6 | 14 00 | 14 30 | 14 45 | 15 00 | 15 15 | 15 30 |
| 7 | 16 20 | 16 55 | 17 12 | 17 30 | 17 47 | 18 05 |
| 8 | 18 40 | 19 20 | 19 40 | 20 00 | 20 20 | 20 40 |
| 9 | 21 00 | 21 45 | 22 07 | 22 30 | 22 52 | 23 15 |
| 10 | 23 20 | 24 10 | 24 35 | 25 00 | 25 25 | 25 50 |
| 11 | 25 40 | 26 35 | 27 02 | 27 30 | 27 57 | 28 25 |
| 12 | 28 00 | 29 00 | 29 30 | 30 00 | 30 30 | 31 00 |

INTERVAL IN MINS.

| | m. s. | m. s. | m. s. | m. s. | m. s. | m. s. |
|---|---|---|---|---|---|---|
| 10 | 0 24 | 0 24 | 0 25 | 0 25 | 0 25 | 0 26 |
| 20 | 0 47 | 0 48 | 0 49 | 0 50 | 0 50 | 0 52 |
| 30 | 1 11 | 1 12 | 1 14 | 1 15 | 1 16 | 1 17 |
| 40 | 1 35 | 1 37 | 1 38 | 1 40 | 1 42 | 1 43 |
| 50 | 1 59 | 2 01 | 2 03 | 2 05 | 2 07 | 2 09 |

| INTERVAL IN HOURS | MOTION OF THE MOON | | | | | |
|---|---|---|---|---|---|---|
|  | 10°0′ | 10°30′ | 11°0′ | 11°30′ | 12°0′ | 12°30′ |
|  | ° m. | ° m. | ° m. | ° m. | ° m. | ° m. |
| 1 | 0 25 | 0 26 | 0 27 | 0 29 | 0 30 | 0 31 |
| 2 | 0 50 | 0 52 | 0 55 | 0 57 | 1 00 | 1 02 |
| 3 | 1 15 | 1 19 | 1 22 | 1 26 | 1 30 | 1 34 |
| 4 | 1 40 | 1 45 | 1 50 | 1 55 | 2 00 | 2 05 |
| 5 | 2 05 | 2 11 | 2 18 | 2 24 | 2 30 | 2 36 |
| 6 | 2 30 | 2 37 | 2 45 | 2 53 | 3 00 | 3 08 |
| 7 | 2 55 | 3 04 | 3 12 | 3 21 | 3 30 | 3 39 |
| 8 | 3 20 | 3 30 | 3 40 | 3 50 | 4 00 | 4 10 |
| 9 | 3 45 | 3 56 | 4 08 | 4 19 | 4 30 | 4 41 |
| 10 | 4 10 | 4 23 | 4 35 | 4 47 | 5 00 | 5 12 |
| 11 | 4 35 | 4 49 | 5 02 | 5 16 | 5 30 | 5 44 |
| 12 | 5 00 | 5 15 | 5 30 | 5 45 | 6 00 | 6 15 |

INTERVAL IN MINS.

|  |  |  |  |  |  |  |
|---|---|---|---|---|---|---|
|  | m. s. | m. s. | m. s. | m. s. | m. s. | m. s. |
| 10 | 4 10 | 4 22 | 4 35 | 4 47 | 5 00 | 5 12 |
| 20 | 8 20 | 8 45 | 9 11 | 9 35 | 10 00 | 10 25 |
| 30 | 12 30 | 13 07 | 13 46 | 14 22 | 15 00 | 15 37 |
| 40 | 16 40 | 17 30 | 18 22 | 19 10 | 20 00 | 20 50 |
| 50 | 20 50 | 21 52 | 22 55 | 23 57 | 25 00 | 26 02 |

| INTERVAL IN HOURS | MOTION OF THE MOON | | | | | |
|---|---|---|---|---|---|---|
| | 13°0′ | 13°30′ | 14°0′ | 14°30′ | 15°0′ | 15°30′ |
| | ° m. | ° m. | ° m. | ° m. | ° m. | ° m. |
| 1 | 0 32 | 0 34 | 0 35 | 0 36 | 0 37 | 0 39 |
| 2 | 1 05 | 1 07 | 1 10 | 1 12 | 1 15 | 1 17 |
| 3 | 1 38 | 1 41 | 1 45 | 1 49 | 1 53 | 1 56 |
| 4 | 2 10 | 2 15 | 2 20 | 2 25 | 2 30 | 2 35 |
| 5 | 2 42 | 2 49 | 2 55 | 3 01 | 3 07 | 3 14 |
| 6 | 3 15 | 3 23 | 3 30 | 3 38 | 3 45 | 3 53 |
| 7 | 3 48 | 3 56 | 4 05 | 4 14 | 4 23 | 4 31 |
| 8 | 4 20 | 4 30 | 4 40 | 4 50 | 5 00 | 5 10 |
| 9 | 4 52 | 5 04 | 5 15 | 5 26 | 5 37 | 5 49 |
| 10 | 5 25 | 5 38 | 5 50 | 6 02 | 6 15 | 6 27 |
| 11 | 5 58 | 6 11 | 6 25 | 6 39 | 6 53 | 7 06 |
| 12 | 6 30 | 6 45 | 7 00 | 7 15 | 7 30 | 7 45 |

INTERVAL IN MINS.

| | m. s. | m. s. | m. s. | m. s. | m. s. | m. s. |
|---|---|---|---|---|---|---|
| 10 | 5 25 | 5 37 | 5 50 | 6 02 | 6 15 | 6 27 |
| 20 | 10 50 | 11 15 | 11 40 | 12 05 | 12 30 | 12 55 |
| 30 | 16 15 | 16 52 | 17 30 | 18 07 | 18 45 | 19 22 |
| 40 | 21 40 | 22 30 | 23 20 | 24 10 | 25 00 | 25 50 |
| 50 | 27 05 | 28 07 | 29 10 | 30 12 | 31 15 | 32 17 |

| INTERVAL IN HOURS | MOTION OF THE PLANETS | | | | | |
|---|---|---|---|---|---|---|
|  | $0°1'$ | $0°10'$ | $0°20'$ | $0°30'$ | $0°40'$ | $0°50'$ |
|  | m. s. | m. s. | m. s. | m. s. | m. s. | m. s. |
| 1 | 0 02 | 0 25 | 0 50 | 1 15 | 1 40 | 2 05 |
| 2 | 0 05 | 0 50 | 1 40 | 2 30 | 3 20 | 4 10 |
| 3 | 0 07 | 1 15 | 2 30 | 3 45 | 5 00 | 6 15 |
| 4 | 0 10 | 1 40 | 3 20 | 5 00 | 6 40 | 8 20 |
| 5 | 0 12 | 2 05 | 4 10 | 6 15 | 8 20 | 10 25 |
| 6 | 0 15 | 2 30 | 5 00 | 7 30 | 10 00 | 12 30 |
| 7 | 0 17 | 2 55 | 5 50 | 8 45 | 11 40 | 14 35 |
| 8 | 0 20 | 3 20 | 6 40 | 10 00 | 13 20 | 16 40 |
| 9 | 0 22 | 3 45 | 7 30 | 11 15 | 15 00 | 18 45 |
| 10 | 0 25 | 4 10 | 8 20 | 12 30 | 16 40 | 10 50 |
| 11 | 0 27 | 4 35 | 9 10 | 13 45 | 18 20 | 22 55 |
| 12 | 0 30 | 5 00 | 10 00 | 15 00 | 20 00 | 25 00 |

INTERVAL IN MINS.

|  | m. s. | m. s. | m. s. | m. s. | m. s. | m. s. |
|---|---|---|---|---|---|---|
| 10 | 0 00 | 0 04 | 0 08 | 0 12 | 0 16 | 0 21 |
| 20 | 0 00 | 0 08 | 0 17 | 0 25 | 0 33 | 0 42 |
| 30 | 0 00 | 0 12 | 0 25 | 0 37 | 0 50 | 1 02 |
| 40 | 0 00 | 0 17 | 0 33 | 0 50 | 1 07 | 1 23 |
| 50 | 0 00 | 0 21 | 0 42 | 1 02 | 1 23 | 1 44 |

| INTERVAL IN HOURS | MOTION OF THE PLANETS | | | | | |
|---|---|---|---|---|---|---|
| | 1°00' | 1°10' | 1°20' | 1°30' | 1°40' | 1°50' |
| | m. s. | m. s. | m. s. | m. s. | m. s. | m. s. |
| 1 | 2 30 | 2 55 | 3 20 | 3 45 | 4 10 | 4 35 |
| 2 | 5 00 | 5 50 | 6 40 | 7 30 | 8 20 | 9 10 |
| 3 | 7 30 | 8 45 | 10 00 | 11 15 | 12 30 | 13 45 |
| 4 | 10 00 | 11 40 | 13 20 | 15 00 | 16 40 | 18 20 |
| 5 | 12 30 | 14 35 | 16 40 | 18 45 | 20 50 | 22 55 |
| 6 | 15 00 | 17 30 | 20 00 | 22 30 | 25 00 | 27 30 |
| 7 | 17 30 | 20 25 | 23 20 | 26 15 | 29 10 | 32 05 |
| 8 | 20 00 | 23 20 | 26 40 | 30 00 | 33 20 | 36 40 |
| 9 | 22 30 | 26 15 | 30 00 | 33 45 | 37 30 | 41 15 |
| 10 | 25 00 | 29 10 | 33 20 | 37 30 | 41 40 | 45 50 |
| 11 | 27 30 | 32 05 | 36 40 | 41 15 | 45 50 | 50 25 |
| 12 | 30 00 | 35 00 | 40 00 | 45 00 | 50 00 | 55 00 |

INTERVAL
IN MINS.

| | m. s. | m. s. | m. s. | m. s. | m. s. | m. s. |
|---|---|---|---|---|---|---|
| 10 | 0 25 | 0 29 | 0 33 | 0 37 | 0 41 | 0 45 |
| 20 | 0 50 | 0 58 | 1 07 | 1 15 | 1 23 | 1 32 |
| 30 | 1 15 | 1 27 | 1 40 | 1 52 | 2 05 | 2 17 |
| 40 | 1 40 | 1 57 | 2 13 | 2 30 | 2 47 | 3 03 |
| 50 | 2 05 | 2 26 | 2 47 | 3 07 | 3 28 | 3 49 |

# APPENDIX IV

## CALCULATIONS FOR SYMBOLIC DIRECTIONS

# 1. SECONDARY PROGRESSIONS

Formula:    One year = one day.

Increments:    Annual—24 hours.
              Monthly—2 hours.
              Daily—4 minutes.

Procedure:    (1)    Find progressed date and time.
              (2)    Find progressed positions.

EXAMPLE:    The progressed date and time for a person 24 years 6 months 5 days of age may be found by ADDING the increment of 24 days (24 years), 12 hours (6 months), and 20 minutes (5 days) to the birth date and GMT. The exact progressed positions may be taken from the ephemeris, making any necessary adjustments for GMT, using the progressed date.

# 2. ONE-DEGREE MEASURE

Formula:    One year = one degree.

Increments:    Annual—1°.
              Monthly—an arc of 5 minutes.
              Daily—an arc of 10 seconds.

Procedure:    (1)    Find increment.
              (2)    Add increment to natal factors.

EXAMPLE:    To find progressed positions for a person 37 years 5 months 10 days of age, simply ADD 37 degrees (37 years), 25 minutes (5 months), and 100 seconds (10 days) to natal factors.

## 3. DUODENARY MEASURE

Formula:    One year = two and one half degrees.

Increments:    Annual—2½°.
                         Monthly—12 minutes 30 seconds.
                         Daily—25 seconds.

Procedure:    (1)    Find increment (using table given below).
                        (2)    Add increment to natal factors.

### Table of Duodenary Increments

| YEAR | INCREMENT | MONTH | INCREMENT | DAY | INCREMENT |
|------|-----------|-------|-----------|-----|-----------|
| 1 | 2°30′ | 1 | 12′30″ | 1 | 25″ |
| 2 | 5° | 2 | 25′ | 2 | 50″ |
| 3 | 7°30′ | 3 | 37′30″ | 3 | 1′15″ |
| 4 | 10° | 4 | 50′ | 4 | 1′40″ |
| 5 | 12°30′ | 5 | 1°02′30″ | 5 | 2′05″ |
| 10 | 25° | 6 | 1°15′ | 6 | 2′30″ |
| 20 | 50° | 7 | 1°27′30″ | 7 | 2′55″ |
| 30 | 75° | 8 | 1°40′ | 8 | 3′20″ |
| 40 | 100° | 9 | 1°52′30″ | 9 | 3′45″ |
| 50 | 125° | 10 | 2°05′ | 10 | 4′10″ |
| 60 | 150° | 11 | 2°17′30″ | 20 | 8′20″ |
| 70 | 175° | 12 | 2°30′ | 30 | 12′30″ |

EXAMPLE:    The increment for a person 53 years 2 months 13 days of age
                      is 133°00′25″.

## 4. SEPTENARY MEASURE

Formula:   One year = $4\frac{2}{7}°$.

Increments:   Annual—$4\frac{2}{7}°$.
              Monthly—21′25″.
              Daily—43″.

Procedure:   (1)   Find increment (using table given below).
             (2)   Add increment to natal factors.

### Table of Septenary Increments

| YEAR | INCREMENT | MONTH | INCREMENT | DAY | INCREMENT |
|------|-----------|-------|-----------|-----|-----------|
| 1 | 4°17′ | 1 | 21′25″ | 1 | 43″ |
| 2 | 8°34′ | 2 | 42′50″ | 2 | 1′26″ |
| 3 | 12°51′ | 3 | 1°04′15″ | 3 | 2′08″ |
| 4 | 17°09′ | 4 | 1°25′40″ | 4 | 2′51″ |
| 5 | 21°26′ | 5 | 1°47′05″ | 5 | 3′34″ |
| 10 | 42°51′ | 6 | 2°08′30″ | 6 | 4′17″ |
| 20 | 85°44′ | 7 | 2°29′55″ | 7 | 5′00″ |
| 30 | 128°35′ | 8 | 2°51′20″ | 8 | 5′43″ |
| 40 | 171°26′ | 9 | 3°12′45″ | 9 | 6′25″ |
| 50 | 214°17′ | 10 | 3°34′10″ | 10 | 7′08″ |
| 60 | 257°08′ | 11 | 3°55′35″ | 20 | 14′17″ |
| 70 | 300° | 12 | 4°17′ | 30 | 21′25″ |

EXAMPLE:   The increment for a person 23 years 2 months of age is 99°17′50″.

## 5. POINT-OF-SELF MEASURE

Formula:     One year = $12\frac{6}{7}°$.

Increments:  Annual—$12\frac{6}{7}°$.
                        Monthly—$1°04'17''$.
                        Daily—$2'09''$.

Procedure:   (1)   Find increment (using table below).
                        (2)   Add increment to natal factors.

### Table of Point-of-Self Increments

| YEAR | INCREMENT | MONTH | INCREMENT | DAY | INCREMENT |
|------|-----------|-------|-----------|-----|-----------|
| 1 | 12°52′ | 1 | 1°04′ | 1 | 2′ |
| 2 | 25°43′ | 2 | 2°09′ | 2 | 4′ |
| 3 | 38°35′ | 3 | 3°13′ | 3 | 6′ |
| 4 | 51°22′ | 4 | 4°18′ | 4 | 9′ |
| 5 | 64°14′ | 5 | 5°22′ | 5 | 11′ |
| 10 | 129°31′ | 6 | 6°26′ | 6 | 13′ |
| 20 | 258°02′ | 7 | 7°30′ | 7 | 15′ |
| 30 | 27°33′ | 8 | 8°35′ | 8 | 17′ |
| 40 | 157°04′ | 9 | 9°39′ | 9 | 19′ |
| 50 | 284°35′ | 10 | 10°44′ | 10 | 21′ |
| 60 | 66°06′ | 11 | 11°48′ | 20 | 43′ |
| 70 | 215°37′ | 12 | 12°52′ | 30 | 1°04′ |

EXAMPLE:   The increment for a person 30 years 6 months of age is
                      33°59′15″.

# APPENDIX V
## BIRTH DATA FOR SAMPLE CHARTS

## BIRTH DATA FOR SAMPLE CHARTS

ROBERTO ASSAGIOLI:   February 27, 1888; Venice, Italy; Noon. Source: Dane Rudhyar.

BABA RAM DASS:   April 6, 1931; Boston, Mass.; 10:40 A.M.

ALICE BAILEY:   June 16, 1880; Manchester, England; 7:32 A.M. Source: Dane Rudhyar.

SARAH BERNHARDT:   September 25, 1844; Paris, France; 8:00 P.M. Source: *Sabian Symbols in Astrology* by Marc Jones.

ANNIE BESANT:   October 1, 1847; London, England; about 6:00 P.M.

WILLIAM BLAKE:   November 28, 1757; London, England. Source: *1001 Notable Nativities* by Alan Leo.

JOHN BRZOSTOSKI:   July 1, 1926; near New York City; 5:00 P.M.

LEWIS CARROLL:   January 27, 1832; Daresbury, England; 3:48 A.M. Source: *Sabian Symbols in Astrology* by Marc Jones.

MARIE CURIE:   November 7, 1867; Warsaw, Poland; 8:45 P.M. Source: *Sabian Symbols in Astrology* by Marc Jones.

ADELLE DAVIS:   February 25, 1904; Union Township, Ind.; 3:00 A.M.

ISADORA DUNCAN:   May 27, 1878; San Francisco, Calif.; 2:25 A.M. Source: *Sabian Symbols in Astrology* by Marc Jones.

BOB DYLAN:   May 24, 1941; Duluth, Minn.; birth time unknown. Chart is speculative.

SIGMUND FREUD:   May 6, 1856; Freiberg, Moravia; 6:30 P.M. TLT. Source: *The Life and Work of Sigmund Freud* by Ernest Jones.

GEORGE GURDJIEFF:   January 13, 1877; Alexandropol, Russia; 12:39 A.M. Source: R. Davidson.

HERMANN HESSE:   July 2, 1877; Calw, Swabia; 6:30 P.M. Source: *Portrait of Hesse* by Bernhard Zeller.

MARC EDMUND JONES:   October 1, 1888; St. Louis, Mo.; 8:37 A.M. Source: His book *Sabian Symbols in Astrology*.

JANIS JOPLIN:   January 19, 1943; Port Arthur, Tex.; 9:45 A.M.

C. G. JUNG:   July 26, 1875; Kesswill, Switzerland; 7:20 P.M.

KARL KRAFFT:   May 10, 1890; Basel, Switzerland; 12:50 P.M. Source: *Urania Children* by Eric Howe.

J. KRISHNAMURTI:   May 12, 1895; Madanapalle, South India; 12:25 P.M. Source: *Sabian Symbols in Astrology* by Marc Jones.

TIMOTHY LEARY:   October 22, 1920; Springfield, Mass.; 10:45 A.M.

MEHER BABA:   February 25, 1894; Bombay, India; 4:35 A.M. Source: *Sabian Symbols in Astrology* by Marc Jones.

MARIA MONTESSORI:   August 31, 1870; Chiaravalle, Italy; 1:20 P.M. Source: Dane Rudhyar.

RICHARD M. NIXON:   January 9, 1913; Yorba Linda, Calif.; 9:30 P.M. Source: *Sabian Symbols in Astrology* by Marc Jones.

GEORGE SAND:   July 1, 1804; Paris, France. Source: *Sabian Symbols in Astrology* by Marc Jones.

BOBBY SEALE:   October 22, 1936; Dallas, Tex.; 10:30 P.M.

THEOSOPHICAL SOCIETY:   November 17, 1895; New York, N.Y.; 8:00 P.M.

# APPENDIX VI

## ASTRONOMICAL DATA

# 1. RETROGRADE MOTION

Planets do not actually change their direction of motion; they simply appear to, from the point of view of the earthbound observer. This phenomenon is brought about by the relationship existing between the position of the earth on its orbit to the positions of other planets on their respective orbits. Let's take the case of Mars for an example. The earth occupies a position in the solar system nearer the Sun than Mars, and because of this it requires less time to complete one orbit around the central solar body (365 days for earth, 687 earth days for Mars). When in the course of its orbit earth approaches the position of Mars, the apparent daily motion of Mars begins to decelerate (see Figure 1, point 1); several weeks later Mars appears stationary (point 2); Mars then begins its retrograde phase, as earth overtakes it in space (point 3), remaining in retrograde for 58–81 days.

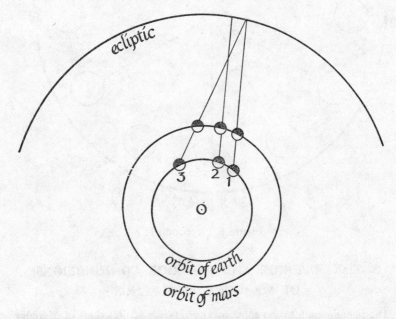

Figure 1 (Appendix)

## 2. EARTH'S REVOLUTION AROUND THE SUN
## AND THE PHENOMENON OF THE ECLIPTIC

As discussed in Part Two of the text, the ecliptic of the zodiac represents the apparent path of the Sun around the earth. The Sun, however, is actually stationary, or at least relatively so, in space, while the earth actually revolves around the Sun. This actual revolution produces the apparent solar motion and the ecliptic of the zodiac (see Figure 2).

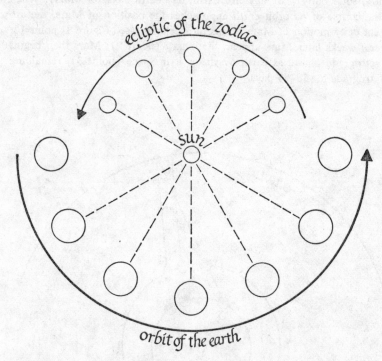

Figure 2 (Appendix)

## 3. THE SUPERIOR AND INFERIOR CONJUNCTIONS
## OF MERCURY AND VENUS

The phenomenon of the superior and inferior conjunctions of Mercury and Venus is illustrated on page 353, in Figure 3.

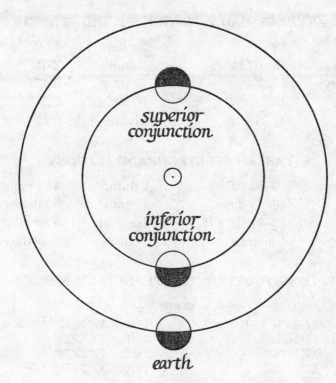

Figure 3 (Appendix)

## 4. MAXIMUM PLANETARY LATITUDES

| | | | |
|---|---|---|---|
| Moon: | 5°–6° | Jupiter: | 1½° |
| Mercury: | 4°–5° | Saturn: | 3° |
| Venus: | 7°–8° | Uranus: | 1° |
| Mars: | 3° | Neptune: | 2° |
| | | Pluto: | 18° |

## 5. AVERAGE DAILY MOTION OF THE PLANETS

| | | | |
|---|---|---|---|
| Sun: | 59'08" | Jupiter: | 4'59" |
| Moon: | 13°10'35" | Saturn: | 2'01" |
| Mercury: | 1°23' | Uranus: | 0'42" |
| Venus: | 1°12' | Neptune: | 0'24" |
| Mars: | 31'27" | Pluto: | 0'15" |

## 6. TABLE OF RETROGRADE MOTIONS

| | | | |
|---|---|---|---|
| Mercury: | 20–24 days | Saturn: | 4½ months |
| Venus: | 40–43 days | Uranus: | 5 months |
| Mars: | 58–81 days | Neptune: | 5 months |
| Jupiter: | 4 months | Pluto: | 6 months |

## 7. LONGITUDES OF THE PLANETARY NODES

MERCURY:        annual increment 42.6"

| | | | | | |
|---|---|---|---|---|---|
| 1900: | 17°10'48" | Taurus | 1940: | 17°38'12" | Taurus |
| 1910: | 17°16'54" | | 1950: | 17°45'18" | |
| 1920: | 17°24'00" | | 1960: | 17°52'24" | |
| 1930: | 17°31'06" | | 1970: | 17°59'30" | |

VENUS:          annual increment 32.4"

| | | | | | |
|---|---|---|---|---|---|
| 1900: | 15°45'36" | Gemini | 1940: | 16°08'16" | Gemini |
| 1910: | 15°51'16" | | 1950: | 16°13'56" | |
| 1920: | 15°56'56" | | 1960: | 16°19'36" | |
| 1930: | 16°02'36" | | 1970: | 16°25'16" | |

MARS:           annual increment 27.7"

| | | | | | |
|---|---|---|---|---|---|
| 1900: | 18°57'22" | Taurus | 1940: | 19°15'40" | Taurus |
| 1910: | 19°01'59" | | 1950: | 19°20'17" | |
| 1920: | 19°06'36" | | 1960: | 19°24'54" | |
| 1930: | 19°11'03" | | 1970: | 19°29'31" | |

JUPITER:              annual increment 36.7"

| | | | | |
|---|---|---|---|---|
| 1900: | 9°28'12" | Cancer | 1940: | 09°52'40" | Cancer |
| 1910: | 9°34'19" | | 1950: | 09°58'47" | |
| 1920: | 9°40'26" | | 1960: | 10°02'56" | |
| 1930: | 9°46'33" | | 1970: | 10°09'03" | |

SATURN:              annual increment 31.4"

| | | | | |
|---|---|---|---|---|
| 1900: | 22°47'05" | Cancer | 1940: | 23°07'01" | Cancer |
| 1910: | 22°52'19" | | 1950: | 23°12'15" | |
| 1920: | 22°57'33" | | 1960: | 23°17'29" | |
| 1930: | 23°02'47" | | 1970: | 23°22'43" | |

URANUS:              annual increment 18.0"

| | | | | |
|---|---|---|---|---|
| 1900: | 13°29'24" | Gemini | 1940: | 13°41'24" | Gemini |
| 1910: | 13°32'24" | | 1950: | 13°44'24" | |
| 1920: | 13°35'24" | | 1960: | 13°47'24" | |
| 1930: | 13°38'24" | | 1970: | 13°50'24" | |

NEPTUNE:             annual increment 39.4"

| | | | | |
|---|---|---|---|---|
| 1900: | 10°40'51" | Leo | 1940: | 11°07'07" | Leo |
| 1910: | 10°47'25" | | 1950: | 11°13'41" | |
| 1920: | 10°53'59" | | 1960: | 11°20'15" | |
| 1930: | 11°00'33" | | 1970: | 11°26'49" | |

PLUTO:               annual increment 48.8"

| | | | | |
|---|---|---|---|---|
| 1900: | 18°57'21" | Cancer | 1940: | 19°29'53" | Cancer |
| 1910: | 19°05'29" | | 1950: | 19°38'01" | |
| 1920: | 19°13'37" | | 1960: | 19°46'09" | |
| 1930: | 19°21'45" | | 1970: | 19°54'17" | |

# BIBLIOGRAPHY

# I. ASTROLOGY

HARRY F. DARLING. *Organum Quaterni* (Lakemont, Ga.: CSA Press, 1968).

MARGARET E. HONE. *The Modern Text-Book of Astrology* (London: L. N. Fowler & Company Ltd., 1st ed., 1951; 4th ed. 1968).

MARC EDMUND JONES. "Arabian Astrology," a study course (Stanwood, Wash.: Sabian Publishing Society, 1932–33).

——. *Astrology: How and Why It Works* (Stanwood, Wash.: Sabian Publishing Society, 1945, 1969).

——. *Essentials of Astrological Analysis* (New York: Sabian Publishing Society, 1960).

——. *The Guide to Horoscope Interpretation* (Stanwood, Wash.: Sabian Publishing Society, 1941, 1969).

——. *How to Learn Astrology* (Stanwood, Wash.: Sabian Publishing Society, 1941, 1969).

——. *Problem Solving by Horary Astrology* (Stanwood, Wash.: Sabian Publishing Society, 1943, 1966).

——. "Pythagorean Astrology," a study course (Stanwood, Wash.: Sabian Publishing Society, 1929).

——. *The Sabian Symbols in Astrology* (Stanwood, Wash.: Sabian Publishing Society, 1953, 1969).

——. *Scope of Astrological Prediction* (Stanwood, Wash.: Sabian Publishing Society, 1969).

——. "Symbolical Astrology," a study course (Stanwood, Wash.: Sabian Publishing Society, 1931).

DANE RUDHYAR. *The Astrological Houses: The Spectrum of Individual Experience* (New York: Doubleday, 1972).

——. *An Astrological Study of Psychological Complexes and Emotional Problems* ('S Gravenhage, Netherlands: Servire N.V., 1969).

——. *Astrological Timing* (New York: Harper & Row, 1972).

——. *The Astrology of Personality* (New York: Lucis Press, 1936; New York: Doubleday, 1970).

——. *The Lunation Cycle* ('S Gravenhage, Netherlands: Servire N.V., 1967; Berkeley, Calif.: Shambala Publications, 1971).

——. *My Stand on Astrology* (Palo Alto, Calif.: The Seed Center, 1972).

——. *Person-Centered Astrology* (Lakemont, Ga.: CSA Press, 1973).

——. *The Practice of Astrology* ('S Gravenhage, Netherlands: Servire N.V., 1968; Baltimore: Penguin Books, 1970).

——. *The Pulse of Life* (New York: David McKay, 1943; 'S Gravenhage, Netherlands: Servire N.V., 1963; Berkeley, Calif.: Shambala Publications, 1970).

——. *Triptych* ('S Gravenhage, Netherlands: Servire N.V., 1968).

——. Various articles in *Horoscope* and *American Astrology*, 1942 to date.


# II. PSYCHOLOGY

ROBERTO ASSAGIOLI. *Psychosynthesis* (New York: The Viking Press, 1965).

ROBERT S. DE ROPP. *Sex Energy* (New York: Dell Books, 1969).

VIKTOR E. FRANKL. *The Doctor and the Soul: From Psychotherapy to Logotherapy* (New York, Alfred A. Knopf, 1955; New York: Bantan Books, 1971).

——. *Man's Search for Meaning: An Introduction to Logotherapy* (Boston: Beacon Press, 1959; New York: Pocket Books, 1963).

JOLANDE JACOBI. *The Psychology of C. G. Jung* (New Haven: Yale University Press, 1943, 1968).

ANIELA JAFFÉ. *From the Life and Work of C. G. Jung* (New York: Harper & Row, 1971).

C. G. JUNG. *Analytical Psychology* (New York: Random House, 1970).

——. *Memories, Dreams, Reflections* (New York: Random House, 1961).

——. *The Spirit in Man, Art, and Literature,* Bollingen Series (Princeton University Press, 1966).

——. "Synchronicity: An Acausal Principle." In *The Interpretation of Nature and the Psyche,* Bollingen Series (New York: Pantheon Books, 1955).

——, ed. *Man and His Symbols* (New York: Doubleday, 1964).

A. H. MASLOW. *The Farther Reaches of Human Nature* (New York: The Viking Press, 1971).

——. *The Psychology of Science* (Chicago: Henry Regnery, 1969).

——. *Religions, Values, and Peak-Experiences* (New York: The Viking Press, 1970).

——. *Toward a Psychology of Being* (New York: Van Nostrand-Reinhold, 1968).

ROLLO MAY. *Man's Search for Himself* (New York: W. W. Norton, 1953).

OLA RAKNES. *Wilhelm Reich and Orgonomy* (Baltimore: Penguin Books, 1971).

WILHELM REICH. *The Function of the Orgasm* (New York: Farrar, Straus & Giroux, 1942).

CARL R. ROGERS. *On Becoming a Person* (Boston: Houghton Mifflin, 1961).

# III. PHILOSOPHY

FRATER ACHAD. *The Anatomy of the Body of God* (New York: Samuel Weiser, 1969).

ALICE A. BAILEY. *Esoteric Astrology* (New York: Lucis Publishing Company, 1951, 1970).

———. *A Treatise on Cosmic Fire* (New York: Lucis Publishing Company, 1925, 1962).

H. P. BLAVATSKY. *The Secret Doctrine,* 2 vols. (Pasadena, Calif.: Theosophical University Press, 1963).

JOHN BLOFELD. *The Tantric Mysticism of Tibet* (New York: E. P. Dutton, 1970).

CLAUDE BRAGDON. *A Primer of Higher Space (The Fourth Dimension)* (Tucson, Ariz.: Omen Press, 1972).

TITUS BURCKHARDT. *Alchemy* (Baltimore: Penguin Books, 1971).

MANLY P. HALL. *The Secret Teachings of All Ages* (Los Angeles: The Philosophical Research Society, 1928, 1971).

FRANZ HARTMANN. *Paracelsus* (New York: John W. Lovell, 1891, 1963).

E. J. HOLMYARD. *Alchemy* (Baltimore: Penguin Books, 1957).

JOLANDE JACOBI, ed. *Paracelsus: Selected Writings,* Bollingen Series (Princeton University Press, 1951, 1958).

LAURA DEWITT JAMES. *William Blake & the Tree of Life* (Berkeley: Shambala Publications, 1971).

MARC EDMUND JONES. *Occult Philosophy* (Stanwood, Wash.: Sabian Publishing Society, 1948, 1971).

MAX KALTENMARK. *Lao Tzu and Taoism* (Palo Alto, Calif.: Stanford University Press, 1969).

JOHN MICHELL. *City of Revelation* (London: Garnstone Press, 1972).

———. *View over Atlantis* (London: Sago Press, 1969; Ballantine Books, 1972).

L. GORDON PLUMMER. *The Mathematics of the Cosmic Mind* (Wheaton, Ill.: Theosophical Publishing House, 1970).

ARTHUR E. POWELL. *The Solar System* (Wheaton, Ill.: Theosophical Press, 1930, 1957).

OLIVER L. REISER. *A New Earth and a New Humanity* (New York: Creative Age Press, 1942).

DANE RUDHYAR. *Directives for New Life* (Railroad Flat, Calif.: Seed Publications, 1971).

———. *The Planetarization of Consciousness* (New York: Harper & Row, 1972).

GERSHOM G. SCHOLEM. *On the Kabbalah and Its Symbolism* (New York: Schocken Books, 1965).

*The Secret of the Golden Flower,* translated and explained by Richard Wilhelm (New York: Harcourt, Brace & World, 1931, 1962).

JAN CHRISTIAAN SMUTS. *Holism and Evolution* (New York: Macmillan, 1926; New York: The Viking Press, 1961).

ARTHUR WALEY. *The Way and Its Power* (New York: Grove Press, 1958).

HERBERT WEINER. *9½ Mystics: The Kabbala Today* (New York: Holt, Rinehart & Winston, 1969; Macmillan, 1971).

HOLMES WELCH. *Taoism: The Parting of the Way* (Boston: Beacon Press, 1957, 1965).